"AN ORGANIZED, LIVELY SO ☐ P9-AOS-472
ENCOURAGEMENT AND PRACTICAL TIPS FOR
WORKING MOTHERS . . . VERY HELPFUL."
— *Publishers Weekly*

For working mothers who sometimes (or often) feel stress,
guilt, or just a bit of conflict; who want fresh inspiration
and time-saving advice; who are concerned about the
implications of their lifestyles for their children . . .
HERE'S HELP!

In this comprehensive and compassionate sourcebook,
you'll find supportive, real-life stories of hundreds of
working mothers who have found ways to be *good mothers*
and have *satisfying careers* at the same time.

The Working Mother's Complete Handbook

"The authors have literally countless
ideas for making life easier for
working mothers. . . . The format in
which this information is presented is
never dull; Norris and Miller refer to
real situations and include quotations
from interviews with working mothers
all over the country."
— *Baby Talk*

ABOUT THE AUTHORS: Both GLORIA NORRIS and
JO ANN MILLER are editors and writers closely associated with
books by and for women. Ms. Norris, a native of Mississippi, lives
in New York City. Her short stories have appeared in two
O. Henry Prize collections. Ms. Miller, who divides her time
between her family and her career, also lives in New York City.

The Working Mother's Complete Handbook

BY

Gloria Norris and Jo Ann Miller

REVISED EDITION

A PLUME BOOK

NEW AMERICAN LIBRARY

NEW YORK AND SCARBOROUGH, ONTARIO

NAL BOOKS ARE AVAILABLE AT QUANTITY DISCOUNTS WHEN USED TO
PROMOTE PRODUCTS OR SERVICES. FOR INFORMATION PLEASE WRITE TO
PREMIUM MARKETING DIVISION. NEW AMERICAN LIBRARY,
1633 BROADWAY, NEW YORK, NEW YORK 10019.

Grateful acknowledgment is made to the following for permission to
quote from previously published material:

Baby and Child Care, by Benjamin Spock, M.D. Copyright © 1945, 1946, 1957,
    1968, 1976 by Benjamin Spock, M.D. Reprinted by permission of Pocket
    Books, a Simon and Schuster division of Gulf & Western Corporation.
Burnout: The High Cost of High Achievement by Dr. Herbert J. Freudenberger,
    Ph.D., with Geraldine Richelson. Copyright © 1980 by Herbert J. Freuden-
    berger, Ph.D., and Geraldine Richelson. Reprinted by permission of Double-
    day & Company, Inc.
Daycare, by Alison Clarke-Stewart, Cambridge, Mass.: Harvard University Press,
    Copyright © 1982 by Kathleen Alison Clarke-Stewart. Reprinted by per-
    mission.
How Was School Today, Dear? Copyright © 1977 by Sara Ann Friedman. Pub-
    lished by Reader's Digest Press.
*Working Mothers: An Evaluative Review of the Consequences for Wife, Husband,
    and Child,* by Lois Wladis Hoffman and F. Ivan Nye. Copyright © 1974 by
    Jossey-Bass, Inc., Publishers. Reprinted by permission of Jossey-Bass, Inc.

 PLUME TRADEMARK REG. U.S. PAT. OFF. AND FOREIGN COUNTRIES
REG. TRADEMARK—MARCA REGISTRADA
HECHO EN HARRISONBURG, VA., U.S.A.

SIGNET, SIGNET CLASSIC, MENTOR, PLUME, MERIDIAN and
NAL BOOKS are published *in the United States* by
New American Library, 1633 Broadway, New York, New York 10019,
in Canada by The New American Library of Canada Limited,
81 Mack Avenue, Scarobrough, Ontario M1L 1M8

Library of Congress Cataloging in Publication Data

Norris, Gloria.
    The working mother's complete handbook.

    Includes index.
    1. Mothers—Employment—United States. 2. Mothers—
United States. 3. Parent and child. I. Miller, Jo Ann.
II. Title.
HD6055.2.U6N67 1984   646.7'8'024042   84–2062
ISBN 0–452–25523–6

First Plume Printing, June, 1984

1 2 3 4 5 6 7 8 9

PRINTED IN THE UNITED STATES OF AMERICA

Contents

CONTENTS

A Word on Words

The use throughout this book of "working mother" is something of a misnomer, of course. All mothers work. We might have said more precisely the "wage-earning" mother. But since "working mother" has come to mean, in public and private usage, the woman who holds a job outside the home, we have stuck to this instantly recognizable term.

As for pronouns, we have alternated "he" and "she" arbitrarily throughout when what we have to say can apply to children of both sexes. Because the people who care for children while their parents are at work—housekeepers, baby-sitters, day-care teachers—are most often women, we have chosen to refer to these caregivers with the feminine pronoun. We hope we have managed to avoid cumbersome language without offending the growing body of dedicated male caregivers we have met. We can only hope that in future editions of this book, the concept of men caring for children will have taken hold so firmly that we will have to revise our language to reflect a new reality.

Acknowledgments

Many people helped us in creating this book. Our thanks go first to the busy women who so generously shared their feelings and experiences as working mothers. We are grateful to them for their candor and for the many good ideas that we hope will inspire women everywhere.

We received valuable support from the following people: Helen Barer, Suzanne Bernstein, Linda Blachman, Stella Chess, Gloria Davis, Dana Friedman, Ellen Galinsky, Judith Langer, James Levine, Marilyn Machlowitz, Susan Moore, Nancy Samalin, Lucy Scott, Barry Silvergold, Carol Spero, Marcia Storch, Carol Weiss, and Susan Weissman.

We would like to thank our agent, Berenice Hoffman, for her diligent efforts on our behalf, and Elaine Koster, Carole Hall, and Arnold Dolin of New American Library, for sound guidance and for making this book possible.

Finally, we thank each other for a collaboration that has been stimulating, rewarding, and, most of all, fun.

—G. N. and J. A. M.

I am grateful to my children, Michael and Nicholas, and my husband, Lou, for displaying admirable patience during the many hours I disappeared to "work on the book about mommies who work." My gratitude goes to Helen Plowden, who has been a mother to my children—and to me. Her devotion has helped me be a successful working mother. Lynette Ransome helps to run our household calmly and efficiently, for which I am most appreciative. My special thanks to Betsy Kovacs for a very special friendship.

—J. A. M.

A Good Mother Is . . .

Have you ever asked yourself: Is this the best a working mother can manage? Am I doing right by my family? Am I doing right by my job? Every working mother breathing (and many a father too) suffers these moments of doubt at low times—when the babysitter falls sick for two weeks, nothing goes right at work, or the children come home with surprisingly low grades on their report cards.

Fortunately these doubts have spurred mothers not to despair but to inventive new solutions. That was what we discovered as we interviewed over 150 working mothers across the country, holding such various jobs as stockbroker, hairdresser, teacher, secretary, librarian, boutique owner, accountant, and computer operator. By daily experience, by experiment and blind luck, but most of all by force of the love that these mothers bear for their children, they are pioneering a new style of mothering, new ways of being good mothers while holding jobs. Information about how they're doing it, and how their families are changing, is what we share in these pages.

You'll find three kinds of guidance here. First, practical information—all the specific knowledge, tips, and tested advice to steer you successfully through the arenas of your home, job, and family. For example, we tell you where to look for childcare in your community, what to ask a prospective housekeeper, how to write an ad for a babysitter, what you can learn from parenting resource groups (the wonderful, new source for working mothers who must miss out on the old park-bench exchange) about a wide range of problems—from coping with colic to disciplining with love. We provide specifics like dinners your kids can cook, a maternity-leave checklist, five ways to make the most of your time with your children, job fields that promise a strong market for your talents in the 1980s, rules for latchkey children, daycare licensing agencies state by state, three ways to stop money quarrels with your husband, six stress relievers.

But working mothers face other problems that are not answered by advice on three-ways-to-make-a-meat-loaf-last—essential though planning and good information are. That leads to our second kind of guidance. How much independence is good for a child? How do you convince your boss you're committed to your job although you can't ever work as late as your coworkers do? How can you pace your career, taking time off when your children demand your full attention, without losing your place on the job ladder? Should you wait until you're thirty-five and established to have a baby? If you're married, how can you keep your marriage strong despite limited time for your husband? If you're single, how can you manage a personal life separate from work and kids?

There are no quick answers to these new dilemmas, so we've set down the stories of women who've successfully faced them. Their collective experience will light the way for other women. You can take heart that others have found good answers, and you can use their experience to work out the ways that will be right for you.

Third, you'll find a section devoted to that most overlooked person—you. While you're straining never to let down as a mother and never to let down on the job, you're likely to take all the give from yourself. Don't. You need and deserve *self-time*—as we call those restorative moments—time that can be only fifteen minutes in a hot bath while you get back in touch with your own person. Stress and burnout (the numbing exhaustion that finally consumes a person who forces herself too far) have become the battle fatigue of the working mother. You need not fall victim if you know what to watch for and take some precautions.

Readers of the first edition of our book may wonder how this extensively revised edition differs. First of all, approximately 60 percent of this edition is new material. But a more important difference is *experience*. The first edition, reflecting the state of the art for most working mothers, emphasized how to *get started*. Now we are happy to provide more advice on how to *keep succeeding* as a working mother and handle situations farther along in time. For example, you'll find extensive advice not only on how to *find* good childcare but on *how to keep it good.* And we also talk about the critical and, in some ways more difficult, problem of staying in touch with teenage children.

Most of all, this new edition reflects a new acceptance of working mothers. Today more than half of all children have a working mother. For a child, *it's more usual to have a working mother than not to have one.* Difficulties do persist. Government still has little commitment to the needs of children with working parents. Business is just awakening to the potential assets of working mothers and fumbling toward ways to help these valuable employees. But a growing body of professionals and the real experts—mothers themselves—are redefining what a good mother is.

Women like you have proved through their own experience that "mother" does not necessarily mean you must handle your child's every need, every daily question personally. The fact that your child's daycare teacher can soothe his tears or quiet him when his aggressive impulses get out of hand doesn't mean you are losing your place in his life as mother.

Being a good mother does mean showing your unwavering love and concern by staying in touch with your children's feelings. It means showing your children the model of a woman who feels competent both in the world and in the home. While being a working mother need not have any feminist significance for you—after all, divorced mothers who are forced to support their families are the largest-growing category of working mother—being a good mother for many women means living new roles for women so that our daughters and sons will not be caught in the same shoulds and can'ts that we have grown up with. We are the products of our past, but our children—as every mother dreams—need not be the products of that same past.

"Mother" also means passing along values and commitments that are concerned with a larger world than that immediately around us. Many mothers hope to inspire their children with a vision, however misty or incomplete, of how the world might be better for women, men, and children, and that such a vision will be part of the legacy they leave their children. And they are convinced, as Betty Friedan has written, that only by participating in the mainstream of society will women and mothers reap the training and experience and skills to understand the complex society we call home.

The
Working Mother's
Complete Handbook

Part One

Your Family

Chapter One

Succeeding with Your Children

"Remember, darling," says a mother to her four-year-old, "I'm a working mommy, but I'm a mommy first." No matter how devoted she is to her job, the typical working mother reserves her deepest feelings for her family. Loving her children, and getting their love in return, helps to soften the blows of the world out there. And children need to know that they matter to their parents. When you praise their accomplishments, when you show them you appreciate them—and especially when you tell them they're terrific, for no reason at all—you help to quiet the doubt that sometimes creeps into every child's consciousness: "If she really loves me, why does she leave me so much?"

Children need our love throughout their lives, but they also have special needs that change as they grow. Understanding how these needs relate to your working is a first step in succeeding as a working mother right from the start.

Timing Your Return to Work

In a pleasant switch to unanimity, developmental psychologists generally agree on the timetable of a child's evolving psychological needs. A mother's return to work takes on different meanings at various stages of her child's life. Fortunately, at each stage, there are steps a mother can take to make her transition from being at home full-time easier and more positive for the child. We will discuss each of these steps more fully later. But first, we want you to know what the initial working-mother issues and answers tend to be—from a child's-eye view.

Remember that children develop at different rates; the ages given here are meant to be approximate rather than exact.

Early Infancy (up to six months). If you definitely plan to work, taking only a brief leave does have its advantages. During this period the baby forms a close attachment to the mother—by about four or five months he can distinguish her from others—but he can attach successfully to other loving figures as well and tolerate your absence more easily than the older child can.

The baby's task during these months is to satisfy his need for physical comfort and nourishment and to develop a trusting, warm relationship with the people who care for him. Your task is to put these needs above all others. Hire a caregiver as far in advance of your return to work as possible, and plan to overlap with her, so that the baby can get used to her while you're still around. Look for someone who you think will last—constancy is very important during this period—and who is loving and attentive. Changing diapers and giving bottles is not enough; make sure the person you hire is sensitive to your baby's developing social and cognitive needs; that she cuddles him, plays with him, and talks to him. Most people who have raised children of their own or who have training in child development do these things easily and naturally.

Observe the caregiver while you are at home; check in with her by telephone after you've returned to work. Most important, try to spend as much time as you can with the baby; the intimate relationship you and he develop will help you both tolerate later separations.

If your baby seems unnaturally apathetic and unresponsive, if he doesn't begin to smile somewhere between two and three months or suffers an unusual amount of eating and sleeping problems, a change in the caregiving situation may be in order. But don't rush to this conclusion: Babies often have eating and sleeping difficulties in the early months, and the caregiver may not be the problem at all. Be sure to examine your own feelings about leaving the baby during this time. The mother-infant bond is a two-way process, and if you have not made your peace with returning to work, your ambivalence may be creating tension at home.

Six Months to Three Years. During this period the child who is used to having mother around all the time may cling and cry if she is separated from her. And somewhere between six and twelve months she may become frightened of strangers, typically clinging fearfully to mother if a stranger approaches. These signs of separation distress are normal; they are a good indication that your baby has formed a strong loving attachment, a relationship that will give her the trust and confidence to form other enduring relationships throughout life.

To introduce your child to a new caregiving situation at the height of this phase can be difficult. Part-time work is ideal between six months and two-and-a-half to three years, after which separation distress will likely wane. Of course, this is not an option for many mothers. If you do begin working full-time during this period, make every effort to get your child used to the caregiving arrangement while you can be around. These phases pass, and if you have given her warmth and security from the beginning and gotten her used to substitute care gradually, the chances are she will accommodate to your absence without too much difficulty. Be patient, though, and be sure to monitor the care very carefully after you return to work.

If you begin working when your child can talk and understand language, around the age of two, you will be able to reassure her that "Mommy will be back soon." And she will feel more confident because she can express herself to you and others. Walking also gives a child a needed sense of control. By this time, too, she has developed a sense of herself separate from you and, unlike the infant, she can be comforted by knowing that you still exist even though you are out of sight.

Despite their growing independence, it is not uncommon for toddlers to regress if you begin working during this period. Don't be alarmed if your child goes back to the bottle or slips up on toilet training. Let her hang on to babyhood a little longer until she becomes confident that your absences are only temporary. Be prepared, too, for temporary problems like waking at night, crying, perhaps even a brief period of apathy. Remember, children are resilient. If you give your child loving, consistent care, if she is played with and talked to, the joy she experiences from her own rapid growth will soon outweigh the pain of separation.

It is especially important to preserve a sense of stability during this period, so that the child learns that the world is a safe and reliable place. Try not to have an array of caregivers; stay home as much as possible in the evenings. Avoid introducing anything new —unfamiliar foods, toilet training, weaning—right around the time you begin working.

If you are satisfied with your caregiver but you feel your child could use more stimulation, why not invite visitors during the day? Toddlers and babies are always glad to see Grandma or Grandpa, and they seem to get special pleasure from being entertained by teenagers.

Three to Six Years. It's no accident that nursery schools begin taking youngsters at age three, for children at this stage of development need socialization with others. With your three- to five-year-old in gainful activity away from you during part of the day, he will usually be able to adjust to your working. Remember, though, that starting group care is a big adjustment for a young child. And if you return to work at the same time, he may have trouble coping with the two new situations. A child who has never been away from his mother for any prolonged period can suffer separation distress even at this age.

A lot depends on your attitude. If you are confident, cheerful, and firm, his anxiety is not likely to last long. Be prepared to help him start gradually. Talk to him at home about the school or center, explaining carefully what will take place there. If the school permits it, you can hang around for a few days or even a week or two until he is secure enough for you to leave. Again we recommend you accomplish this before you begin to work full-time.

If your child doesn't adjust readily—if he seems unhappy at home, reluctant to return to school in the morning, and in general shows signs of distress—trust his reactions. He may not be getting the stimulation or attentive care he needs. Changing the caregiving situation can help: perhaps a larger group for a very active child, a combination of half-day group care and at-home baby-sitting for a shy or withdrawn child. Remember, as a parent you have options. You do not have to stay with an arrangement if your child is not thriving in it.

Six to Eleven Years. Now your child has a "job" of her own— school—and you may be dismayed to find her so embroiled in her own activities and friends that you see less and less of her. Both from the child's viewpoint and a time-management angle, most mothers find these are the best years to return to work.

Some cautions: Children at this age think of themselves as very grown up and may be reluctant to tell you about their concerns or fears. A child who begins school just as you return to work may worry that she can't manage without you. She may fear that the after-school sitter won't show up or that she will forget where she is supposed to meet the sitter. She may be afraid that you won't remember to return home in the evening. Keep these possibilities in mind when making after-school arrangements; check to be sure that sitters are not late (this is a very common cause of fear in young children), and try to keep afternoon activities simple and consistent. It is a good idea to arrange for schoolmates to visit in the afternoon so that your child will feel less lonely. And when you are with her, listen to her attentively and acceptingly; make sure you give her the chance to open up to you about any worries she might have.

Eleven to Fourteen Years. This might seem the ideal time to you, with your adolescent more and more self-sufficient, but beware. Although your teenager may appear mature enough to tolerate your absence, the sudden change in family life can throw him into a tizzy. If you're concerned about your teenager partying in the empty house after school, set firm limits about visitors. Many youngsters are so involved in extracurricular activities that contact with you may decline to touching base now and then. But see that those bases are touched; even these near-adults need your attention and involvement.

Getting Off on the Right Foot

"Never apologize to your kids for the fact that you're working," cautions a successful film producer. "Let them know that they are important to you, but that your job is important, too." Regardless of your child's developmental stage, if he realizes that your going to work is a non-negotiable reality, he will be much better able to accept it.

When you first start working, however, smooth the transition with a few precautions:

Get your child used to the childcare arrangement you've chosen gradually. Hiring and trying out a sitter or enrolling your child in a day-care center two months before you start your job may seem like unnecessary expense and trouble. But you'll be well repaid by less friction—and less worry on your part—when you do start. Both you and the child will gain from a dress rehearsal.

Minimize disruption of usual home routines. If your family has always eaten dinner together at six, try to keep to this schedule, at least in the beginning. Keep reading bedtime stories, if that's what you've always done. But watch out for overcompensation. If you've never allowed TV treats after dinner, don't start now. Remember, you don't want to give the message "I'm doing something that's hurting you and so I'll make it up."

Don't let your new enthusiasm for your work life take over your home life. Talking about your exciting new life and new friends may only rub salt into the wounds of a resentful youngster. There'll be plenty of time later to share your experiences with the children. If you must bring work home, handle it after the children are in bed.

Anticipate and encourage questions. Not only the easy ones like "What do you do at your office?" or "How much do you get paid?" but also the hard ones like "Do you like the kids you teach better than you like me?" or "Will you ever be here when I get home from school?" Dealing openly with a child's apprehensions, if she has them, is the best reassurance you can offer.

ATTACHMENT AND SEPARATION—THE THEORIES

Many of our fears about the effects of separation on an infant stem from early, exceedingly limited studies of childhood attachment carried out two decades ago by John Bowlby in England and René Spitz in America. They direly concluded that children who do not "attach," that is, form an intimate, caring relationship with one specific person, preferably the biological mother, will almost inevitably develop gross pathology, growing up with "affectionless characters" unable to give or receive love, since they have never known the delicate reciprocity of a constant loving relationship. Investigators then declared that in order for this warm relationship to develop, the child must have the benefit of unbroken mothering during the first two-and-a-half to three years of life.

But the flaw in this argument is that the studies were performed on hospitalized infants separated traumatically from their families, an environment far removed from that of babies whose mothers go off to work and return home each evening. Unfortunately, many professionals and lay people have been generalizing from these investigations and making grim predictions for the children of mothers who work during their children's early years.

The fact is that *few systematic studies support the contention that unbroken mother-presence is necessary for the development of later relationships.* Researcher Barbara Tizard, who studied children reared in institutions before being adopted, found no appreciable ill effects of their early lack of one-on-one mothering. In fact, Bowlby himself was unable to locate any inability to form deep relationships in adolescents who suffered hospitalization during their early years. Moreover, today, experts are questioning the *exclusiveness* of the mother-infant bond.

Jerome Kagan, the distinguished professor of developmental psychology at Harvard University, has concluded on the basis of extensive study that children can be attached both to their caregivers *and* to their mothers. Citing the importance of quality rather than quantity of time spent with the child, he contends that attachments can be formed between parent and child even if they see each other only a short time each day.

Pediatrician T. Berry Brazelton echoes this view. If the parent is basically loving, even an hour in the morning and an hour in the evening may be sufficient for attachment to take place.

Rudolph Schaffer, professor of psychology at the University of Strathclyde, Glasgow, has found that children can make *multiple attachments* (29 percent of the infants he studied formed several attachments at the same time; 87 percent had formed multiple attachments by the age of eighteen months).

The conclusion being drawn today is that if the baby can indeed successfully become attached to a number of people, he can receive comfort from them, too. Thus, if there is consistency of care—if there is a small core of constant caregivers, including the parents—the child will develop a number of emotional investments and will be able to build the trust necessary for healthy emotional growth. Or, as one young mother said, "I've discovered there's no limit to a baby's love. The more people he has to love, the better."

Explaining Why You Work

How your child reacts to your working is strongly colored by his conception of *why* you're going off to a job. You'll want to give careful thought to explaining it to him—but don't make the mistake of getting overly involved in explanations beyond his grasp. The eleven-year-old has little trouble understanding "We need a second income to help pay for your brother's college education and for your summer camp." She may even be able to sympathize with her mother's need for a life separate from that of the family.

But let a mother who is the sole support of her three-year-old son tell him that she's working because she needs the money and he might make her a present of $100 in play money as an inducement to stay home (one inventive youngster did just that, and gift-wrapped the package, too!). Instead, the preschooler will accept the entire concept better if you present it matter-of-factly and with as little explanation as possible: "Mommy goes to work, Johnny stays home and plays with the baby-sitter. . . ."

The school-age child isn't swayed by lengthy explanations, either, but will respond easily to the fruits of her mother's labors. Says one woman, a long-time victim of guilt despite her financial need to work: "I only started to feel better when Joanie was old enough to understand that the $35 ice skates, the skiing trips—all the extras that she was enjoying—were coming from my salary."

Fortunately, older children can understand our need for fulfilling work, and some can even identify with it. Belinda, a talented commercial artist, confided her discouragement over a difficult project one bleak day to her twelve-year-old daughter and was gratified to hear her say, "But Mom, you know you love your work . . . it's so creative." A few years earlier, the same complaint would probably have only confused this youngster, who was still grappling with the reality of her mother's absence.

THE POWER OF POSITIVE THINKING

It is always gratifying to learn that your child is comfortable with your working. A school librarian tells this story about her four-year-old son:

"One of Ethan's favorite books is *Are You My Mother?* the story of a tiny bird that is hatched while his mother is out gathering food for his arrival. Never having seen his mother, the bird goes about asking all sorts of unlikely creatures—a cow, a dog, even a huge derrick—'Are you my mother?'

"Ethan loved the gentle repetition and also the tension he felt confronting that most fearsome of calamities—a missing mommy. Each time the bird's puzzled question was greeted with another disdainful no, Ethan squealed with delight . . . and pressed a little closer to me. Finally, the baby bird stands up, yellow wings akimbo, and cries out, *'Where is my mother?!'* at which point Ethan piped up calmly, 'Don't worry, little birdie, she's at work, she'll be home soon.' "

The Working Mother's Challenges: Five Critical Areas

Learning to Be a Parent.   Women who return to work shortly after their babies are born miss out on the park-bench networks from which mothers have historically learned not only which baby foods to buy or how to toilet train, but also how to cope with their own and their children's emotional needs. Parent groups can fill this vital gap. They come in a variety of formats—from ongoing interactive workshops to formal courses—and there are programs for parents of all age groups, from infancy through adolescence. There are daytime groups sponsored by corporations or professional organizations, and some mothers have even organized their own leaderless support groups that meet regularly at members' homes. You can locate a parent group through hospitals, Y's, childbirth classes, and university extension programs.

These support systems are a boon to working mothers. Discovering that yours is not the only child given to midnight walks (maybe even finding a solution to the problem) or that you are not the only mother who has fallen asleep at her desk will help you fight the isolation that often goes along with parenting and working. One mother says simply, "My parent group saved my life. I feel I have a team of consultants to call on."

In a group or workshop you can learn about the stages of child development and have the chance to share your experiences and solutions to child rearing problems. Most working mothers agree that being in a group that *doesn't* include nonworking mothers makes it easier for them to discuss "their" subjects—work-family conflicts, guilt, childcare options—in a safe and supportive atmosphere.

A good parent group should *not* aim to teach any particular "right" way to bring up children. At the heart of an effective program is the belief that parents are the true experts and that they can learn from one another to become confident problem-solvers. Says Carol Spero, co-founder of New York City's Association for Parent Education, "Parents must be taught that they know more about their children—they live with them. They must see information from experts as resources to help them do their work. I always tell parents that when they listen to an expert or pick up a book, they have to ask if this person ever had the responsibility of full-time childcare for at least a week. If the answer is no, then you really have to raise questions."

PARENTING RESOURCES

- Family Resource Coalition. This grass-roots organization of resource programs across the United States and Canada operates a clearinghouse and will put you in touch with programs and workshops in your community. Contact Family Resource Coalition, c/o Family Focus, Inc., 2300 Green Bay Road, Evanston, IL 60201.

- BANANAS, a childcare information and referral service in Oakland, California, offers an astonishing variety of low-cost handouts and pamphlets, ranging from dealing with child molestation to how to start a parent group. Call or write for a complete listing: BANANAS, 6501 Telegraph Avenue, Oakland, CA 94609. 415–658–7101.

- Parent Effectiveness Training (PET) stresses day-to-day parental coping skills and conducts courses nationwide. Write: Parent Effectiveness Training Information, 531 Stevens Avenue, Solana Beach, CA 92075.

- A selection of parent centers. *New York City:* Contact the Association for Parent Education, 170 Thompson Street, New York, NY 10012, for a complete listing of parent groups in the tristate area. *Minnesota:* MELD (Minnesota Early Learning Design), 128 East Grant Street, Minneapolis, MN 55403. MELD also operates programs in other states and gladly shares information. *Massachusetts:* COPE (Coping with the Overall Pregnancy/Parenting Experience), one of the oldest and largest support services, 37 Clarendon Street, Boston, MA 02116. *Seattle:* The Parent Place, 1608 East 150th Street, Seattle, WA 98155.

- Helpful books: *Between Generations*, by Ellen Galinsky (Times Books, 1980), a uniquely valuable and supportive account of how parents change and grow throughout the stages of their children's development. *How to Grow a Parents Group*, by D. Mason, G. Jensen, and C. Ryzewicz. Order from CDG Enterprises, P.O. Box 97, Western Springs, IL 60558. Excellent guides to child development: *The Magic Years*, by Selma Fraiberg (Scribners, 1959) and *Your Baby & Child: From Birth to Age Five*, by Penelope Leach (Knopf, 1982).

- Newsletters: *Salk Letter*, published monthly by psychologist Lee Salk, 941 Park Avenue, New York, NY 10028. *Sesame Street Parents' Newsletter* (monthly), Sesame Street, P.O. Box 2889, Boulder, CO 80322. *Practical Parenting*, published every other month by Vicki Lansky, best-selling author of *Feed Me! I'm Yours* and *The Taming of the C.A.N.D.Y. Monster*. Practical Parenting, 18326B Monnetonka Boulevard, Deephaven, MN 55391. *Growing Child* tracks a child's development every month for six years. Growing Child, 22 North Second Street, P.O. Box 620, Lafayette, IN 47902.

Career-Family Conflicts. No matter what contortions you go through to avoid these dilemmas, you are sure at some point to come up against the school play that coincides with your annual sales conference, the stomachache that befalls your son on the first day of an important business trip. These kinds of career-family conflicts are a fact of life for every working mother. But if you handle them sensibly and honestly, they'll be a lot less troublesome to you and your children.

If you must leave your child at a time when both of you would prefer to be together, sharing your own feelings about the conflict is often the best course of action. You can say: "I know how you feel. I wish I could stay home with you. But this is one day I can't do that. And I understand you feel bad about this. But I think you will feel better by tomorrow." Assuring your son or daughter that this will not happen all the time will also help. So may a promise of spending some extra time alone with your children. You might add: "How about if, on Saturday, you and I go downtown and go shopping, just the two of us, and have lunch in a restaurant?" If this plan is made out of your own real desire to be with your child, rather than from guilt or obligation, you will usually find that he will harbor little resentment.

Never underestimate the power of unsolicited hugs, lunchbox love notes, spontaneous phone calls. Children are unabashedly sentimental. They thrive in the warmth of our affection and admiration. You can be sure your teenage daughter appreciated that heartfelt letter you wrote her last summer, even though she'd die before she'd tell you so. Your eight-year-old may squirm and blush when you say, "I think you're a wonderful boy," but he'll love it all the same.

Bringing a present from the office is another way of telling a child you care about him. (Don't make the mistake of thinking a goody from Mommy is an admission of guilt. No one suggests that your son is guilt-ridden when he brings home his latest collection of finger paintings.) Keep the gifts simple—a puzzle, a comic book, some colored pens; but don't fall into the pattern of bringing something home every day, or you'll wind up like the poor woman whose children's outstretched hands and cries of "What did you bring me?" greeted her before she could even pull her car into the garage.

If you are afraid that your child will be frustrated or resentful because you work, remind yourself that children whose every need is always met never have the opportunity to find their own solutions to problems. If, for example, you take a day off from work every time your daughter seems to miss you, she will never learn to deal with these uncomfortable emotions. Nor will she learn how to use her own resources to make herself feel better. Children grow from experiencing stress, and they are reassured by learning that they can deal with it well.

Fostering Independence.   There is no doubt that, whether out of conviction or necessity, most women find themselves being less overprotective and more encouraging of their children's independence once they start working. This development is usually all to the good in a society where the trend has been to make full-time mothers their children's full-time servants—and children often grow up to be overly dependent young people, clinging to mothers who are reluctant to let go. A thirty-six-year-old social worker remarks: "Now that I have more control over my life, I've stopped needing to control my kids. I tended to be a dominating, over-organized force in their lives; there was too much input from me. Working's really forced me to let go."

Some women say that their working encourages the children to seek out other adults in their lives—to good effect. Occasionally seeking help from neighbors, sitters, or other children's parents teaches youngsters to cope successfully with the world about them, not just with their own families.

The fact that working mothers are usually happy to see their kids' growing independence contributes to the children's confidence. Say researchers Lois Hoffman and Ivan Nye in *Working Mothers:* "To the non-working mother the move from protector and nurturer to independence trainer is often difficult. For the working mother, however, the child's growing independence eases her role strain."

With a little thought, you can help your child get used to his new independence. Following in a second bus when your daughter takes her first bus ride alone . . . making a few phone calls to the child who stays home alone . . . entrusting a child with a long supermarket list (and being tolerant about mistakes)—show your child that you trust and can depend on him while at the same time giving him your support and love.

Independence, of course, is a relative matter. Children must be allowed to be dependent before they can learn to be independent. Mothers who have given their children a firm base of security—whether by staying home for the first years, by establishing a pattern of consistent, attentive care from other adults, or by making every effort to be available to their children on a regular basis—report that the move to increasing independence comes with very little difficulty.

Don't be too quick to force independence on your child. Be realistic about his capabilities. Allowing a four-year-old to walk a mile to school alone is foolhardy, no matter how much time it saves you and how willing he is to do it. On the other hand, you can say to an eight-year-old: "You are old enough now to go to the dentist by yourself." And you can help him by adding, "I will show you exactly how to get there and how to get home." The first time your youngster goes to the dentist alone, you may both feel uneasy. The second time, he'll probably regard it as routine. And by the third time, he'll turn his nose up at his friends who are still escorted by their mothers.

BOOKS FOR CHILDREN

Introduce young children, through these words and pictures, to the idea that women can hold satisfying and useful jobs and be wives and mothers as well. In these books, youngsters will meet women in diverse fields and also will see how other young children cope with having a mother who works.

Ask Me What My Mother Does, Katherine Leiner (Watts, 1978)
Mommies at Work, Eve Merriam (Scholastic, 1973)
Mothers Can Do Anything, Joe Lasker (Whitman, 1972)
Sonya's Mommy Works, Arlene Alda (Simon & Schuster, 1982)
Waiting, Nicki Weiss (Greenwillow, 1981)
Women at Their Work, Betty Lou English (Dial, 1977)

Hurried Children.   Independence is only part of the story. In a provocative new book, child psychologist David Elkind talks about what he calls the "hurried child."* "Unlike spoiled children who remain children too long," he says, "hurried children grow up too fast, pushed in their early years toward many different types of

* *The Hurried Child: Growing Up Too Fast Too Soon*, by David Elkind (Addison-Wesley Publishing Company, 1981).

achievement and exposed to experiences that tax their adaptive capacity." Working mothers, stressed by the pressures of their busy lives, are in danger of passing this pressure on to their children. "We hurry our children because we hurry ourselves," observes Elkind.

One has only to see a tight-lipped mother dragging a cranky toddler through the supermarket to understand what Elkind means by "emotional overload." Witnessing a tense fourteen-year-old caring for a younger sibling and being her single mother's confidante makes us painfully aware of the consequences of "responsibility overload."

Elkind explains that how children respond to hurrying depends somewhat on their developmental stage. Children under the age of eight tend to see it as a rejection; they reason that if a parent really cared about them as they are, the parent wouldn't need to push them into achievement or rush them through the day. We can lessen their stress by reacting sensitively to their feelings, says Elkind, rather than dealing with them strictly on a thinking level.

School-age children begin to like hurrying—it makes them feel grown-up—but they also want to retain their childishness. For this age, says Elkind, it is important "that we communicate our appreciation for all that they do for us . . . but also that we know they are still children and that there are some things they should not be burdened with." Adolescents, notes Elkind with some irony, "not only blame their parents for hurrying them as adolescents, but also for hurrying them as children." They see themselves as being exploited, "of being used by parents who put their own needs ahead of their children's." (See pages 150–155 for a discussion of adolescents.)

By calling our attention to the stress of the "hurried child," David Elkind performs a valuable service for all parents. If we recognize our own hurrying and the stress it produces, if we take the time to learn what we can realistically expect of children at various stages, and if we pay close attention to our own sons' and daughters' needs, then we are more likely to raise relaxed and emotionally healthy children.

Emotional Problems.   If your child misbehaves or seems unhappy, it may well be his way of telling you he wants more attention from you. And remember that kids deliver their emotional messages in all sorts of ways. There was no mistaking the meaning of two-and-a-half-year-old David's howls of "Me! Me! Me!" as he grabbed the telephone out of his mother's hand. Or of seven-year-old Lisa's simple request: "Why can't you take me to school? I want to be a walking child, not a busing child." Sulking, misbehaving, and acting out can be subtler indications that a young child needs more attention from his mother. Nightmares, toilet-training difficulties, and eating problems should also be a warning to you that something is amiss. Here are some general danger signs to watch out for:

- any persistent change in eating or sleeping habits
- aggressive or destructive behavior
- excessively obedient behavior
- listlessness or a tendency to withdraw
- excessive fearfulness or timidity.

Children require more than attention, though; they also need limits. And here is where many working mothers fall down on the job. Eager to compensate to their children for the time not spent with them, they sometimes fail to make clear that they are firmly in charge—with unfortunate results. Children to whom "I said no, and that's final" is a foreign language, eight-year-olds who stretch "five more minutes" to a two-hour sprawl in front of the television set—in short, children who have turned their mothers' guilt into a powerful weapon of their own—make life difficult for themselves and everyone around them.

Don't wait for problems to become full-blown before you take action. If your daughter keeps saying, "I wish you could stay home with me today," take a good look at your childcare arrangement. Maybe a change is in order. If your son keeps complaining about school, don't wait for him to start cutting classes. Have a talk with the teacher. Right now.

Be on guard for what your kids *don't* say, too. The school child who withdraws and the baby who never cries (but rarely smiles, either) may be telling you a lot more than the screamers and complainers. If you set aside time just to play or talk with an uncommunicative child, you will most likely find out what's bothering him.

You may find you have few unusual problems with your children's behavior. Part of the reason is that priorities shift slightly when both parents work. As one mother says, "I'm more able to tolerate my children's little behavior problems because I'm not with them all day."

Working Mothers <u>Are</u> Succeeding With Their Children

Deep in their hearts working mothers know they *are* succeeding, that their children are developing as normally as those whose mothers do not work outside the home. And it is reassuring that experts are reaching the same conclusion. Says famed developmental psychologist Urie Bronfenbrenner: "Taken by itself, the fact that a mother works outside the home has no universally predictable effects on the child."

Of course, having a working mother can rarely be "taken by itself." Many other ingredients go into the mix of child development: the quality of the substitute childcare; how the mother and child interact when they are together; the child's age and social class; his relationship with his father; and, most important of all, *how the mother feels about her chosen role*. It is this mix of variables that makes research on the children of working mothers so difficult.

More finely tuned studies are sorely needed to address our many questions. But until then, here are some encouraging answers that researchers have right now:

Do children of working mothers develop more social and school problems? To start with worst fears first, studies do not support that old theory of the "experts": The mother works, so the children get in trouble. "There is no evidence that the children of working mothers are more likely to be delinquent," say Lois Hoffman and Ivan Nye, who sift through a mass of findings in their definitive *Working Mothers*. And no evidence suggests that children perform less well in school when their mothers work. Indeed, some studies indicate that children of working mothers have higher academic aspirations (usually measured by desire to go to college) and that many seem to be more highly motivated to achieve, particularly at the grade-school level. More controlled studies are needed to probe the validity of these findings.

The impact on daughters is more definite. Hoffman and Nye report, "There is evidence that college-educated daughters of working mothers have higher career aspirations and achievements than do college-educated daughters of nonworking mothers." As we observed from our interviews, children of working mothers fail algebra and so do kids whose mothers are home all day. The nine-year-old whose mother works may be apprehensive at school, but so may his classmate whose mother waits for him at home with milk and cookies. Recent studies also show no difference in school attendance between children of working and nonworking mothers, an impression that was certainly confirmed by our interviews. In fact, while an at-home mother may allow her child to take an occasional day off for "rest and recreation," working mothers are understandably disinclined to do so.

Do working mothers' children have more emotional problems? Pediatrician Mary Howell, in her authoritative article "Effects of Maternal Employment on the Child," points out that the emotional problems of children *"have been found repeatedly to be related not to the mother's employment, but to her own emotional state."*

Do children raised with the help of caregivers grow up to be unresponsive adults, unable to relate warmly to others? Probably the keenest fear working mothers experience is worrying about the effect that having a surrogate mother will have on a young child.

With infants, the growing body of psychological opinion is that a child can "attach" successfully to a number of people, and indeed that this variety is normal and desirable. (See pages 4–6 for the meaning of attachment.) Rudolph Schaffer, professor of psychology at the University of Strathclyde, Glasgow, and author of *Mothering* (Harvard University Press, The Developing Child series, 1977), found that children can make multiple attachments by the age of eighteen months. And Schaffer adds this reassurance on the meaning of such multiple attachments: "Being attached to several people does not necessarily imply a shallower feeling toward each one, for an infant's capacity for attachment is not like a cake that has to be shared out. Love, even in babies, has no limits."

Will a child come to love the caregiver more than the mother? In study after study the same conclusion is reached: Mom is still Number One. The emotional intensity between mother and child creates a special relationship that is uniquely personal and intimate. Children in day care centers, as well as those cared for by sitters at home, consider their mothers the most important person in their lives, and turn to her more than anyone else for comfort and affection.

What effect does a mother's working have on her children's concept of sex roles—of what men and women do in life? Hoffman and Nye offer four important findings:

1. *"The effect of maternal employment was to raise the estimation of one's own sex—that is, each sex added positive traits usually associated with the opposite sex; daughters of working mothers saw women as competent and effective, while sons of working mothers saw men as warm and expressive."* The sharing of child-rearing and housekeeping tasks that usually results when a mother is working helps break down the stereotypes of passive mother/breadwinning father for children of both sexes. For those of us committed to non-sexist child-raising, this is indeed heartening.
2. *"Elementary-school daughters of working mothers see women as less restricted to their homes and more active in the world."* Allied to this finding is a more surprising one: When asked to describe which activities they thought women liked or disliked, the daughters of working mothers report more liking and less disliking of all activities—household, work, and recreation! This suggests that these children come to feel that working contributes to a woman's sense of self-esteem and pleasure in *all* activities in life.
3. *"Daughters of working mothers view work as something they will want to do when they are mothers."* If the mother enjoys her job, it is not surprising that her daughter will want to emulate her. But, report several women we spoke to, many

young girls need to see themselves as mothers before they can even envision themselves as having a career. "I'd ask her, 'What do you think you'll want to be when you grow up?'" one woman recalled. "And she'd always say, 'A mother.' I'd feel very disappointed, and I'd try to tell her about all the professions a girl can have nowadays. But finally I realized that she had to deal first with the basic need to be a mommy."

4. *"For girls, maternal employment seems to contribute to a greater admiration of the mother, a concept of the female role that includes less restriction and a wider range of activities, and a self-concept that incorporates these aspects of the female role."* For boys, the results are not that clear. "Maternal employment might influence their concept of the female role, but what the effects are on their attitudes toward their father and themselves depends very much on the circumstances surrounding the mother's employment."

To learn what the experts have to say specifically about day-care children versus those reared at home, see pages 93–94.

FROM INFANCY TO ADOLESCENCE— WHAT THE EXPERTS SAY

Having a working mother affects children differently at different ages (see also pages 3–7 on Timing Your Return to Work). Here are some professional observations:

Infancy and Preschool. Overall, the research is cautiously optimistic. Psychologist Claire Etaugh says: "A reasonably cautious conclusion that can be drawn from the available data is that high-quality nonmaternal care does not appear to have harmful effects on the preschool child's maternal attachment, intellectual development, social-emotional behavior, or physical health." But despite the flood of pronouncements in the popular press, scientists still know very little about how maternal employment affects the very young child. Data tend to be scant and the tie between cause and effect flimsy at best.

School-age. At this age, children of working mothers are more likely than those of at-home mothers to thrive on their growing independence and to respond well to household rules. Having household responsibilities has been shown to help children feel effective and competent, and to contribute to their self-esteem throughout their lives.

Adolescence. Not only do studies find few negative effects on teen-age children as a result of Mother working, but *most find positive effects.* Adolescent daughters of working mothers are more outgoing, more highly motivated, and do better in school. Sons, too, show better social and personality adjustment. Notes psychologist Lois Hoffman, commenting on these findings: "the overall picture suggests that maternal employment is better suited to the needs of adolescents than is full-time mothering."

Chapter Two

Childcare at Home—Mary Poppins and Other Possibilities

Once you take a job, the first—and maybe the most crucial—decision you will make is: How will my child be taken care of? Experts and mothers agree that *the success of a working mother hinges on how satisfactorily she manages to arrange for surrogate childcare.*

More than half of the children under the age of six with mothers in the work force are cared for at home. A number of advantages *do* come with this kind of setup: Keeping a child in his own environment can be less disruptive to him, especially when he's first getting used to your working. You won't have to agonize about what to do when your daughter has the sniffles or your son comes down with a stomach virus (although you may worry about the caregiver getting sick). Most important, your youngster will bask in the attention of someone whose major job is caring for her and her alone. She will have what child-development specialists consider the most important advantage: the chance to develop basic trust in a one-to-one relationship. Although these relationships can develop in group care as well, experts tend to agree that, when it is possible, very young babies are best cared for at home. And since few day-care centers or family day-care homes accept babies under six months, most infants are, in fact, cared for at home.

On the minus side: An at-home caregiver will cost you more than a day-care center, and she may offer less stimulation or companionship than your child would receive in a group situation. Says a bank teller who chooses a different solution—to have her four-year-old daughter cared for, along with three other children, in the home of

24

a neighborhood woman: "I feel it's very important for her to be part of a family, since I'm divorced. They're a surrogate family, and an enormous help to me."

Another drawback of in-home care can be the lack of supervision. When you send a child to a reputable center, you're at least assured that the people in charge of him are not, as one woman complained from bitter experience, "talking endlessly on the phone while the kids are eating potato chips and watching TV."

If you decide to have your child cared for at home, either by a relative or a paid caregiver, you will no doubt have a lot of questions, among them:

- Will my child be lonely at home? Will she miss me?
- What exactly is a "substitute mother"? How do I go about finding one?
- Will my child get too attached to the caregiver?
- What about values . . . discipline . . . daily routines?
- How can I be sure my own child-rearing style is maintained?
- How much will it cost? Can I afford it?

There are no easy answers to any of these questions. Like parenting itself, childcare arrangements are rarely perfect, and what works well for one family can be terrible for another. But experts and mothers agree on one vital point: *Consistency of care is the single most crucial factor for a child's well-being.* Noted child psychiatrist Stella Chess assures us that this does not mean you can never, never change caregivers once you've found one, or that you can't have a couple of people who alternate caring for your child. Warning against a "constantly changing array," Dr. Chess reminds us, however, that children are resilient and, in fact, that it is important for their growth to learn to deal with more than just a parent as caregiver. "Part of what children have to learn in this world," she says, "is that people are different and that you behave in one way in one situation and another way in another."

To provide predictable, consistent care, you will be looking for a caregiver who has a proven track record of reliability, who will be warm and friendly toward your children, and who will do her best to give them the kind of care you yourself give them.

What Are Your Options?

Depending on where you live and what your financial situation is, a number of choices are available to you—from the starched nanny dispatched by the big-city domestic agency, to the college drop-out who winds up mothering the children and you. Whatever the options in your own community, arm yourself with the following facts, based on what other working mothers have experienced, about what to look for and what to expect.

Care by Relatives

It seems like a perfect solution. Your mother says she'd love to take care of your son while you're at work. Or, your mother-in-law has been thinking of going to work herself but can't find an interesting job; what better opportunity for her than watching over her own granddaughter! You'll have lots of company if you choose this solution: 40 percent of children under the age of six are cared for by a relative. That special warm feeling that can exist between grandparent and grandchild, or between a child and any loving relative, is what draws so many parents to this type of childcare arrangement.

If your mother or aunt or sister-in-law agrees to take care of your child but refuses to accept anything for her services, override her generosity. *Insist on paying her.* Even a small sum (avoid paying in gifts) will put your relationship on a better basis. Paying your relative will repay you in two ways: She'll learn to appreciate your role as a working mother; and you'll feel less uneasy about sharing maternal responsibilities.

You can still run into trouble if you don't take the time to come to an agreement on the basic issue of your working. Laments the mother of an eighteen-month-old: "My mother is proud of my career, but she can't stand that her grandchild is not being cared for by his own mother." If your relative constantly makes you feel guilty—if she sees herself as the protector of your children, rather than as your helper—you may have more headaches than help. Seek out a different arrangement, no matter what hurt feelings result.

Sometimes the best relative to be in charge of your child is her own father. And many a graduate student, at-home worker, or househusband (whose wife is taking her turn at supporting the family) has found caring for his children an enriching experience.

If your children are of school age, you may have a childcare solution right under your own roof. Leaving a younger child in the care of his older brother or sister can work out fine, *if* the older child is reasonably responsible and mature. But be sure you take a few precautions. Watch out for resentment, which can quickly lead to problems. An eleven-year-old who's missed batting practice because he's had to mind his little sister can make life miserable for everyone around him.

Be realistic in your expectations; remember that not every child considers himself his brother's keeper. And don't forget that some youngsters are afraid to complain about helping out because they have an investment in pleasing their parents. Show your appreciation and respect by paying the older child, either in cash or extra privileges. Explain exactly what you want him to do—which days he's expected to cover, what the house rules are when he's in charge —and don't violate your agreements. (See also pages 53–56 for advice on handling children home alone.)

Housekeepers

At the very top of the list, both in expense and service rendered, is the woman (or occasional man) who often becomes a "substitute mother"—the housekeeper. This is the person whose role most closely approximates your own. The full-time housekeeper's tasks may vary from so-called light housekeeping (what one woman calls "everything I would do if I ever got around to it") to such heavy-duty chores as cooking for twenty-guest dinner parties, ironing shirts, and running the household while you and your husband are traveling in Europe. All this in addition to assuming full care of the children. Look behind any supermom career woman and you are likely to find this supersurrogate.

A housekeeper may live in or out, but either way you must be prepared to pay her more than you would a person who just takes care of children—a minimum of $125 a week in smaller cities or suburbs, up to $250 or more a week in large metropolitan areas. Salaries for live-in help are usually lower, since you are providing room and board.

Expect also to provide such benefits as two weeks' paid vacation, sick leaves, social security payments (many employers pay both their own and their employee's share), and regular salary review. Many housekeepers work a 5½-day week, which usually means they will work for you every other Saturday ("If she hesitates for a second on the telephone when I mention Saturdays," says one determined mother, "I don't even bother to set up an interview").

Who hires a full-time housekeeper? Money, of course, is the major consideration. Only people with substantial income can afford to part with a good portion of it in exchange for the peace of mind that comes with round-the-clock coverage. But don't assume that high-ticket help is necessarily a guarantee of security. A lot of mothers who employ competent housekeepers live in a perpetual state of terror that the housekeeper will quit. Many mothers have been known to make concessions that range from full summers off with pay to allowing the housekeeper to bring along her own children. And most have learned the hard way to maintain a list—the longer the better—of reliable backup help.

Families with very young children often find housekeepers a worthwhile investment. Kids under the age of six still need a lot of supervision; they can't yet be counted on to bathe, feed, or pick up after themselves. And riding herd on them and the household chaos that accumulates around them demands a lot of attention. The luxury of coming home to a house that is not strewn end to end with toys, to a roast in the oven and no dishes in the sink, has inspired many a working mother to sacrifice a hefty chunk of her salary to pay a housekeeper. "It's as if I hired a wife," one formerly married woman says with relief.

Baby-sitters

Next in responsibility to a housekeeper is a baby-sitter, who might be defined as anyone from your neighbor's teenage son to the middle-aged woman down the block whose primary responsibility is caring for your child. Most people agree that the term "baby-sitter" is an unfortunate one. Whether she lives with you or comes in each day while you're at work, *a sitter should not just sit.*

Beyond the routines of childcare—diapering, feeding, playing with children, helping with homework, transporting kids to and from lessons—what can one reasonably expect of this kind of care-giver?

Sitters are paid less than housekeepers—anywhere from $1.50 an hour for a young teenager to $3.35 an hour or more for a mature person who lives in a large city—and thus are usually not expected to do major household chores. But just as you yourself would not simply sit with your children if you were at home, so you can ask a sitter to take on many time-consuming tasks that don't really fit into the category of housework (these can be done while her charge is napping or playing by himself). Consider how much time you would save if you asked your sitter to:

- cut up celery and cheese for after-school snacks
- pick up milk and bread
- mail a package (while out wheeling the baby carriage)
- take clothes to the cleaner
- empty the dishwasher
- fold laundry
- put a casserole (which you've prepared) into the oven
- sew on name tapes
- make the cupcakes you promised to bring to the school fair.

You can easily double this list without abusing the working relationship. But be sure to define the job clearly at the beginning (be specific: don't just mention vague household chores).

Au pairs and **mother's helpers** are among the kinds of baby-sitters you might hire. Both of these terms refer to a person who usually lives in your home and helps care for your children in exchange for room and board and (sometimes) a modest salary (between $35 and $65 a week is customary).

A typical arrangement is twenty hours of light housekeeping and baby-sitting in exchange for full room and board.

The *au pair*, a term that originated from the custom of cultured young ladies of two different countries switching with one another as governesses, has now generally come to mean a foreign student or other young man or woman who exchanges domestic and childcare services for the chance to experience another style of life for a limited period, usually a year. In the last few years, the Department of Labor has cracked down on importing this kind of help and, except in rare instances, will not grant a prospective *au pair* the necessary work visa. Still, in those large metropolitan areas where there are domestic agencies and an abundance of foreign-language newspapers, it is sometimes possible to import an *au pair* (you must pay the fare both ways) or to hire one whom another family has sponsored. Sometimes having a family or other personal connection with officials in another country can help you locate and bring in an *au pair*.

A mother's helper can be a high school student who might welcome the chance to change his or her living situation or to earn a little extra money. A typical candidate is the oldest child from a large family whose experience with younger children and housekeeping skills will stand him or her in good stead in your home. College students are a natural for mother's-helper positions, particularly those who attend a school that offers no housing facilities. So are would-be actors, writers, musicians, artists—men and women who do the kind of low-remuneration work that lends itself well to a live-in childcare situation.

One problem with mother's helpers and *au pairs* is that young people who seek these jobs often tend to need a lot of mothering themselves. Many a busy woman has found herself acting as therapist-cum-mother-substitute to a youngster escaping from an unhappy family situation. (One woman nursed an eighteen-year-old through morning sickness and an abortion, only to find the mother's helper pregnant again three months later!) Avoid this type of relationship if you are not willing to cope with a certain amount of dependency.

The Right Person for You

There are, of course, as many varieties of caregivers as there are mothers. But one quality is essential: A caregiver must care. Successful caregivers genuinely like and enjoy children. Beyond the other basics of reliability and warmth, many women admit that they look for a friend, someone on their own wavelength whom they feel will then relate to their children the same way they do. Says one: "I figure if I like her, the kids'll like her, and we'll all get along better."

Are you seeking that certain someone "just like me"? Be more realistic: Find a person whose attitudes and style will mesh comfortably with your own. In fact, there is a virtue in hiring someone not at all like you. Your children may find a happy-go-lucky type a nice contrast to your own seriousness. And you may all flourish better with a keep-everything-tidy sort than your own once-a-week, tear-the-house-apart brand of housekeeping.

When choosing a caregiver, decide on your own priorities and then be prepared to compromise on what is less important to you. If you care more about developing your child's independence than maintaining a spotless house, forget about the woman who insists on spoon-feeding your three-year-old, even though your kitchen never looked cleaner. If you absolutely have to leave the house at eight o'clock, don't even interview someone who must travel an hour or more to your home (no matter how good her intentions, she's bound to disappoint you too often).

Trust your own instincts; they're more reliable than someone else's advice. Consider the unfortunate experience of Marcia, a young teaching assistant in an eastern college town who had always fared well with "a kind of flower child, hippie-type baby-sitter" for her son, Ethan. She allowed herself to be persuaded by an overcritical mother-in-law to hire instead Darlene, a kindly but "incredibly dull" housekeeper. For only slightly more money Darlene would take care of both child and house.

The results were disastrous. "Ethan was used to having college girls around him, people whose heads were in a place he understood. Along came Darlene, uneducated, not concentrating on him, actually more interested in the dishes, the laundry, and the cooking. One night Ethan came into my room in the middle of the night and just screamed at me, 'I hate Darlene!' "

Marcia admits that she, too, hated having Darlene in the house. She would certainly have done better sticking to her original priority of hiring people on her own wavelength.

Here are the choices you'll have to think out when you are looking for a caregiver:

Live-in or Live-out? If you have the room and are willing to sacrifice a certain amount of privacy, a caregiver who lives with you can be just the ticket. Her salary will be lower, she is available evenings and early mornings (an important plus for nurses, teachers, and other women whose jobs have irregular hours), and she may even be prevailed upon to work some weekends.

If you are a divorced mother with small children, a live-in person —especially someone who's willing to exchange her services for room and board and only a token salary—can really ease the stress of working and raising children alone. Having someone on the premises all the time will give both you and your children a sense of security and continuity. And it will let you go out in the evenings or work late in the office without the hassle of arranging for sitters in advance.

Because a live-in person is sharing your home, it's essential that you establish personal rules of conduct that are acceptable to you both. Is she to use the telephone? Is she free to invite friends to your home, and if so, at what hours? (You don't want to deprive a teenager of a normal social life, but you also don't want to wind up playing hostess to an ongoing party.) Will you all eat together or will you expect her to feed the children ahead of time? Will she join you on family vacations or weekend holidays?

Don't be afraid to set down firm rules such as no smoking, no boyfriends in the house, no drinking (again, these are your personal decisions to make). Be sure you both agree to these prohibitions right in the beginning. You can always relax them later on.

Male or Female?   Young men can make wonderful caregivers for both boys and girls. As living examples of males in nurturing roles, they help break down the sex-role stereotyping that so many families are trying to combat. An added bonus: They are often much more relaxed than young women about doing housework.

One of the most successful situations we came across involved a man. Sally, a busy lawyer who has two children in school and who describes herself as working "seventeen hours a day," has managed beautifully with the help of Robert, a "lovely out-of-work actor . . . and a marvelous cook." She comments that she deals much better with him than with the women she had hired, probably because "the women were overqualified (I wanted only creative, bright people around my kids) and resisted doing things."

It is sad but true that overqualified women may resent domestic duties. The question of what constitutes "overqualified" when it comes to childcare is a painful issue (can anyone really be "too capable" to care for our most valuable resource?); but the fact is that some women avoid this controversial subject entirely simply by hiring a man and not "exploiting their sisters."

Do children cared for by a male gain a different perspective on sex roles? Research on families in which the father is the primary parent is still too new to offer conclusive results, but informal observation suggests that the more contact boys and girls have with males in nurturing roles—as caregivers, primary-school teachers, homemakers—the broader and richer will be their concept of their own options in society.

Old or Young?   Older women have traditionally worked as sitters; many a grandmother who has raised her own children will find caring for yours a perfect way to supplement her pension or social-security income. And hiring a grandparent as a sitter can be a marvelous means of giving your children experience with another generation—especially if they have no grandparents of their own nearby.

Besides checking that the person you choose is healthy enough to chase after your active youngster, you'll want to make sure she can successfully bridge the generation gap. When you interview her or observe her with your child, watch out for telltale traces of a bygone age of child-rearing. These needn't be as extreme as the elderly lady who proudly reported that her one-year-old charge had stopped sucking his thumb after she tied his hands to the crib. Or the woman who left a two-year-old on the potty for an hour, telling him to "be a good boy and surprise Mommy." Or even the well-meaning grandmother who couldn't spend the morning in the park with the children because she had to put up baked potatoes for their lunch.

But if an older woman seems unable to adjust to today's more casual style of childcare—if she won't tolerate a little paint on an overall or she is afraid to let your nine-year-old ride his bike—you and she had better not sign on for any full-time commitment.

Another problem with older people is the feeling described by twenty-eight-year-old Nina: "I thought of her as my grandmother. But how do you tell your grandmother what to do each day? She's older; she's supposed to know more than you do." If you feel this way, better hire someone closer to your own age.

A Non–English-Speaking Caregiver? If you live in a large coastal city, a university community, or any area in which there is a substantial foreign community, you may want to hire a non–English-speaking person to care for your child. Recent immigrants (many of whom can find no other work here) may be well educated in their own country, come from middle-class backgrounds, have fewer master-servant hangups, and thus treat their jobs with a high degree of professionalism. Elizabeth, a California history professor who wanted a sitter comparable to herself in values and intellectual capacity, found this need well served by hiring the wives of foreign graduate students. Describing a woman caregiver who had been trained as a pharmacist in her native Chile, she comments, "Her English was not perfect, but I'd rather have someone whose English is not perfect because they speak a foreign tongue than someone who uses language that I wouldn't want used in my home."

Hiring someone who speaks virtually no English at all is another matter (we are still marveling at the New Jersey psychotherapist who engaged a Bulgarian woman to care for her newborn son, and then called home twice a day, "so that David can hear English spoken while he's up").

If you are thinking of hiring a caregiver who is not fluent in English, the age of the children is an important consideration. Dependability and a pleasant disposition may be all the person you hire needs to see that your nine-year-old and your seven-year-old don't get into trouble after school. But you would certainly think twice about leaving a toddler who is just beginning to express himself verbally with someone he can't talk to easily.

Making things work with a foreign-speaking person can simply be a matter of buying a dictionary and having a little patience. If the person possesses other desirable qualities, the inconvenience may be well worth it. One mother hired Maria, "a fat old lady, very motherly, who spoke hardly any English." She was supposed to do housework and start dinner, but "her idea of housework was washing the dolls' faces and giving the children lots of kisses. I overlooked a lot, though, because the kids loved her dearly." In fact, Maria's arrangement with the family worked out so well—and her English improved so speedily—that she continued working for them long after they no longer needed full-time help.

For Now or Always? Be prepared to make changes. Even after you've found the right person for you and your family, remember that what works now may not work forever. Children's needs change as they move through different developmental stages. The kindly grandmother who happily bounced your baby boy on her knee may not look so cheerful when at age two-and-a-half he turns the house upside down. Your fourteen-month-old may be content to play alone in his playpen under the eye of a neighborhood teenager, but in another few months, he'll need a group situation part of the time.

Just because you are relieved to find any solution at all to the childcare problem does not mean you should cling to an arrangement after it's outlived its usefulness. This can happen when a second child is born and the sitter is unable or unwilling to care for a baby. Or when a child clearly needs the company of other children—true of all children beyond eighteen months—and the sitter is reluctant to play hostess to a handful of toddlers. This is often a problem with the kind of older caregiver who loves babies but lacks the imagination or playfulness to deal successfully with an older child. If your caregiver does not seem able to grow with your child, you may have to make new plans at some point. Don't wait for your son or daughter to become actively unhappy; keep a watchful eye on the situation, and take prompt action if you feel it's necessary.

Finding a Caregiver

You've got before you your own private image of Mary Poppins, that near-perfect right arm who will help you perform the delicate balancing act of working motherhood. Now how do you go about making her (or him) materialize in your own home?

For starters, accept the fact that there is no surefire formula for success in this arena. Although it's possible that one phone call will miraculously produce an energetic grandmother whom your children adore, you are more likely to sweat it out for a few weeks on the phone with friends, neighbors, and assorted employment services before the right person comes along. The most important thing to remember is: *Don't panic and, above all, don't settle for someone you don't really like.* Better to press your mother or other relative into temporary service while you explore all possibilities of finding permanent help.

Another very important thing to keep in mind is that people who are looking for jobs usually want to start right away. If you begin searching for a caregiver sometime before you need her full-time, be prepared to pay her even before she starts working. If you do this, it makes sense to have her come in part-time for a while and get acquainted with you and your child.

We find that old standby, word of mouth, is still the best way to locate your baby-sitter or housekeeper. Asking around can mean making a pest of yourself on supermarket lines and at dinner parties, but it may also be the only way you'll ever hear of Mary Jane's sitter's sister who's moving here from Ohio and needs a job.

If you find yourself in the pediatrician's office or a playground or any other place where mothers and children gather, keep your ears open for possibilities (one woman latched onto a first-rate housekeeper by eavesdropping on a waiting-room conversation). And by all means ask the sitters of people you know if they have friends or relatives looking for work. Be persistent; take the initiative. Follow up with phone calls rather than waiting for someone to get in touch with you.

Tacking up notices on neighborhood bulletin boards is another way of finding help. Type or write your message clearly, and write your phone number vertically a number of times along the bottom of the notice so that interested applicants can tear it off.

Encourage your pediatrician (or even your obstetrician) to serve as a clearinghouse for childcare information. Suggest that he or she hang up a bulletin board on which parents can post notices.

Placing an advertisement in a local newspaper involves a small investment, but it's usually worth it. Be as specific as possible. And be sure to say "References required." If you expect the person to work Saturdays or some evenings, say so; and indicate whether or not the job includes housework ("light housekeeping" and "plain cooking" are good, unambiguous terms).

It is usually best to specify the number and ages of the children: While it's true that "two preschoolers" or "four children" might scare off some applicants, you will be left with fewer but stronger

(a newspaper advertisement)
Help Wanted

Responsible, warm person to care for 2-year-old girl and 7-year-old boy. Live in or out, 5½ days (every other Saturday). Light housekeeping. Recent references required. 555-6410 (days); 555-3345 (eves.).

(a bulletin-board notice)
Energetic Housekeeper Wanted

Pleasant, mature person needed by working couple to care for large house and 3 school-age children. 11 A.M. until after dinner, 5 days. Must have recent references and driver's license.

555-6410	555-6410	555-6410	555-6410	555-6410	555-6410

candidates. Leave your options open by not specifying the salary in the ad.

When placing an ad, keep an eye on the readership of the paper in which it appears. If, for example, you don't want a hippie-type unemployed actress or a part-time sculptor, steer clear of a counterculture newspaper.

By all means, follow up any likely billboard notices or advertisements that appear under "Situations wanted." People who go to the trouble of advertising themselves can often be counted on to be responsible and mature.

Interviewing a Caregiver

Judging a person in an interview calls for a combination of intuition and careful evaluation. Gut reactions are indeed important; how a person looks, talks, even the way he or she enters the room

HELP—AND WHERE TO FIND IT

- Employment offices of colleges and nursing schools (those without living quarters are especially good for live-in help, and most have good screening services)
- Foreign-language newspapers (especially if you speak the language or would like to learn it)
- Small-town newspapers (if you live in an urban area, ads here may help you uncover eager and capable helpers who want to try the big city)
- Notices in high schools (a good source of after-school help) and in the pediatrician's office
- Senior-citizen centers (an excellent source of part-time help)
- Employment agencies specializing in domestic help (note, too, that some locales have agencies for mother's helpers and other temporary help)
- Your state employment office (check here too about government-funded training programs, which may supply well-trained household help at a fair price)
- Social welfare agencies, including Family Service Association, Catholic Charities, Federation of Protestant Welfare Agencies

reveal a lot immediately. But a carefully structured face-to-face meeting can tell you both a good deal more about each other. Here are some guidelines that will help you make the most of each interview.

1. *Exchange basic information on the telephone before even scheduling an interview.* "I was amazed how many people you can weed out right away," one woman told us. "So many people just don't read ads carefully or maybe don't really know what they want themselves. My notice clearly said 'sleep-in' and three women called who only wanted sleep-out positions."

2. *Ask for recent references, and be sure to check them.* Many a mother, happy to find that the prospective employee has worked steadily for the last few years, neglects to actually talk to previous employers and to find out about the appli-

cant's past performance. Information like "she's a marvelous cook and wonderful with kids, but you have to get after her about coming in on time," can be extremely helpful. Be sure, too, to find out why the applicant left her last job.

3. *Describe the job in detail, using as a general rule "the worst comes first."* If watering the plants and feeding the cat are included in the duties, this is the time to say so. Try not to fall into the gratitude trap ("As long as the kids are safe . . . I don't really care about anything else") and don't be ashamed if the list of duties is a long one, as long as you are paying fairly for the work.

Be specific about the salary, raises, hours, holidays, sick leave, and any other details you haven't covered on the telephone. Enumerate any childcare responsibilities that you think might pose a problem (give some thought to these in advance; try writing them down).

4. *Have your children present for at least part of the interview.* As one woman put it, "If they stick around, chances are that person has something." Children are uncanny at sensing people's interest in them; watch them smell out the gushing "child lover" even as you're trying to convince yourself that her phoniness is just nervousness.

The response of very small children can be particularly revealing. Says the mother of a two-and-a-half-year-old about her interview with a grandmotherly baby-sitter: "She sent out such loving signals that Rebecca simply walked over and climbed into her lap. I'm glad she stayed in the room. She really made the decision for me."

5. *Ask specific questions that will encourage the applicant to express herself honestly rather than to try to second-guess you.* For example, you will learn more from asking, "What would you do if David hit Martin while they're in the park?" than you will by inquiring, "What are your feelings about discipline?"

6. *Give the applicant plenty of time to answer your questions and to ask ones of her own.* (If none are forthcoming, you can say, "Do you have any questions?" or "What would you like to ask me?") Be an active listener, and be encouraged if you and she feel comfortable talking to each other.

"WHAT WOULD YOU PLAY WITH A FOUR-YEAR-OLD?"

Some Interview Questions

- "Josh is about ready for toilet training. How would you go about that?" (Here's a chance to discover her attitude about a sensitive issue.)
- "How many days were you sick on your last job?" (*Not* "How is your health?")
- "What games would you play with a four-year-old?" Give her an A+ for proficiency in games like Candyland or Trouble; any skill whatsoever in arts and crafts, especially if you're weak in those areas; an honest answer such as "I'm willing to play anything they want." Remember, too, that older children also need companionship. Says one anxious mother: "Every time it rains and I know the kids are home alone with Hilda, I worry they'll either be fighting with each other or watching TV. I'd give anything to have someone who'll drop everything and organize a game of checkers."
- "What would you do if one of the children had a nosebleed?" (Or cut himself? Or burned herself?) Once the person is hired, you will make clear rules for safety. At this point, you want to get some feeling for her ability to handle everyday mishaps.
- "What do you like to cook?" (A better question than "How is your cooking?") Again, give credit for honesty. If a responsible-seeming person confesses that she can't do much more than broil a hamburger, give her points for credibility and think about simplifying your meals.

Watch for direct eye contact, for enthusiasm that seems genuine and not likely to burn itself out in a few months. Look for a real appreciation of children, for a professional attitude toward working, for signs of enough flexibility and intelligence to adjust to the unpredictability of daily life around youngsters.

7. *Finally, remember that the purpose of the interview is not to see how many questions the applicant can answer successfully.* Rather, it's a chance for you and her to size each

other up. Keep in mind that you are not looking for someone to bring up your children. That's your job. What you can expect from a good caregiver is the support that will help both you and your children grow as independent human beings.

Chapter Three

Managing Childcare at Home

I wanted to work but I didn't want to have a servant.
It went against my grain. I ended up calling the
baby-sitter Mrs. Mullins and she called me Nina.
— A TWENTY-EIGHT-YEAR-OLD MAGAZINE EDITOR

Nina is not alone. Indeed, women who can successfully manage whole departments in an office are often thrown by the prospect of employing a person in their own home. Grown women have been tyrannized by teenagers; thirty-year-olds are intimidated by women twice their age.

Whether you have hired a grandmother or a teenager, *establish a businesslike relationship right from the start.*

Salary and Benefits

At present, few government guidelines about salary and benefits exist for domestic workers. Legally, domestic workers have been covered since 1974 by federal minimum-wage legislation (before that time, their median annual income was under $2500, and their benefits were strictly at the caprice of their employers). By law, any sitter who works more than twenty hours a week must be paid the minimum wage ($3.35 in 1984). In practice, however, wage and benefit standards for household workers are nearly impossible to enforce, and a great many workers continue to suffer from unconscionably low salaries and virtually nonexistent benefits (for example, it's not unheard of for a family to "lay off" a housekeeper in the summer when the children go to camp).

You can enjoy a dignified relationship with your caregiver by sharing the wisdom of experienced working mothers: *Don't exploit the situation.* Maintain the same standards of professionalism you would expect on your own job. Agree in advance on a set number of sick days and holidays (many women base this on the benefits given by their own employers). Set up a schedule of regular salary review. Outline the hours, duties, and privileges clearly at the outset (see below for a code of standards that covers all these issues). You may even want to establish these terms in writing.

If you are not sure what to pay, ask friends who have hired babysitters. Or be guided by the current federal minimum wage. And when in doubt, overpay.

If you only need help a few hours each day—say, from three o'clock, when the children come home from school, through the dinner hour—overpaying can be a fine way of assuring yourself the best possible people at what amounts to the least cost. Carol, a California mother of three school-age children, pays $6.00 an hour (three times the going rate in her community) to a twenty-five-year-old faculty wife to supervise the children's activities and generally manage the household during the after-school hours. The $80 a week she pays for this service is still less than she would have to pay for full-time help.

STANDARDS FOR HOUSEHOLD EMPLOYMENT*

Wages

- Salary should conform to local cost of living (at least minimum wage, higher in expensive areas) and wages should be increased at least once a year.
- Specialized skills—for example, gourmet cooking, tutoring children, altering clothing—should command a higher wage.
- Gifts of food, clothing, or household goods should not be considered part of the wages.

- Pay periods should be regular and means of payment should be agreed upon in advance.

Hours

- Live-in workers should earn one and a half times their hourly rate for work done in excess of forty hours a week; two times the rate after forty-eight hours.
- Full-time, live-out workers should earn one and a half times the hourly rate after forty-eight hours.

Benefits

- Employers must report earnings and make payments toward Social-Security insurance. They should also file quarterly statements with the IRS. Check your local Social Security office for further information.

Sick Leave and Holidays

- There should be a minimum of one day of paid sick leave a year for each day per week worked—in other words, a five-day-a-week person would be entitled to five days of paid sick leave a year.
- Live-in employees should have at least eight legal holidays a year. Full-time, live-out workers are entitled to six such holidays; day workers, at least one paid holiday a year.

Vacations

- Two weeks with pay is the rule for full-time employees (families who have longer vacations often elect to give their employees the same time off). Vacation time for part-time employees should equal at least two days a year for each day per week worked.

* Based on *Standards for Household Employment*, by the National Committee on Household Employment.

Good Childcare Can Be Taught

Remember that it is up to you to see that the caregiver handles the children in a way that is acceptable to you. "What many women don't realize," says a psychologist who conducts parent-education groups, "is that baby-sitters can be *taught* to care for children in certain ways, just as mothers and fathers can be taught to be more effective parents."

Go over with the caregiver everything you can think of about your own and your children's likes and dislikes—their favorite games, lunch menus, when and where they should go outside, even what they should wear.

In the beginning, leave little to chance: Don't expect the caregiver to know intuitively that Debbie can't fall asleep unless the closet door is closed or that Jason is allowed to take his bear into the bathtub or that Nicky is the only child in the world who loathes French fries. Laying down a firm foundation of *your* values and preferences will help her use her own judgment as she gets more accustomed to the job. Unless you're an incurable optimist or your caregiver has signed a lifetime contract in blood, it pays to write down all these instructions; you never know when you may be breaking in someone new.

As the weeks go by, take a good look at how the person interacts with your children; listen carefully to the children's reports; ask direct questions. If you don't agree that your children should wash their hands five times a day, simply state what you expect along these lines. ("Please have the kids wash up before meals, or if they've played with mud and it looks like they're going to smear it on the walls.")

If your sitter or housekeeper is given to watching soap operas all afternoon, assign her specific chores that will occupy her during that time. If you worry that she will use the television as an instant sitter—a fear of many working parents—consider forbidding television entirely. Or lay down firm limits as to which programs the children can watch and for how long. If you like to see your children more actively involved, plan a trip to a museum or library and have the sitter accompany them. Watch your local newspaper for announcements of interesting events they might enjoy.

If you are committed to nonsexist child-rearing and you overhear your sitter telling your five-year-old son that "big boys don't cry," sit her down and explain carefully your own attitude about what boys do or don't do. If her feelings differ markedly from your own on important matters like this, consider replacing her with someone more sympathetic to your point of view.

Discipline is another sensitive issue. Make it clear to the caregiver and to the children that she is in authority when you are not there, but be sure that you and she see eye to eye on how that authority is to be enforced. Be as specific as possible. Saying "The next time Jeff throws a ball at his sister make him sit on his bed for half an hour," is more effective than the vague "You have my permission to punish him if he misbehaves." Be on guard against the caregiver who enforces no discipline at all to show you how kindly and loving she is. Or for the one who tries to impress you with her rules and regulations.

Watch out, too, for the unsociable caregiver. The parents of eight-year-old Mike, for example, were puzzled when he suddenly refused to stay with the sitter, insisting that she didn't like him. It turned out that Mike's budding sense of humor was being squelched because the sitter didn't laugh at his jokes or listen to his stories. "She never cares about anything I tell her," Mike complained. And he was right. This kind of unresponsiveness can be as harmful to a child's development as out-and-out unkindness.

Physical stimulation is also important. Cuddling and kissing a baby, giving a hug to a toddler, a friendly pat on the back to a ten-year-old—all the everyday expressions of affection—these are acts that you can expect and encourage in the caregiver.

The Trial Period

Some experts recommend an actual tryout period—say, a day or a weekend during which you try out a few sitters—but this can be time-consuming and impractical. Instead, hire carefully and make it clear that the first few weeks will be a trial period. Set a date for a meeting at the end of that time, when you can both air your beefs and renegotiate if necessary.

The trial period is also the time for your children to adjust to the new person in their lives—and for you to keep tabs on that adjustment. Try to take a few hours off to observe the caregiver in action. Make your leave-taking as casual as possible, and impress upon your child that the caregiver is in charge while you are away. It helps to remind your son or daughter of exactly when you will be home. If you express confidence that you are leaving your youngster in good hands, chances are he will be comfortable. Do not be overly concerned if your child cries or is otherwise upset when you leave; this is natural in the beginning, and should only become a source of real concern if the crying doesn't stop soon after you leave or if it persists for more than a week or so. (For a further discussion of children's adjustment, see pages 4–7.)

Spies

No matter how trustworthy the sitter is, regardless of how happy your child seems, it is a good idea to get firsthand reports about the caregiver's conduct. A neighbor, your child's teacher, the parent of a child who visits yours, a relative—ask any of these people who see the sitter with your child to let you know how they appear to be getting along. Don't wait for volunteered reports; ask specific questions. Was she talking to the child? Did he seem occupied happily? Was she on time picking him up at school?

"EVERYTHING'S FINE . . ." AND OTHER DANGER SIGNS

No matter how carefully you choose a caregiver, there will be times you can't help worrying. You'll probably have no trouble spotting evidence of neglect, abuse, or indifference, but there are subtler danger signs you may not have thought of.

1. The "everything's fine" syndrome. Remember, the sitter has a stake in issuing only good reports to show she's doing a good job. If that's all you get, encourage her to share with you some of the day's events, including any problematical incidents, no matter how insignificant they seem to her. Remind her that you want to take an active interest in what goes on in your home and with your children. If she persists in painting only rosy pictures, you may have to replace her with someone more realistic.
2. A busy signal on the phone every time you call. One mother who tried to rationalize this as "just bad timing" paid a surprise visit to her house and found the housekeeper chatting merrily on the phone to a friend while her children were glued to the TV.
3. Your children seem consistently subdued when you arrive home. Most young children are excited and even boisterous at this time.

The sitter may be exerting too much control. A serious talk with her can help ease the situation.

Safety

Make sure that anyone in charge of your children knows how to stop bleeding (applying direct pressure on the wound or cut will stop bleeding from all but the deepest lacerations, yet a surprising number of adults don't know this and will just keep mopping up the flow until they and the child panic) . . . what to do if a child is choking . . . how to handle a burn, and so on. Consult your local Red Cross chapter for information on first aid and home nursing courses. You'll find straightforward easy-to-understand first-aid instructions, as well as valuable general childcare advice, in the handy booklet *Dear Baby-sitter,* by Vicki Lansky (Meadowbrook Press, 1982).

Paste a list of poisons and their antidotes on the inside of your medicine-cabinet door (you can photocopy this from a home medical guide, or write to your local board of health). Be sure to paste the phone number of the nearest Poison Control Center right next to your telephone; a Poison Control official will give emergency telephone instructions on how to deal with any harmful substance your child may have ingested. These and other numbers—pediatrician, internist, dentist, and so on—can be incorporated into a "Baby-sitter's Card" (see below).

Post your own card in a prominent place in your kitchen or in another room that has a telephone:

Baby-sitter's Card

Mother's office:
Father's office:
Julia Brown (grandmother):
Leslie and James Stonier (neighbors, apt. 5C):
Sally's school:
Jerry's school:

After-school playgroup (Tuesdays and Thursdays):
POLICE:
FIRE DEPARTMENT:
TAXI SERVICE (call for emergency transportation):
Dr. Lipsett (children's doctor):
Mercy Hospital:
POISON CONTROL:
Martell's Pharmacy (they will deliver):
Reliable Grocery (will deliver in an emergency):
Plumber:
Electrician:
Washer/Dryer Repair Service:

Have on hand an easy-to-read children's home medical guide. *A Sigh of Relief* (Bantam Books, 1977) is a good choice.

Tell your sitter exactly how she should handle an emergency that requires she go to a hospital. For example, you may want to be sure she calls you or your husband first so that you can meet her at the emergency room. Make sure always to leave enough money in the house for a taxi ride to a doctor or hospital.

If you travel or are otherwise inaccessible during the day, it is a good idea to leave a release letter authorizing the person in charge of your children to give permission for emergency surgical procedures (some hospitals will not even remove a splinter or set a broken bone without written permission from a parent). Check with your local emergency room for the exact wording they would prefer on a release letter.

To avoid unnecessary accidents, child-proof your home even more diligently than you would if you were there all the time. And be sure to stock your medicine chest with antiseptics, Band-Aids, aspirin, and other staples.

A CHECKLIST OF CAREGIVER CAUTIONS AND PRECAUTIONS

1. Are all important phone numbers posted clearly near the telephone? (Your office number and your husband's and any other key rela-

tives'; the pediatrician; pharmacy; trusted friends' and neighbors' numbers; your children's school; Poison Control Center)

2. Is the sitter familiar with your home? (Does she know how to use the appliances? Where to find the children's rain boots? Where you keep the fuses—and how to change one?)

3. What are the ground rules for the caregiver? (Can she entertain guests? Use the telephone? Watch TV?)

4. What about the children? (Can they invite friends over without checking with you first? Are they permitted to call you at the office?)

5. Are rules for safety clearly spelled out? (Is your four-year-old allowed to plug in an appliance? Is your six-year-old allowed to stay alone for fifteen minutes?)

When the Caregiver Is Absent

The truth is *you* may drag yourself into the office with the world's worst migraine, but the person you hire to care for your children won't necessarily have the same blind devotion to her job. Baby-sitters get the flu. Housekeepers leave suddenly to nurse ailing relatives in far-off lands. *Au pairs* come down with the chicken pox and take to their beds in your house.

How can you best handle these unexpected absences? First of all, expect them. Keep a list of backup sitters or neighbors who will not flinch at an early-morning phone call. Don't be shy about asking a friend to pinch-hit for you; you can always repay the favor on the weekend. Second, make it clear to your caregiver right from the start that you expect her to give you as much early warning as possible if she's going to be absent or late. You and she have agreed on a fair number of sick days; encourage her not to abuse this agreement. Finally, consider this novel idea: Have the sitter herself be responsible for backup—with the backup person subject to your approval, of course.

Your community may be a source of last-minute baby-sitting help. In Berkeley, California, for example, the Sick Child Care Program, financed by a combination of city, state, and federal monies, supplies trained caregivers for a sliding-scale fee. Although it is intended as a resource for parents whose children must stay home

IN CASE OF ACCIDENT . . .

If your housekeeper breaks her leg putting away the groceries, if your cocker spaniel bites the baby-sitter, you may wind up losing more than just a trusted household employee. At-home accidents have been known to cost employers the equivalent of a year or more in salary, particularly if the injured person is unable to work for any length of time.

To be sure that you—and your employee—are protected, check your homeowner's insurance policy very carefully. Most liability clauses cover only a modest fixed payment, usually under $1000, although some insurance policies provide for much higher sums if the injured person should sue for negligence.

A good development is the expansion in most states of workmen's compensation laws. Workmen's compensation, long a staple benefit for factory and office workers, provides payment to an injured party without that person having to prove negligence. Essentially a form of no-fault insurance, it varies in premiums and coverage from state to state. Most states require that any household employee who works more than forty hours a week be covered by workmen's compensation insurance. Your insurance agent or the state's workmen's compensation board can give you the information you need to make sure you are covered.

---

from school or day care on account of illness, this kind of program can also serve as a backup when the sitter is ill.

Firing a Caregiver

She's tippling from your best Scotch . . . your children simply hate her . . . you and she have turned out to be worlds apart in child-rearing styles. So why does your heart go into your throat when you say tonight's the night to fire her? Remind yourself that if you hire for professional competence, on occasion you must fire for professional incompetence.

Don't Procrastinate. The experience will be worse for you, the children, and the sitter herself if you allow your displeasure to linger on. Simply summon up the same skills you practice all day on your job and tell her she will have to go, and why. Depending on the circumstances, you may want to give her two weeks' notice and/or severance pay to tide her over. Try to apply the same rules of fair play you would expect of your own employer.

If you do find yourself firing a caregiver, ask yourself how you might have avoided getting into that predicament. And try to learn from your own mistakes. Did you, for example, fall into the trap of being so grateful that someone was "doing your job" that you never made any demands at all? This kind of misguided guilt practically guarantees that you'll be disappointed.

Amy, a Chicago school librarian with two small boys, describes how when she first began working, she would say to the sitter, "I just want you to watch over the baby and love him." And that's what each sitter did—leaving Amy to be greeted each evening by unwashed lunch dishes, an obstacle course of Tinker Toys and building blocks in the front hall, and the unhappy prospect of dinner to prepare from scratch. Eventually she discovered that she could, for the same $2 an hour, find a sensitive, loving baby-sitter who would also take responsibility for certain basic housekeeping chores. "Now when I interview," declares Amy self-assuredly, "I say, 'This is a very hard job. I want dishes done, I want all the toys picked up, I want you to start dinner some days.' And I've had no trouble finding terrific people."

A Word About Jealousy

The intimacy that develops when a child and the person who cares for him interact warmly is, we believe, a necessary and important quality to be nourished by parents and caregivers alike. And it is reassuring to know that all research points to the fact that children almost invariably prefer their parents, no matter how attached they are to a caregiver. But if you find yourself resenting the person who takes care of your son or daughter, it's a good idea to take a hard look at your own relationship with your youngster.

Is your son clinging to the caregiver because she is actually warmer and more loving to him? Does your daughter perhaps sense a tension in you about your own qualities as a mother? Sometimes just making an effort to spend more time with your child—without the distractions of your job, your marriage, your household responsibilities—will help ease feelings of competitiveness you may have with others who care for him.

What you call jealousy may really be regret at having missed out on some important event in your child's life. "My baby-sitter saw his first steps and I was heartbroken," says one woman. But she quickly adds that the feeling passed when she realized that there are few one-shot experiences in a child's development, and that she would have many chances to share in other events.

Jealousy and competitiveness can sometimes be tricky feelings to confront and work through. If you persistently resent your housekeeper or baby-sitter, don't give notice at the office; instead, consider seeking professional guidance to help you cope with these complicated emotions.

LATCHKEY CHILDREN—PLANNING AND PRECAUTIONS

More than three million children under the age of thirteen are latchkey children—they come home to a house in which there is no adult supervision at all. If your child is one of these, be sure to listen carefully to what he says and does. Ask him directly how he feels, and be wary if he is evasive. Assure him that you can help make his experience more comfortable.

Recent studies have shown that latchkey children are often worried, fearful, or just plain lonely and bored. What's more, they usually don't share these feelings with their parents because they don't want to make their parents feel bad about a situation they can't do anything about.

You may find that the ten-year-old who snuggles in bed after school is relishing her privacy, not cowering in fear. On the other hand, the twelve-year-old who talks a lot about his pet dying (a common fear of latchkey children) may be expressing more deep-seated worries. Only by staying tuned in can you know what your own child is experiencing.

If your child is very uneasy, try to plan change-of-pace activities like visits to other children, or to programs at the Y or at the library. Having plans for even one or two days a week can make all the difference. Another possibility is to hire, usually at very low cost, a "homework helper," an older teenager who accompanies your son or daughter home, helps with homework, and generally offers companionship until you get there.

Finally, look into the possibility of after-school programs run by your child's school or by a community agency (see box, page 38).

Here are the most important precautions to keep in mind if your son or daughter is unsupervised at home:

1. *Fire safety.* Parents voice this fear more than any other. Some solutions: Do not let even an older child use the stove when you are not home. Tell your child exactly what to do if she smells smoke or suspects a fire emergency. If you're not sure yourself, ask a representative of your local fire department to pay a visit.

2. *Other emergencies.* Learning the basics of first aid and how to handle simple household emergencies helps a child gain the confidence he needs to deal with any kind of problems that come up. One mother was delighted to hear from her thirteen-year-old son only *after* he had called the plumber, mopped up the flood, and soothed the little sister who had dropped four apple cores and one banana peel down the toilet.

3. *Phone calls.* Teach your child never to say, "My mother isn't home," to a stranger on the telephone, no matter how official the caller sounds. The best thing to say, counsels Kathleen McNamara of Houston's CHATTERS program, is simply, "My mother is busy right now. Can I have her call you back?" Then the child can call the parent and relay the message.

4. *Strangers.* Save your child from having to make hard choices. Instruct her not to open the door to any stranger unless she knows the person by name beforehand.

5. *Signs of crime.* Teach your child to recognize such danger signs as a broken window, unlocked door, suspicious lights on, and not to enter the house. He should go instead to a neighbor's house or to a nearby store and call a parent or the police. If you live in a high-crime area, consider installing a burglar alarm.

6. *Keys.* Carrying house keys inside a book bag or knapsack is a lot safer than on the highly visible neck chain. To make keys easier to find inside the bag, attach them to a large pom-pom with a bell inside.

7. *Sibling strife.* Friction and fighting can cause distress for children left in each other's care. Older children complain that younger

ones won't obey them; younger siblings insist they are bullied. And parents resent having to be telephone referees. A solution is to pay children to care for each other, making each of them—regardless of age—accountable to each other and to you. The mother of two sons, 11 and 13, reports success with this system. "I used to dread three-thirty," she told us, "because I knew the phone would start ringing, and I'd hear them killing each other on both extensions. One day I sat down and offered to pay them a dollar each if certain chores were done and only if there was no fighting. The next time they called, and I heard yelling and complaining, I reminded them of the deal and then hung up quickly. My younger boy actually called back five minutes later to say, 'Mom, we just wanted you to know we're getting along better now.'"

8. *Chores and snacks.* A not-too-long list of tasks to do—folding laundry, setting the table, feeding a pet—will help to fight boredom and loneliness, especially if it goes along with a chatty note. One mother leaves a plateful of cut-up vegetables and a favorite dip, along with a note that says "With love, for a tired fifth-grader, from your friendly neighborhood mom."

Latchkey Resources

• CHATTERS (Children's Home Alone Telephone Reassurance Service). Funded by the United Way, this Houston, Texas, program offers telephone assistance, home visits in an emergency, training in safety and home activities (like cooking and crafts), as well as parenting seminars. For information on how to start a similar program in your community, call 713–529–3931, or write Kathleen McNamara, Neighborhood Centers, 5005 Fannin, Houston, Texas 77004.

• "I Can Do It." This eight-week program for children covers practical needs—making snacks, doing chores, handling emergencies, using the phone—as well as psychological issues like dealing with fears and loneliness. Contact Camp Fire, Inc., Program Department, 4601 Madison Avenue, Kansas City, Missouri 64112.

• School-Age Child Care Project. This research and development project is primarily concerned with after-school care within the schools themselves (see pages 83–84), but it is a valuable source of information on all aspects of school-aged childcare. Write to School-Age Child Care Project, Center for Research on Women, Wellesley College, Wellesley, Mass. 02181.

- Two booklets: *Prepared for Today*, available for a nominal fee from your local Boy Scout Council; and *Survival Skills Handbook*, which can be ordered from the Virginia Cooperative Extension Service, Virginia Polytechnic Institute, Blacksburg, Virginia 24061.

- And one book: Simple practical advice on everything from plumbing emergencies to everyday cooking is available in *In Charge: A Complete Handbook for Kids with Working Parents*, by Kathy S. Kyte (Knopf, 1983).

Chapter Four

Childcare Outside Your Home: Daycare, Family Daycare, and Other Options

If you've interviewed dozens of sitters and still feel uneasy, or if you simply think your child will be lonely or bored alone at home, consider having her cared for outside your home.

What are your options if you make this decision? You can send your son or daughter to a public or privately funded *daycare center.* Or you can take him to the home of someone who cares for a small group of children, an informal arrangement known as *family day-care.* Your school-age child can go to an *after-school* or *extended-day program.* Finally, like some 15 percent of all working mothers with children under six, you can bring your child to the home of *your mother or other relative.* With the exception of the last option, each of these choices is a form of *group care,* as distinct from the one-on-one care your child receives in your own home.

If you send your child to a daycare center you will be in the minority of working mothers. Although daycare enrollment has doubled since 1958, it is estimated that fewer than 20 percent of families who would like to send their children to this form of care can find places for them: There are 8 million preschool children of working mothers and only 2 million daycare places.

Whether or not you choose daycare depends on a number of factors. The *age* of your child is important. For example, if you have an infant, you are unlikely to find a center for him. Daycare authority Richard Ruopp, president of the Bank Street College of Education in New York City, estimates that there are currently 1.3 million children under the age of 12 months with mothers in the work force—and of these probably fewer than 5 percent are in group care. Even though infant care is the fastest growing segment of the daycare population (it has increased 70 percent since 1970), good quality care is still a rarity. Providing enough qualified teachers in a well-designed environment costs so much that few centers can afford to do it without government subsidies or extremely high parent fees. Most infants who are in group care tend to be in family daycare homes or centers, rather than in regular centers.

The *kind* of child you have will also determine your choice. The easygoing sunny two-year-old who naps at the same time every day and takes happily to new toys and new people will adapt better to the constraints of group care than the child who naps irregularly, is easily frustrated when he doesn't get his way, and cries when placed in new situations. On the other hand, the child who drives you crazy at home climbing on the sofa and pulling clothes out of the dressers may thrive in the stimulating and less restrictive environment of a center.

Whether or not to use group care, like all choices you make for your family, is a highly individualized matter. Decide carefully, and only after considering both advantages and disadvantages:

The Pluses.   Daycare offers some definite advantages:

1. At best, a center can provide programs and facilities—as well as sensitive, trained teachers—that are more stimulating to children than the kind of care they receive from a sitter at home. A special plus in some centers is the presence of male caregivers, as well as elderly or teenage volunteers.
2. Because daycare centers must be licensed by the state, you can usually be assured of at least minimum standards of safety and health.
3. Unlike a caregiver in your home, a daycare center can always be counted on to be there. And even if some of the staff is absent, you can still rely on adequate supervision.
4. Many centers offer support in parenting to inexperienced mothers. Moreover, they offer working parents a chance to meet other parents, which in itself is supportive.
5. Most daycare centers maintain long enough hours—typically staying open from 8 A.M. to 6 P.M.—to accommodate all sorts of parental working schedules.

6. Children in daycare centers enjoy the company of others their own age and don't suffer from the isolation that a child in his own home may experience. If you are divorced, the contact of your child with another "family" may break up the tight dependency of single parent and child.

The Minuses. Those who see daycare as less-than-ideal or even harmful point to a number of drawbacks:

1. Because staff members usually work in shifts, children are cared for by a number of different adults during the day. Critics point out that this diversity prevents children from developing close attachments to the people around them. However, the validity of this point of view is being challenged by investigators who feel that children can actually benefit from learning to deal with a variety of adults as caregivers. Moreover, research has shown that children's positive relationships with their parents are unaffected by personal attachments they form in a daycare center; they invariably prefer their parents and do not see teachers as substitutes for them.
2. A daycare center is an institution rather than a personalized system, and so it just may not deliver the kind of individualized care you would like your child to have. Even the most "liberal" centers must operate on fairly fixed schedules, which can present very real problems for the child who doesn't want to nap or go to the bathroom or drink juice at the same time as everyone else.
3. Good daycare is a very expensive proposition. Government-supported centers are in constant danger of losing funding; private, for-profit centers run the risk of not filling up, and therefore are often prone to cutting back drastically on facilities and services.
4. Daycare children are exposed to more colds and other childhood infections, as well as to contagious diseases like diarrhea that flourish in group settings. Most centers cannot accommodate sick children, and finding and paying for backup is a big problem for daycare parents. Some whose kids are sick a lot find that keeping a backup sitter "on re-

tainer" is a better, albeit costly, solution than making frantic phone calls at the last minute.

Kinds of Daycare

The largest percentage of preschool children in group care—some 20 percent—are not, strictly speaking, in daycare centers at all, but rather in family daycare homes, in which a provider cares for a group of children in his or her home. Although much of what we'll be saying about evaluating a daycare center applies to family homes as well, we've included a separate section on family daycare (pages 78–82) to highlight some of the special features of this growing form of group care.

Approximately 13 percent of children under six are cared for in what can properly be called "daycare centers." These vary in size, price, and quality, and can be roughly divided into *public* centers, which are supported at least in part by public monies, and *private* centers, which receive no government funding.

Public Centers. These represent a mere 9 percent of daycare centers in the United States and are usually available only to families that can show financial need—with requirements differing widely from state to state. On the average, these centers offer more services (including medical and social support for families), better trained personnel, and more clearly defined educational goals than the broad range of private centers. This does not mean, of course, that any one public center is necessarily better than a particular for-profit one: As one expert commented, there are terrible centers run by churches and there are wonderful ones in which the proprietor actually makes a profit.

Distinct from government-supported centers are those nonprofit ones run by churches, Y's, or other community organizations. These account for 35 percent of the daycare centers in this country. Church centers are often surprisingly nonsectarian. Even when the walls are festooned with crosses or Stars of David, these symbols tend to be ceremonial rather than indoctrinating. And children love the festivities that go along with religious holidays.

Another type of nonprofit group care is the center run by a corporation or other business or institutional enterprise (actually, half of such centers are operated by hospitals, which find them a necessary inducement to recruit nurses). Although on-site employer-run centers are rare, there is some evidence that more employers may be willing to involve themselves *indirectly* in childcare (see pages 165–168). It is possible that parents will someday be reimbursed for daycare expenses as routinely as they are now paid for their children's orthodontia. A growing form of on-site care is the center run by a university for its students and employees; it is estimated that 40 percent of four-year and two-year colleges offer some form of childcare.

On-site care at the place where you work offers the obvious advantage of letting you visit your child during the day, but it has the drawback of requiring that you travel into commercial districts at rush hour with children in tow.

Private Centers. Here the picture becomes more complicated. It is the contention of many people in the daycare movement that the needs of small children simply do not jibe with making a profit, and that services must be cut if a center is to operate in the black. The large chains, such as Kinder Care or Children's World, have been accused of turning out "Kentucky Fried Children." Like their cousins in the fast-food business, they use a standardized approach to offer a product—in this case, childcare—at an attractive price. The costs to parents are lower than the typical nonchain private center, and the buildings and equipment are impressively showy.

Where these centers usually cut costs is in staff. It is unlikely that any preschooler—and certainly not an infant—can get good care when there is only one adult for eight or ten children. And when that adult is poorly paid, the situation becomes bleaker. Although not every commercial center suffers from these faults to the same degree, it is worth keeping these precautions in mind when evaluating a chain-operated center.

A much more prevalent type of private care is offered by the *proprietary center*: about half the centers in this country are this type of small "Mom and Pop" operation. The better ones tend to cost more than the chains. If child-adult ratios are to be low and teachers are to have some training in early childhood education or childcare, parent fees, of necessity, must be fairly high.

The quality of these centers varies widely. We have seen centers in which the proprietor's profits are relatively low and parent fees are used to hire well-trained teachers, to purchase high-quality equipment, to develop excellent educational programs. Other centers offer loving care but pay scant attention to children's intellectual or social development. Some centers are little more than child-minding services. Because daycare centers do vary so, we've devoted the rest of the chapter to unraveling some of the complexities, and to giving you the specific information you need to make the choice that's right for you and your child.

Daycare—The Basics

Here are the main issues to keep in mind when you consider group care:

Philosophy and Goals.   Roughly speaking, we can divide centers into those which focus on the needs of the children and those that cater more to the needs of the parents. For example, a center that offers drive-in drop-off and pickup facilities, instead of encouraging parents to accompany their children morning and evening, might be said to be thinking more of working parents' time pressures than of children's emotional needs.

Centers can also be characterized as *developmental* or *custodial.* In reality, any good center offers a little of both: Children can't help but "learn" in even the most loosely structured noneducational setting, and all centers should provide the consistent loving care that small children need in order to learn. So-called "developmental centers," however, have as their expressed goal fostering children's cognitive, social, and emotional development. At least some of the teachers in these centers will have advanced training in early childhood education; there is likely to be a formal curriculum and set of goals geared to each age group; equipment will be designed to encourage mastery and skill-building. In addition, teacher-student communication will be encouraged, and written records may be kept on each child's progress.

Throughout this and the next chapter we will be talking mostly about programs that have at least some educational-developmental component. By "developmental" we mean the capacity to stimulate a child's ability to solve problems, to get along with other children, to get pleasure from personal relationships and from his own growing competence. Good daycare offers unique opportunities for these qualities to flourish that may not be available in every child's home.

Ratios and Group Size. Although the federal government has determined the optimum number of children per adult, these Federal Interagency Daycare Regulations (FIDCR) have never been enforced. Instead, the states have been made responsible for this aspect of regulation. The result is a confusing array of standards, with some states allowing as many as ten three-year-olds per adult and others adhering more closely to the federal government's standards. When evaluating a center it is useful to keep in mind the FIDCR regulations concerning adult-child ratios: For infants and toddlers (up to age two), 1:3; two- to three-year-olds, 1:4; three- to six-year-olds, 1:8.

Group *size* is as important as child-staff ratio. It has been found that children interact more productively and are more secure in small groups than in large ones. In other words, a group of 12 three-year-olds with three teachers works better than a group of 24 children with 6 teachers, although both have the same 1:4 ratio. The federal guidelines for group size are: 6 for up to age two; 12 for two- to three-year-olds; 16 for three- to six-year-olds.

Age of Children. Children in daycare centers are usually grouped by age. Research has shown that they fare best, in both family daycare homes and regular centers, when there is no more than a two-year range, although mixed age groups can work if the group is very small with a high adult-child ratio. Children of all ages tend to mix at some points in the day at most centers; in one we visited, older children regularly helped put the babies to sleep by patting their backs and singing to them.

If you are concerned about your child being the oldest or youngest in a group, discuss this with the director, who can evaluate the situation and recommend the best placement for your child. Be careful, though, about enrolling your child in a center where there are no others her age, since she will then always be at the bottom or the top.

Costs.   Costs vary significantly from center to center and from state to state, tending to be higher in urban areas and in both the Northeast and Northwest. The younger the child, usually the higher the fees, with toilet training often a break-point in price. As of this writing, full-time care for infants and toddlers in a licensed daycare center ranges from a low of $160 a month in some states that permit high adult-child ratios, to a high of $600 a month or more in several states in the Northeast. Family daycare tends to be less expensive throughout the country.

Some things to keep in mind when figuring costs:

1. Even the most expensive daycare, as much as $720 a month for a 6-month-old in a private center in New York City, costs less than a sitter for the same number of hours earning the minimum wage.
2. Be sure to consider whether or not the center provides diapers, lunches, transportation (if you'll have to travel to the center, figure those costs in).
3. You may be eligible for partial federal subsidy; once again, this varies from state to state. To find out, contact your local Social Security office or, if there's one in your area, an Information and Referral Service (see pages 66–67).

Licensing.   Daycare centers are licensed by the state, which sets regulations about group size, ratios, safety standards, and so on. Each state's licensing agency is different (see list on pages 67–70).

Rules and Regulations.   All daycare centers operate better when parents and proprietors agree on rules and regulations. In some centers these are stipulated in a formal contract. Among the issues are:

- Hours. Be sure you're clear on regular hours, "extensions," and late fees. It is not uncommon for centers to charge for lateness (usually with a 15-minute leeway).
- Absences. Since each child is taking up a "slot" that might be occupied by another, daycare centers often charge even when children are absent for vacations or illness.
- Schedule of payments. Most centers ask that you pay monthly.

Late payments are the bane of daycare directors' existences. Try to treat the center with the same businesslike respect that you give the phone company and your landlord.

- Medical releases. Centers should have on file a full medical history of your child, as well as a "release form" that allows him to be treated medically in your absence. Be suspicious if the center does not require these.
- Meal, snacks, diapers. If the center provides meals, be sure you check up from time to time to see that standards are maintained: food is a typical area for cost-cutting. Find out, too, if you can supplement meals with a special treat or an extra sandwich (some centers frown on this).
- Other services. Large nonprofit centers typically offer other social and health services—job assistance, counseling, parent education—rarely provided by smaller private establishments. However, it pays to ask about these services when investigating any center. One small center we visited used its well-equipped kitchen to provide low-cost take-out meals for parents. Another invited evening speakers to address parents about child-rearing issues.

TAX RELIEF FOR CHILDCARE

Childcare is expensive, but tax credits can help to relieve the burden. Here's how the current law works:

If your *adjusted gross income* is $10,000 or less, you can claim a credit of 30 percent of eligible childcare expenses. The maximum is $720 for one child, $1,440 for two or more children. Above $10,000 and up to $28,000, you lose a percentage point for every $2,000 you make. If your income is *more than $28,000* you get a flat 20% of costs, up to $480 for one child, $960 for two or more.

In addition, the IRS puts a ceiling on the expenses that can be used to figure the credit. The "eligibility expense limit" is $2,400 for one child, $4,800 for two.

Some things to keep in mind:

- Children must be under the age of fifteen.
- There is no distinction between expenses paid for childcare inside

or outside your home: daycare center; nursery school through kindergarten; after-school program; vacation or summer programs.

- The credit applies even if you are a student or work part-time.
- Payments to a relative entitle you to a credit even if the person lives with you, as long as the relative pays Social Security tax and is not your dependent.
- You must use the long federal tax form 1040, even if you take the standard deduction. The childcare expenses are filed on form 2441, "Credit for Child Care Expenses."
- If you are married, you must file a joint return.
- Be sure to save all receipts.

How to Find a Daycare Center

If you think a center will be a possibility for your family, start looking at least six months before you'll need one. It's not uncommon for families to register their children before they are born, and one daycare director told us that women frequently check out her center before they make the decision to become pregnant!

As with home caregivers, word of mouth is your most reliable source. If no suggestions are forthcoming from friends, you can check the Yellow Pages under "Childcare" or "Day Nurseries" or the ads of a community newspaper. The agency that licenses centers in your state may also be able to provide you with a list of possibilities in your neighborhood (see pages 67–70).

Make a list and begin by phoning the likely-sounding choices. Don't make the mistake of scheduling a visit without thoroughly screening the center on the telephone. Location, fees, whether or not they accommodate children your child's age, and number of children are among the questions that will narrow your choices.

You may also be able to locate a center through an *Information and Referral Service* (I & R). In some states these are part of the Community Coordinated Child Care (4-C's). There are an estimated 6,300 I & R's in the United States, run by community organizations and by private or government agencies; about 4 percent are run by corporations (see pages 165–168). Some, like BANANAS in Oakland, California, not only help parents find daycare but can also help qualified families pay for it by administering government subsidies. Other I & R's, like PAWS in New York City, maintain registries of centers but do not play any part in funding. Many I & R's, like the Child Care Network in Pittsburgh, Pennsylvania, or the YMHA Family Day Care Network in New York City, offer training and technical assistance to daycare providers.

STATE DAYCARE AGENCIES

ALABAMA
Department of Pensions and
   Security
64 N. Union Street
Montgomery, AL 36130

ALASKA
Department of Health and Social
   Service
Division of Social Services
Pouch H-05
Juneau, AK 99811

ARIZONA
Child Day Care Health Consultant
Arizona State Department of
   Health
1740 W. Adams Street
Phoenix, AZ 85007

ARKANSAS
Day Care Specialist
Department of Human Services
P.O. Box 1437
Little Rock, AR 72203

CALIFORNIA
Department of Social Services
744 P Street
Mail Station 19–50
Sacramento, CA 95814

COLORADO
Department of Social Services
1575 Sherman Street
Denver, CO 80203

CONNECTICUT
Day Care Licensing
Department of Health
79 Elm Street
Hartford, CT 06115

DELAWARE
Chief, Day Care Licensing
Bureau of Child Development
P.O. Box 309
Wilmington, DE 19899

DISTRICT OF COLUMBIA
Department of Human Resources
Washington, D. C. 20003

FLORIDA
Department of Health and
   Rehabilitative Services
1317 Winewood Boulevard
Tallahassee, FL 32301

GEORGIA
Child Care Licensing Unit
618 Ponce de Leon Avenue
Atlanta, GA 30308

HAWAII
Department of Social Services
and Housing
Day Care Licensing Unit
Public Welfare Division
1319 Miller Street
Honolulu, HI 96813

IDAHO
Day Care Licensing
Department of Health and Welfare
Statehouse
Boise, ID 83720

ILLINOIS
Day Care Licensing
Department of Children and
Family Services
1 North Old State Capitol Plaza
Springfield, IL 62706

INDIANA
Day Care Supervisor
Department of Public Welfare
141 S. Meridian Street, 6th Floor
Indianapolis, IN 46225

IOWA
Day Care Supervisor
Department of Social Services
Lucas State Office Building
Des Moines, IA 50319

KANSAS
Day Care Supervisor
Department of Social and
Rehabilitation Services
State Office Building
Topeka, KS 66612

KENTUCKY
Department of Human Resources
Bureau for Social Services
275 E. Main Street
Frankfort, KY 40621

LOUISIANA
Department of Health and Human
Resources
P.O. Box 3767
Baton Rouge, LA 70821

MAINE
Department of Human Services
Statehouse
Augusta, ME 04333

MARYLAND
Child Day Care Center
Coordinator
Department of Health and Mental
Hygiene
201 W. Preston Street
Baltimore, MD 21201

MASSACHUSETTS
Office for Children
Director of Day Care Licensing
120 Boylston Street
Boston, MA 02116

MICHIGAN
Department of Social Services
300 S. Capitol Avenue
Lansing, MI 48926

MINNESOTA
Department of Public Welfare
Licensing Division
Centennial Office Building
St. Paul, MN 55155

MISSISSIPPI
Day Care Supervisor
Division of Family and Children's
Services
P.O. Box 1700
Jackson, MS 39205

MISSOURI
Department of Social Services
Division of Family Services
Broadway State Office Building
P.O. Box 88
Jefferson City, MO 65103

MONTANA
Social and Rehabilitation Services
P.O. Box 4210
Helena, MT 59601

NEBRASKA
Day Care Welfare Consultant
Department of Public Welfare
P.O. Box 95026
Lincoln, NE 68509

NEVADA
State Department of Health
Department of Human Resources
505 E. King Street
Carson City, NV 89710

NEW HAMPSHIRE
Day Care Licensing
Division of Welfare
Concord, NH 03301

NEW JERSEY
Division of Youth and Family
    Services
Bureau of Licensing
1 S. Montgomery Street, #400
Trenton, NJ 08625

NEW MEXICO
Child Care Licensing
725 St. Michael's Drive
P.O. Box 968
Santa Fe, NM 87503

NEW YORK
Department of Social Services
40 N. Pearl St.
Albany, NY 12243

NORTH CAROLINA
Office of Child Day Care Licensing
Department of Social Services
P.O. Box 10157
Raleigh, NC 27605

NORTH DAKOTA
Supervisor of Children and Family
    Day Care Services
State Capitol Building
15th Floor
Bismarck, ND 58501

OHIO
Department of Public Welfare
Division of Social Services
30 E. Broad Street
30th Floor
Columbus, OH 43215

OKLAHOMA
Children's Day Care Services
State Department of Public
    Welfare
P.O. Box 25352
Oklahoma City, OK 73125

OREGON
Department of Human Resources
Children's Service Division
198 Commercial Street, S.E.
Salem, OR 97310

PENNSYLVANIA
Licensing Supervisor
Children and Youth
1514 N. Second Street
Harrisburg, PA 17102

PUERTO RICO
Puerto Rico Department of Social
   Services
P.O. Box 11697
Santurce, Puerto Rico 00908

RHODE ISLAND
Department of Social and
   Rehabilitative Services
610 Mt. Pleasant
Providence, RI 02908

SOUTH CAROLINA
South Carolina Department of
   Social Services
P.O. Box 1520
Columbia, SC 29202

SOUTH DAKOTA
Department of Social Services
Illinois Street
Kneip Building
Pierre, SD 57501

TENNESSEE
Day Care Licensing
Department of Human Services
111 Seventh Avenue North
Nashville, TN 37203

TEXAS
State Department of Public
   Welfare
105 W. Riverside Drive
Austin, TX 78704

UTAH
Division of Family Services
150 W. North Temple, Room 370
P.O. Box 2500
Salt Lake City, UT 84110

VERMONT
Department of Social and
   Rehabilitation Services
State Office Building
Montpelier, VT 05602

VIRGIN ISLANDS
Department of Social Welfare
P.O. Box 539, Charlotte Amalie
St. Thomas, Virgin Islands 00801

VIRGINIA
Division of Licensing
8007 Discovery Drive
Richmond, VA 23288

WASHINGTON
Bureau of Children's Services
Department of Social and Health
   Services
Mail Stop, OB-2, 41-D
Olympia, WA 98504

WEST VIRGINIA
Day Care Unit
State Department of Welfare
1900 Washington Street, E.
Charleston, WV 25305

WISCONSIN
Department of Health and Social
   Services
1 West Wilson Street, Room 384
Madison, WI 53702

WYOMING
Day Care Supervisor
Division of Public Assistance
State Office Building
Cheyenne, WY 82002

Your state licensing agency may itself function as an I & R; in any case, it is a good place to begin seeking out a referral agency. When you telephone an I & R be sure to give the service complete information about your needs so they can narrow the selection appropriate to you.

Evaluating a Daycare Center

Choosing childcare is one of the most critical decisions you will be making, so take the time to do it carefully. Plan to visit at least two centers. If possible, have your husband accompany you. Evaluating daycare is a confusing business, and two sets of impressions are usually better than one. A group of mothers we met found it most efficient to check out four centers together and then meet to compare reactions.

Don't ever ignore gut reactions. But learn to bolster your impressions by zeroing in on specifics. After setting up an appointment to visit a center, make a careful list of key points to observe. Or use the checklist on pages 76–78. Carry your list with you and don't be self-conscious about making notes or referring to it while you're at the center.

Try to spend about a half-hour with the director, ten to fifteen minutes with the teacher, and at least one hour observing in the classroom. During these periods, you will have a lot to find out about the center's philosophy and regulations, its facilities and the qualifications of the staff, the kinds of families that send their children there, and, most important, whether or not the center can provide a warm and stimulating environment for your child.

The Director. Ask him or her about costs, hours, schedule of payments, whether or not the center can accommodate your child when she is sick (many centers have sick bays for children who don't have serious or contagious illnesses). Question the director about his and his staff's professional qualifications. Ask about the caregiver-to-child ratio and the size of groups. Ask, too, about staff turnover (be wary if it's more than 60 percent) and about the benefits given to staff.

Some things you can ask the director to show you:

- center's license (this will probably be displayed)
- parent contract, if they have one
- a typical menu
- a daily or weekly program
- written records of a child's development.

Get the feel of the place by asking open-ended questions (see box of sample questions below). Finally, request the names and phone numbers of parents whose children are close to your child's age; most satisfied parents will be glad to share their experience with you on the telephone.

"CAN HE BRING HIS BEAR FROM HOME?"

Questions to Ask a Daycare Director

1. *How do you go about hiring a teacher?* The qualities and qualifications she looks for—education, experience, warmth, maturity—will reveal both her philosophy and her administrative skills. Many good directors actually "test out" teachers by having them work for a day.

2. *What do you do when children bite or hit?* Biting and hitting are common in centers, so be suspicious if she insists that "our children never bite." Instead, expect a nonpunitive plan that considers the age of the child and that doesn't allow the aggression to continue.

3. *What if my child doesn't want to nap?* This is a sticky question, since all centers have some kind of rest period. A good director might ask *you* a few questions: Does your child nap at home? Does he need a special toy or blanket? Is his bedtime so early that he's never tired at nap time? For inveterate non-nappers, the director should try to make an alternate plan, such as quiet play in another room.

4. *What do you do if a child cries when her mother leaves?* The director's answers and the ways she deals with "separation anxiety" will reveal not only her understanding of this normal developmental phase, but also her experience in dealing with parents' anxiety about leaving their children. Expect a detailed answer to this question.

5. *Can my child bring his toy bear (or bunny or blanket) from home?* A sensitive director knows how comforting these objects are to very young children. Be wary if she says something like "The children have enough toys here."

6. *Can you tell me about a typical day?* If the director allows it—and you have the time—you can go through an entire day yourself. But asking her to describe it has the added advantage of letting you hear how well she's thought through the day and what she herself thinks about the various activities.

The Caregiver. The men and women who care for your child directly are the most important people in his daycare experience. You are looking for responsiveness to children, a sense of competence about their activities, and a relaxed attitude that will get the caregiver through a day that invariably is peppered with accidents and incidents. Does she look directly at a child and listen to him carefully, or is she glancing nervously around the room to see how the group is doing? Watch for the caregiver who gets on her knees to talk to a child at his level. This is a good sign. Research has shown, too, that in a good program caregivers make a point of talking to every child every day.

When she intercedes in an argument, does she offer comfort to both the "wrongdoer" and the "injured party"? Is she sensitive to the needs of the loner or withdrawer? Check to see that the caregiver looks for opportunities to teach the children as she works with them. For example, serving lunch is a good time to engage children in a conversation about how foods grow.

Does the caregiver know all the children's names, and does she treat them with respect? As an observer, you have an interesting opportunity to judge this. If she comes over to you at the expense of paying attention to the children, be suspicious. Watch, too, how she treats boys and girls or minority children. Can you detect any prejudice or any sign of sexism? (Does she, for example, make any comment when a little boy wheels a baby carriage or a girl plays with a gun or a truck?)

Is the caregiver basically accepting rather than judgmental? Do you hear her rewarding positive actions rather than issuing a lot of don'ts and no-nos?

In the course of your visit, she is likely to come up against at least one discipline problem. Focus your attention on this and ask yourself if you feel comfortable about the way she handled the situation.

Do the caregivers work well together? Nothing can upset a child more than conflict among the adults who care for him.

Finally, childcare authority Ellen Galinsky, of the Bank Street College of Education in New York City, co-author with William Hooks of *The New Extended Family* (Houghton-Mifflin, 1977), suggests a particularly revealing way to evaluate a caregiver. Ask her to describe one of the children to you; you'll learn a lot about how she feels about her job and about the children and parents she deals with.

The Children.   Do the children seem happy and relaxed? Do any of them cry when their parents leave? Do they settle down quickly? Do the children seem actively engaged with each other and with the activities of the center? *The New Extended Family* quotes daycare director Betty Van Wyck, who suggests that if several children turn their attention to a visitor, there is probably not enough going on for them in the classroom.

Focusing on one or two children for a half-hour or so is a good way to catch the general mood. Are the kids learning to experience self-control, to deal with their peers? Do they have a chance to rest and withdraw from social interaction? Are they learning to respect the equipment and materials in the room?

Look, too, for close attachments between children: Studies have shown that, contrary to what had been thought of most under-threes, daycare children form close friendships and are capable of playing well together. Be wary if children do not seem to know each other's names (not uncommon in some poorly run centers).

Activities.   Is there a regular schedule of active play, quiet play, rest period, snacks, meals? Do children move from one activity to another smoothly? How is going out handled? Is there a workable system for having children put on coats, boots, and hats? Are they encouraged to handle this themselves? Are the activities absorbing and likely to foster growth and development? Do the children seem interested, or are they bored and restless? Are children given a choice of activities or is everything handled as a group? (Many youngsters will cry or misbehave when they find total group activity too demanding.) Are field trips to nearby places of interest planned?

In general, daycare research suggests that the best centers offer a balance of structured activities and free choice. Too much rigor is stifling to children. Not every child, for example, wants to drink juice when others do, and some good centers solve this problem by having a juice bar available all day.

If the daycare program is combined with a half-day or 9 A.M. to 3 P.M. preschool, be sure that the daycare schedule is not simply tacked on to the shorter program. If all the interesting activities take place earlier in the day, and many children leave the center at noon or three, the daycare program can feel like a weak extension. Children may become restless or cranky if the rhythms of the day are not geared to their schedule.

Materials and Environment. Are materials accessible to even the smallest children, and are they arranged so that children can keep them neat? Is the equipment safe; is the room accident proof (watch for sharp edges on tables, exposed nails on shelving, no-slip surfaces on floors)? Is the room well lit and cheerful? Are the materials plentiful and appropriate to the age of the children? If there are not enough, you will find children fighting over favorite items. Are they in good condition? (Check that puzzles are intact, that paints and clay are not dried out, that books are not missing pages or games missing pieces.) Are there little nooks or corners in the room where children can retreat for privacy, resting, or small-group play? (Even the most underfunded center can make imaginative use of limited space to provide these areas.) Is the children's artwork on display around the room?

Two positive signs: Snapshots of parents around the room can be comforting to children; so can toy telephones (or discarded real ones) on which children can pretend to call Mom or Dad.

And finally . . . After you have looked over a daycare center carefully, come back to your gut feelings. Daycare director Betty Van Wyck suggests that you ask yourself if you would like to spend a day there. Or a week. Or a year. Your answers may surprise you.

Try to be flexible. As in choosing a baby-sitter, try to concentrate on those qualities most important to you and your own child. For example, most women would agree that plenty of fresh air is important for all growing children. Yet one intelligent and devoted mother was willing to trade that off for the comfort of an on-site daycare center located within the graduate school she attended. The school was located in a busy downtown section, so the children rarely went outdoors. But she was happy to sacrifice this because she knew her son was receiving high-quality care in a place that she could visit during the day.

A DAYCARE CHECKLIST

This checklist is based on guidelines from research and applies to both daycare centers and family daycare homes. Items on it can be observed in a half-hour visit.

Health and Safety

- Adults do not smoke when with children
- Floors are clean and carpeted or have nonskid covering
- Children's eating area is clean and attractive
- No children with soiled diapers or pants
- At least one adult present at all times with children
- Detergents, medicines, and drugs out of reach (high shelf or locked cabinet)
- Electrical outlets covered with safety caps
- Toys and equipment in good repair (no sharp edges, splinters, paint chips, electrical wires, loose parts on toys)
- Heavy furniture (lockers, bookcases) secure, cannot tip over
- Woodworking or kitchen tools and other sharp objects used only with adult supervision

Physical Space

- Individual cubby space for each child
- Dark and quiet space for napping
- Individual cots or cribs for each child
- Storage space available for children to return toys and equipment to shelves after use
- Windows low enough for children to see out
- A variety of pictures, posters, mobiles
- Toileting area easy for children to get to

- Direct access to enclosed outdoor play area from the building
- Outdoor play area with open space for sunny days
- Outdoor play area with covered space for rainy days
- Outdoor play area easy to supervise (no hidden areas where children cannot be seen)
- Outdoor play area well drained and covered with a soft surface (sand, bark, grass for tumbling, running, sitting) in one place and a hard surface (for riding toys) in another place
- Indoor play area with soft surfaces (pillows, cushions, rugs, easy chairs, couches)
- Physical space not overcrowded (too many children, too much large equipment)

Materials, Equipment, and Activities

- Materials and equipment for quiet play (books, puzzles) and active play (riding toys, climbing structures)
- Enough materials and equipment so that children do not have to wait more than a few minutes to use them
- Opportunities to run and climb both indoors and outdoors
- Choice of several activities (story, music, painting, puzzles) much of the time (except naps, meal times, lessons)
- Full range of activities for both boys and girls
- Some or all of the following materials: paints, crayons, pencils, paste, clay or dough, sand, water, scissors, paper, buttons
- Two or more of the following toys and equipment: riding toys, climbing equipment, pull toys, balance beam, pounding toys, stringing toys, nested boxes
- Two or more of the following toys and equipment: social games (checkers, pickup sticks), musical toys or instruments, toys or materials that teach the three R's (cards, puzzles, books)
- Building or construction materials: wood, cardboard, boxes, blocks, Tinkertoys, Legos
- In outdoor play area two or more of the following: blocks, cartons or boards for building, sandbox and sand toys, slides, riding toys, seesaw, balance beam, tires
- Play area indoors where no furniture or objects are off-limits
- Toys and play materials accessible without asking

Teachers, Adult Staff, and Caregivers

- Enough adults to provide individual attention
- Adults explain clearly what they want in words children can under-

stand, often kneeling or bending over to the child's eye level when speaking
- Adults use encouragement, suggestion, and praise rather than orders, commands, prohibitions, criticism, or reprimands
- Adults respond to children's questions
- Adults are observed to teach children sometimes but not all the time (teaching may be informal, explaining, labeling, reading)
- Adults do not spend all their time with one child while other children have nothing to do
- Male as well as female adults are present
- No physical punishment

Children

- Children appear happy (laughing, joking) around adults
- Children are busy and involved (not wandering aimlessly, just sitting and staring blankly, waiting for a long time)
- Each child spends some time interacting (playing, talking, working together) with other children
- Children seem to enjoy one another (help, smile, show approval, play)
- No fighting (hitting, pinching, kicking, grabbing toys)
- Children are in relatively small classes or groups
- Both boys and girls present
- Age spread of children is about 2 years
- Children are observed choosing a new activity on their own

Adapted from *Daycare,* by Alison Clarke-Stewart, Copyright © 1982 by Kathleen Alison Clarke-Stewart. Reprinted by permission of Harvard University Press, Cambridge, MA.

Family Daycare

It is eight o'clock in the morning. Two-year-old Mark Daniels is leaving his house with his mother, a secretary in a real estate office. He carries a favorite stuffed animal and a sandwich neatly wrapped in a school bag. . . . A fifteen-minute bus ride later, Mark and Mrs. Daniels arrive at the home of Esther Green. She greets Mark warmly and ushers him into her large, comfortable living room, which is fixed up as a playroom, complete with bright-colored toys and child-size furniture. Two other children are already there and are having an early-morning snack. One, seven-year-old Amy, will leave shortly for a nearby school; she has been at Mrs. Green's house since 7 A.M., when her mother, a nurse, left for work. At the end of the school day, Amy will return to Mrs. Green's and be picked up by her mother at 3:30 P.M., when the day shift ends. Mark, however, will remain in Mrs. Green's care for the day, along with three other preschoolers. After 3 P.M., he will be joined by four children who range in age from six to ten. One of them is Mrs. Green's own nine-year-old son.

This is family daycare, a childcare system that accounts for approximately 20 percent of the children cared for outside their homes. Advocates believe it offers a nurturing, homelike environment without the drawbacks of either large-scale, institutionalized daycare or the isolation of an unsupervised baby-sitting arrangement at home. Critics point out that unless the family daycare program is administered by an organizing agency or is in some way committed to higher purposes, it can be nothing more than a child-minding service.

At its best, family daycare can provide a warm, caring, and enriching experience for the children of working parents. Its ability to be responsive to the needs of children and parents makes it a good choice for infant care—especially since babies are usually not accommodated at most large-scale daycare centers. Moreover, these homes can function as drop-in centers for before-school, after-school, and even overnight care. If you work odd hours, this flexibility can be a real lifesaver.

Licensing and Costs. Daycare homes are officially divided into *family daycare homes* (1–6 children) and *group daycare homes* (7–12 children), and in either case they are supposed to be licensed, certified, or registered (the latter two mean they are listed with the appropriate state agency, but no minimum standards are imposed). In reality, however, most daycare homes are neither licensed nor registered, although many of them are run in a very professional manner. There is, in fact, no evidence that licensed homes provide better care than unlicensed ones. What can make a difference, however, is whether or not a home is connected to a supervising agency or network (often part of an Information and Referral service). In those cases, providers may be given courses in child development, nutrition, even music and art education. Some programs provide ongoing professional guidance from childcare experts. Others offer support from the community, including low-cost lunches and toy-lending services. Costs vary according to locale, but you can figure on paying a minimum of about $60 a week for full daycare.

Rules and Regulations.   Because of the lack of supervision in a daycare home, it is especially important that you and the provider have a firm, detailed agreement about both of your needs and obligations. You can make up your own agreement or use a standard family daycare contract (write to BANANAS, 6501 Telegraph Avenue, Oakland, CA 94609 for an excellent sample). Be sure you consider hours, lateness fees, rules about absences (daycare home providers are sometimes more flexible than centers, but most understandably insist on your paying when your child is sick or on vacation), who pays for food, diapers, trips. Like a daycare center, a family center should keep children's medical records and medical release forms on file.

What to Look For.   Choosing the daycare home best suited to your child is a lot like selecting a baby-sitter. Here, however, you are looking not only at the daycare provider herself, but you are also inspecting an ongoing environment, trying to judge whether it will suit your own child.

The daycare mother will also be interviewing you and your child to make sure he will fit into the mix she already has, and to see whether you and she will be able to cooperate together to give him the best care possible.

Be sure to ask the provider what emergency backup she has in case she gets sick or has to deal with her own family problems.

If possible, make two visits, once without your child, when you can observe the activity and talk to the daycare mother without distraction; and once with your child, so that you can see how he reacts to the adults and children. The criteria for observing a daycare center on pages 76–78 apply to family daycare as well. But because a family daycare home is a *home,* you'll want to consider the following:

1. *What is the place like?* Is there a safe outdoor area where children can play freely even in cold weather? Is the indoor area reasonably clean and spacious, and is it safely laid out for the number of children the home accommodates? Are lunch or snacks nourishing and nicely prepared? Look for simple, healthy food like crackers instead of cookies, apple juice rather than soda, fruit instead of sweets.

2. *Is there some separation between the family's living quarters and the area the children will spend most of their time in?* One of the advantages of family daycare is that it gives children the opportunity to participate in family life. However, the children need to feel that certain spaces are their own. Do they have a place to hang up their coats? Are there child-size tables and chairs? Where can they nap or rest? That bed-making, cooking, cleaning go on is a plus—as long as they don't overshadow the children. If the house seems too clean and neat, be suspicious.

3. *Does the daycare mother seem healthy and vigorous enough to handle a group of children?* Watch her in action. Does she get harassed easily? How does she handle a crying child? A dispute over a toy? How does she react when children ask her questions or make demands on her? Does she seem to know the children as individuals, to be sensitive to their particular needs?

4. *If there are other people around—the daycare mother's children, husband, or other relatives—are they positive additions to the group?* If the affairs of the daycare provider's own family take precedence over the children, they will obviously start to feel like outsiders. This can be a real danger in very small groups. One mother was dismayed to discover that the daycare provider's own two children sat at the table at lunchtime, while hers had to sit on the floor.

5. *Are there toys and equipment for all the ages accommodated?* And what condition are they in? One woman was impressed by the shelves full of cheerful-looking toys until she realized that they were all for infants and that there would be nothing stimulating for her three-year-old. Toys need not be expensive; a good caregiver will be able to

improvise with household objects and kitchen materials (it is a rare daycare mother who can't make her own low-cost play dough).

6. *What kind of activities does the daycare provider plan?* Remember, she is much more flexible than the director of a large center and can decide on her own routines. Does she take the children for walks in the neighborhood? Do they go to a park or on trips to nearby places of interest like the firehouse or library? In the house, does she read to the children? Do they listen to music? Can the older ones dress up or put on a play? Are there group activities like baking cookies or building a playhouse?

Extended-day and After-school Programs

If your children are in school all day and you only need coverage early in the morning or from three to five-thirty or six, an extended-day program is a good solution—if you can find one. The public schools themselves are the logical place, but financial problems, conflicts between daycare and custodial staffs, and union disputes make these difficult to get off the ground. Where these programs do exist, however, parents are quick to praise the stability of the arrangement, the fact that the children remain with other children they know, and the enormous advantage of not having to transport them to other programs after school.

INFANT DAYCARE

The guidelines in this chapter apply to infants as well as older preschoolers. However, small babies have very special needs (which is why infant daycare costs so much). If you are fortunate enough to find a center or family home that will accept your baby, here are some questions to keep in mind:

1. *What is the adult-baby ratio?* Many states have no regulations at all for children under one year old. Despite the federal guideline of three infants to one adult, in some states ratios run as high as one

to ten. Researchers have found that babies cannot receive attentive quality care if there are more than three for each adult.

2. *Is the environment safe and stimulating for babies?* Babies are very tactile creatures. Look for soft, carpeted surfaces, spacious enough for a crawler to explore safely without winding up under the kitchen sink or being stepped on by an older child. A baby should not be confined to a crib or playpen unless he is sleeping or unless an adult is playing with him or talking to him.

3. *Does each baby have her own crib?* Babies spend a lot of time sleeping. Avoid the center that allows them to sleep in strollers or on mats on the floor. Cribs should be located in a comfortable, separate sleeping room.

4. *Are babies allowed to lie awake in the dark, or are they picked up promptly?* When there are not enough caregivers, babies are frequently left "safely" in cribs instead of being played with and stimulated. A good caregiver can tell each baby's cry and will go to him promptly. It has been amply demonstrated that infants who do not receive responsive attention eventually become apathetic and unresponsive themselves.

5. *Does the caregiver hold the babies and talk to them when she feeds them or changes them?* Talking, cuddling, and hugging are vital for the baby's cognitive and emotional development. Look for comfortable chairs—a rocker is a good sign—in which adults can feed and hold babies. Be wary of propped bottles.

6. *Are toys and equipment appropriate to a baby's development?* For tiny infants look for mobiles over cribs, brightly colored pictures, soft balls, and rattles they can explore with their hands. Crawling babies need things to climb on and pull up on as well as a good assortment of smaller objects: shape sorters; blocks; pull toys. Take a good look at what the babies are doing when they are not eating or sleeping. Be sure there is enough for them to touch, look at, play with.

The School-Age Child Care Project in Wellesley, Massachusetts, which has studied this issue, recommends that public schools operate in "partnership" with another agency—perhaps a group of parents incorporated as a nonprofit corporation or a civic group in the community—to establish after-school programs. Parents are usually expected to pay a sliding-scale fee; schools can supply space and janitorial services or can lease them to the other arm of the partnership.

Churches, synagogues, community centers, and Y's are now reaching into the community to provide after-school care on a low-cost, nonsectarian basis. When no government funding is available, fees are often based on ability to pay, and, because these centers are not operated for profit, costs are usually within the range of most wage-earning families. Some such centers provide pickup and delivery services to local schools, and most offer after-school snacks and supervised activities.

A drawback of any after-school program is that your child rarely gets to spend time in his own home. For some children, going from one group situation to another, never getting a chance to be alone or to have a school friend visit at home, can be a strain. You can ease this problem by having your child skip the center on the one day a week you have cleaning help, or by actually hiring a sitter one day a week.

When you are choosing an after-school center, look for the same qualities you would seek out in any daycare center. Beyond these, however, make sure that the center is not simply an extension of school itself. Steer clear of structured, heavily scheduled programs.

If you want to start an after-school program in your community, here are some places to contact for information:

School-Age Child Care Project
Wellesley College Center for Research on Women
Wellesley, MA 02181

Day Care Council of America, Inc.
711 14th Street, NW., Suite 507
Washington, D.C. 20005

Children's Defense Fund
1520 New Hampshire Avenue, N.W.
Washington, D.C. 20036

You've selected a daycare program and enrolled your child in it. But your job isn't over yet. In the next chapter we'll show you how to get the most out of group care.

Chapter Five

Getting the Most Out
of Group Care

A daycare center is not like a garage: You cannot park your child in the morning and pick her up at night, as you would your car. Group care that works demands a creative partnership between caregivers and parents; it calls for a community of caring so that children can go back and forth in an atmosphere of affection and trust.

Once you've enrolled your child in a center or family home, make sure you maintain regular contact with the people who are directly responsible for his care. In centers that make few demands on parents for active participation—this is typical of most—it's up to you to keep in touch and to monitor your child's progress. Try to pick up and deliver your child yourself. Don't be afraid to ask questions if something at the center bothers you. For example, if you see a different face every morning you have a right to inquire about staff turnover. If your child comes home with an uneaten lunch every day, you should be asking questions. As one woman commented, a good mother is not a quiet mother.

Group Care Is Special

Daycare kids get dirty; they lose their belongings, despite the best of precautions. Harry may come home with Johnnie's bottle, and a rambunctious toddler may tear Mary's new dress. Of course, you'll want to remove your child from a center where he gets bopped over the head every day (you won't be thrilled either if he's the bopper), but you'll find you'll get the most out of group care if you can adopt a flexible attitude. Your child's good spirits at the end of the day are much more important than the unswept crumbs under the playroom table or even the occasional bruise or bump.

The most important thing to keep in mind is that *you are the parent*. You know more about what's good for your child than anyone else does. New York City daycare director Susan Weissman says, "We want to take the cues from the parents—about feeding, toilet training, how to hold or touch their children—and we want to make sure that parents are always aware of that, that we are taking their cues." A parent must trust both herself and the people who will be caring for her child. Says Weissman: "If the parents don't have trust, really a basic sense of trust in the person who's caring for the child, and if they don't have good feelings about themselves as parents, substitute care is never going to work."

In the Beginning

Prepare your child.   The first experience with daycare is bound to produce some anxiety in nearly all children. Keep this to a minimum by preparing yourself and your child thoroughly for the experience. Find out in advance exactly what will be expected of both you and your child. If possible, visit the center with your child; allow her to meet the teachers and explore the place. Be sure to talk to her about the center before she starts.

Small children can get very distressed if they feel unfamiliar with their environment. Where they hang their coats, park their belongings, go to the bathroom, where and when they will eat, where the parents pick them up—these are some of the things your child needs to know before she can feel comfortable in a new place.

Allow for an Adjustment Period.   Psychiatrist Stella Chess urges us to remember that children can adapt much more easily than parents expect them to. Although children can make the adjustment at any age, it's smart to keep in mind your child's stage of development at the time he's beginning daycare (see Timing Your Return to Work, pages 3–7). It's best not to begin daycare right after the child has had to make another major adjustment, say, to a divorce, a death in the family, or even a change of residence. A crucial factor in helping your child adjust, Dr. Chess says, is understanding his basic temperament. For example, a "slow-to-warm-up" child may always have to take on new experiences slowly and hesitantly; acknowledging this, rather than forcing a quick adjustment, is the best course to follow. By the same token, it helps to understand that the shrieks and howls of the very intense child are simply his way of reacting to *any* new experience, from a skinned knee to a full day away from Mommy. On the other hand, comments Dr. Chess, a child who is "mild in intensity may not make enough of a commotion to make it clear that he needs a little attention to help him through the changes he's experiencing."

Most daycare centers will encourage you to stay on hand in the beginning, at least until the child shows that she can watch you leave without dissolving into tears. If you and the caregiver communicate your confidence that your child will be fine and can indeed handle the separation, his adjustment will be easier.

Don't make the mistake of lying to your child or sneaking out without telling her. A firm "Mommy is leaving now; I'll be back at five-thirty to pick you up," may call forth louder crying than a false promise to come back in a few minutes, but it's bound to smooth your child's adjustment in the long run.

If your child continues to cry at your leaving, ask at the end of the day exactly how long the crying persisted. If it lasts only a few minutes, or if it seems to be lessening each day, the chances are it will stop entirely within a few weeks. If, however, the crying persists for more than two weeks with no signs of abating, if your child shows signs of serious maladjustment, or is going backward in competence (reverting to baby talk, wetting his pants, refusing to dress himself), you should look at the situation more closely. Talk to the director. Watch your child closely at home. Try to evaluate the problem. Before you rush out to find another center or to quit your job, see if assigning your son or daughter to a different teacher or group of children will make a difference.

In fact, experienced teachers report that children help each other work through their separation discomfort. Says one daycare director: "I find that some of the children get nurturing from the other children, not only from the teachers. It doesn't have to be an adult."

Making extra time for your child at home, giving him a chance to chat with you about his new experiences away from the center itself, can also be a big help.

A key to helping children adjust is your own attitude. Sometimes your feelings will have to be bolstered by a little false bravado. But if you have made your choice conscientiously, you can put aside *your own* separation anxiety to help your child get used to his new environment. Says a woman who, with some trepidation, left her two-year-old at a small family daycare home: "I hung in there for a while to help him get adjusted. I wanted him to feel that the daycare mother was someone I knew and liked. So I'd talk to her and I'd give her a hug, letting him know that I thought she was okay. And then I'd grit my teeth and I'd walk out the door. And she'd pick him up and say, 'Go ahead, he'll be fine.' "

It's often the parent who's really having the trouble separating. Some mothers linger behind, waving good-bye endlessly and rushing back for one more hug; it's as if, as one family daycare provider wryly observed, they're waiting for the tears as proof of how important they are to their child. Be honest with yourself: If you think your son or daughter is responding to your ambivalence, discuss this with the staff. Most are so experienced with this sort of problem that they can help you sort out your feelings and speed up your child's adjustment. A sympathetic director will encourage you to call the center to check on how your child is doing and will take the time to discuss his adjustment in detail.

If your own negative feelings persist—one mother, for example, spent her whole day imagining her son mangled under the park carousel—group care may not be for you. When you transmit your worries with anxious good-byes and tearful reunions, you make it impossible for you or your child to adjust successfully.

Daycare Dos and Don'ts

Make Friends with the Caregiver. When you deliver or pick up your child, stop and chat briefly with the caregiver. Try to establish a relationship with her that will help the two of you cooperate in nurturing and guiding your child's growth. Be sure to report important events and situations: Let her know if your son is cutting a tooth (which may explain his crankiness that day), if your daughter slept poorly the night before (she may need a nap), if there is illness or other disruption going on at home.

Encourage the daycare person to report back to you in the same fashion. Like some baby-sitters, daycare personnel may not want to burden you with the ups and downs of your child's day. If you make it clear that you very much want to hear about life at the center, you will be doing yourself and your child a favor.

Forming a good working relationship with the caregivers is the most important and the most delicate task facing you. Expect to feel some rivalry. Sarah, the mother of a two-year-old, was somewhat dismayed to hear her little girl chanting absentmindedly, "Marcella is Mommy; Marcella is Mommy." On the advice of the daycare director, Sarah corrected her daughter gently, reminding her that she was Mommy even though Marcella was her favorite teacher. By sharing her daughter's feeling with Marcella, Sarah supported the relationship, but she didn't try to imitate Marcella's style or to compete with her for her daughter's affections.

It's reassuring to know that your child can love a caregiver without sacrificing her feelings for you. In small family daycare homes especially, children and adults become very attached to each other. But this kind of attachment is not exactly the same as what happens between children and parents. *Attachment means not only closeness, but also the feeling that people have when they know they are very important to one another—as children and parents are.*

Here are some pointers that will help you and the caregiver work well together:

- Treat her with the respect you would give any other professional. Too many parents treat caregivers like servants. Firing questions and demands like "Why is he wet?" or "See that he gets outside tomorrow" creates resentment. Be diplomatic and polite; try to praise her work and trust her judgment.
- Ask the caregiver for her phone number and for the best times that you and she can talk together after hours. Don't burden her with long discussions when she's trying to attend to the children.
- Inviting your child's caregiver to your home will give her a

chance to see how you handle him; observing him in his family environment may help to solve any problems that arise.

- When you talk to the caregiver, ask specific questions: "How long did he nap?"; "Who did he play with?"; "What did he do outside?" Doing this will give you much more information than a vague "How did he do today?"

Make Friends With Other Parents. Although we recommend that you deliver and pick up your child yourself, it's a good idea to have other parents' names and phone numbers in case of an emergency. Some centers make a conscious effort to get parents together; they hand out a parent list and even arrange parties at which families can meet each other. Knowing other parents from the center who live in your neighborhood lets you arrange play dates for your child and also to compare notes about the center.

Pay Special Attention to Transition Times. Mornings are very hard for both parents and small children. Unburdened by your sense of urgency, they tend to dawdle irritatingly, blowing bubbles in their orange juice while you frantically try to wriggle them out of wet pajamas. The only solution is to allow more time. You probably don't feel friendly at 7 A.M., but your toddler may be bursting with sociability. Leave the beds unmade and the dishes in the sink, but be sure to take the time to talk to your child, to answer the slew of questions that have a way of cropping up in the morning, to cuddle your baby as you dress and feed her. Double-parking while you dash in to deliver a half-diapered toddler will not endear you to him or to the center staff.

The transition at the end of the day is equally important. Resist the temptation to rush. To you the most pressing need may be to get your three-year-old into his snowsuit, find the boots he started off with that morning, and make it to the market before it closes, but to that three-year-old, the only thing that matters is seeing you and showing you the picture he made with macaroni. Psychologist David Elkind points out that when we rush a child, we give him the message that other things are more important to us than he is. A big greeting at the end of a day, a hug, and a straightforward "Boy, am I glad to see you" tell a child that you're sensitive to his feelings.

Don't Overschedule Your Child. Remember, ten hours is a long time for a small child to be away from his mother and father. Children are often very stimulated, sometimes overly so, and it's wise not to try to duplicate this atmosphere at home. Quiet evenings, fewer people, the chance to reconnect warmly to parents—these activities round out his day nicely. Try to keep weekends and vacations as unstructured as possible; your child needs to lounge around in his pajamas just as much as you do.

Keeping in Touch

How do you know if group care is working out? Here are some ways to keep on top of the situation.

Your Child Is Your Best Indicator. Watch for changes in mood or behavior. As Stella Chess points out, "Happy children don't turn sour; quiet children don't become irritable and restless without cause." If your child is listless or withdrawn at home, if she doesn't greet you enthusiastically at the end of the day or doesn't want to go to the center in the morning, don't just assume that the problem will pass. It's best to talk to the center staff immediately to see if you can work together to find out the cause. It's important for you to know about changes at the center: a new teacher; a favorite friend leaving; even a minor shift in routine can upset some children.

A child old enough to talk will want to tell you something about her day. If she doesn't chat about the caregivers and the other children, try asking specific questions: "Did you paint?"; "Who did you play with?"; "What did you like best today?" Always take your child's answers seriously but not necessarily literally. One mother, horrified when her three-year-old told her that he "always gets lost in the park," called the center, furious, to complain about the lack of supervision. The caregiver assured her that her son had never gotten lost, that in fact he actually clung to an aide's hand during most of the park outings. What turned out to be true, though, was that the little boy *felt* lost and worried that he would not be noticed in such a large crowd. Keeping him with a smaller group and making a special effort to play with him helped remedy the situation.

Visit the Center.   A scheduled visit will let you observe group care in action and see for yourself how your child is getting along, but don't make the mistake of thinking you're seeing a typical day. Remember how you behaved when your mother sat in the back of the room during Open School Week. Your child may want to crawl into your lap and watch the others, as if he were the visitor. Or he may surprise you by displaying his friends and toys proudly. Generally, the younger the child, the less he's able to integrate your presence. Even so, you can evaluate how he's progressing. Has he moved to harder puzzles over the last few months? Is his range of activities broader than the last time you visited? If the center maintains written records, you can ask to go over them during your visit.

Remember, though, if you visit at the end of the day, that children are not at their best during this period. Many of them get edgy as they watch their classmates being picked up one by one during the last half-hour. Good daycare centers recognize this and encourage quiet storytelling, listening to music, or just cuddling with a caregiver at the end of the day.

Get Involved.   In centers or daycare homes that permit or encourage it, having some say in your child's experience can make you feel closer to him and the group. Being the Thursday Lunch Hour Mommy or the Trip Day Parent are not the only ways you can get involved. Even if you work a fifty-hour week, you may be able to find time to go to board meetings, which are blessedly not called too often and are almost always held in the evenings. It's here that you'll learn about the spirited debate raging between the financial committee, which wants to cut corners by cutting out hot lunches, and the education committee, which is fighting to keep the four-to-one student-teacher ratio *and* the hot lunches. You may even be able to give the board some tips on how to manage this without raising the tuition! Having this kind of say in policy-making is a fine way of sharing meaningfully in your child's experience.

If you would rather participate more directly, why not volunteer to assist during your child's mealtime once in a while? With a little ingenuity, you can probably squeeze this into your own lunch period. Your child will be delighted to see you and show you off to her friends and teachers. The staff will surely appreciate the extra pair of hands. And you'll be rewarded by a valuable glimpse into your youngster's daily life.

How Will They Turn Out?

Parents today are eager for answers. Will a daycare child learn to read sooner than his home-reared cousin? Will he make friends more easily? When he grows up, will he be able to form loving relationships with other people? Unfortunately, as one pair of researchers noted, "the jury is still out on daycare."

Daycare children have not been studied long enough for us to know conclusively how they fare later on in school, much less later on in life. Not only that, the children who have been studied have usually been in "model" centers, with optimum ratios and other conditions, so that conclusions drawn about them do not always apply to the broader range of situations. Then, too, comparing daycare children with home-reared ones is sometimes like comparing apples, oranges, and even bananas, since, as we have seen, both home care and group care can vary tremendously in quality.

Despite these limitations, a number of respected authorities have drawn positive conclusions about daycare. Harvard psychologist Jerome Kagan's intensive six-year study (at a high quality center) found no important differences—in attachment, separation anxiety, social and emotional development—between daycare babies and those being raised at home. Kagan says: "These investigations suggest that if the child comes from a relatively stable family and if the daycare is of good quality, the child's development seems to be normal." Distinguished child psychiatrist Michael Rutter similarly concludes that the right kind of daycare "can be a positive and helpful experience all round for many children." Alison Clarke-Stewart, who surveys a variety of current studies in her excellent and up-to-date *Daycare* (Harvard University Press, 1982), points out that although daycare children may be more aggressive and unruly than children reared at home, they also are likely to be more self-assured with adults and to form closer and deeper friendships with other children. In good developmental centers, she notes, daycare children have been shown to perform better on tests of intellectual ability than children of a similar age cared for at home.

However, it would be foolish to rush out and enroll your child in daycare in the hope of speeding up his social and intellectual performance, since these gains have been shown to disappear after a few years in school, when home-reared children catch up to their agemates. What we can conclude from these findings, though, is that daycare does not *harm* a child's social and intellectual development. And this is good news indeed for concerned parents.

We still have a great many more questions than we have answers. When we watch ten eighteen-month-olds sitting on tiny chairs around a little table, not one of them smearing yogurt on the wall or carrying his sandwich from room to room as he might at home, we wonder what effect such regimentation will have on their later life. Observing two one-year-olds happily sharing a pull-toy—at an age when children were thought never to share—makes us reflect on what will happen to competition and cooperation if more and more people are raised in group care.

It will be some time before we have even the hint of answers to these kinds of questions. For now we can only rely on our own observations and the cautious optimism that most of the mothers we spoke to seemed to feel:

- *An office manager, mother of a toddler in family daycare:* "I have seen my child walk into a room where he has never been before, where there may be other children going into the same room, and my child has absolutely no fear of being in that room."
- *A newspaper editor, about her two-year-old daughter:* "She loves school, she loves me. How can I believe that when she grows up she'll suddenly turn around and never love or trust anyone?"
- *A daycare director:* "They come in here laughing and they cry when they have to go home."

In many circles "daycare" is still a dirty word. But while opponents condemn it as the enemy of children's individuality, a growing army of advocates is opening our eyes to the value of this kind of childcare for all kinds of families. It is not our intention to advocate any particular form of childcare. But we feel that the more high-quality options there are, the better we will be able as a society to support the kind of family life we claim to hold so dear. We agree with Vicki Breitbart, author of *The Daycare Book* (Knopf, 1974), that "New forms of childcare that we create and control can help us begin to change our lives and change the way we feel about ourselves and each other. They can help make us all more human."

Chapter Six

Getting Organized on the Home Front

Successful working mothers learn the skills of the efficiency expert: "I manage our household in one-third the time I used to spend just thinking about the living-room color scheme," says an executive secretary. Getting things done with the least amount of fuss is not a gift but an acquired art. We've discovered that there's no one system that works for everybody. Instead, we've found that women use a variety of shortcuts and stratagems to keep their busy lives organized and free of unnecessary strains.

Being organized doesn't mean turning yourself into a machine. "I just want to flop on the bed at night," confesses the mother of a three-year-old. "I know I should be thinking about making lists, about the next day's schedule. But too much planning makes me nervous."

Don't despair if your idea of home management does not include color-coding the clothes in your closet or making a meatloaf that lasts a week. If you run on a precise schedule at the office, you may very well want to loosen up at home. Managing your home exactly like a business will get the wash done on time, but it won't give you the spontaneity that's at the heart of joyful family life. Try instead to borrow a tip here, a timesaver there—and create a homemaking style of your own, one that can even include unmade beds, unplanned meals, and unsaved time.

Basic Considerations

Must You Commute?   With a full day at the office and a full set of responsibilities waiting for you at home, you may not want to spend a lot of time getting from one place to another. Some mothers find commuting a strain. Says a Connecticut urban planner who used to travel more than an hour each way to her office in New York City: "I began to forget what my children looked like in daylight." But other mothers are loud in their praise of working a distance from home. For one thing, commuting conveniently separates home and office so that they don't interfere with each other. As one woman remarked, "When you're thirty miles from work, you don't just run back to the office."

Of course, in practice you may not have the choice. Your children and husband may be too happily settled to uproot and move closer to your job. Or you may not be able to afford high city rents. The next best thing is to try to make the best use of your time on the road.

Commuting Provides Transition Time. The mother of a six-month-old baby told us: "I have a very exhausting day at the office, and when I get on the train I just sort of feel work peeling off of me. It just sort of peels down, and by the time I get home I'm revived."

Consider the trip part of your workday. If you must bring work home, a train or bus is the perfect place to get it done without interfering with family life. "When I get off the train, I'm done," says a lawyer, "and I try not to think about work again until the morning ride."

Shift into Neutral. If you travel by car, try what one Chicago nurse did: She wrote a series of lectures, caught up on developments in her field, and even took French lessons—all on her car audiocassette.

Commuting will probably mean you'll need to make some shifts in timing; dinner and children's bedtimes will be later. And as commuting parents unanimously stress, you'll need to have support from at-home friends and neighbors who can back you up when the school bus breaks down or your child forgets his keys. If neither you nor your husband gets home before seven o'clock, you can run into some trouble with daycare pickups or baby-sitter schedules. But if you solve these problems—perhaps by hiring a sitter who will pick up your child and keep her company at home until you arrive—the advantages of commuting can far outweigh the drawbacks.

The Right Community for You. Living in a community where children can develop independence is a plus for any working mother. When children can play safely outside, ride to the dentist themselves on bicycles, walk to school or supermarkets or swimming pools, you will find life goes much more smoothly. Cluster-house communities, with their centrally located schools and carefully planned recreational facilities, are ideal. And although urban apartment-house living can be high on price and low on space, it does eliminate the problem of car-pooling, which can plague the suburban parent.

One Chicago mother, faced with the choice between staying in a five-room apartment and moving to a spacious ranch house within an easy commute to her and her husband's jobs, chose to stay in the city after considering all the options. "The building we live in has loads of children my kids' ages and lots of other mothers who work. It's almost a small town. I never have to worry about transportation, since the kids can walk or take a bus to most places." Small towns and communal-type apartment houses have in common the opportunity for trading off baby-sitting and sharing in childcare and even housework.

If you move, the decision about whether you should commute or not, or where your family will live, must take into account everyone's interests. Don't underestimate how much your own state of mind and body contribute to your family's well-being. After a year of commuter fatigue, Laura, a personnel manager, proposed that they move closer to the city where she worked. Her husband was willing to transfer his medical practice, but her nine-year-old son, lacking his father's broader perspective, was horrified. He mounted an antimove campaign. When Laura asked him to pass the ketchup at dinner one evening and he replied, "I will if we don't have to move to the city," she decided that a serious talk was in order. Laura sat her son down and explained to him how traveling nearly four hours each day had left her no energy to go places with him and how very much she wanted to spend more time with him. He was able to look at the brighter side of the move when he realized how much his mother had been missing him and how important her family was to her.

Your Life-style. Not only should you decide *where* you live, but you also must make basic decisions about *how* you live. Take a good look at your priorities. Are you wasting precious time with your children screaming at them to stay off your velvet sofa? Are you spending evenings preparing elaborate meals that leave you exhausted before the last dish is washed? Do you socialize with other adults on weekends and then feel guilty about neglecting your kids?

When you choose to work and raise a family, you have to make other choices as well. This may mean covering that sofa in sturdy brown corduroy or limiting dinner menus to hamburgers and broiled chicken or paring down your social life to one or two close friends. It also means getting a fix on what is really important to you and your family right now . . . and then closing your eyes to everything else. As one especially relaxed mother says, "When I can leave the beds unmade, the dishes unwashed, the living room a mess, and go to the beach with the kids on a sunny Saturday . . . then I know I'm doing something right."

Accepting Help. Another basic prerequisite for successful working motherhood is accepting—even expecting—help from others. Although many of us have graduated from the I-must-do-everything-myself syndrome and have gotten our husbands and children involved in running the household, far too few of us are willing to look for help outside our own front doors.

Learning that paid and unpaid help is just around the corner is a valuable lesson. For example, press your mother-in-law into service as family cook when she comes to stay with you. Take advantage of your mother's weekly visits to get your mending done. Your retired uncle, the one who just adores children, may be delighted to fill in when your sitter is sick.

Don't overlook low-cost help in your community. A neighbor's eleven-year-old will be thrilled to earn a few dollars giving you a hand with dinner and baths for two toddlers—and your children are sure to enjoy a lively and friendly playmate. Local teenagers can be hired at low cost to help with cleaning attics, doing yard work, even painting and repairing. An insurance broker, the mother of three boys under the age of eight, reports that she could not survive without her "army of teenagers" who help her with personal chores like balancing her checkbook, answering the mail, running errands, and shopping for groceries.

Many women consider "having someone else do it" the ultimate timesaver, but there are just as many who don't feel right about hiring a cleaning person, even if they can afford it. For them, a good solution is the professional cleaning service. These are not cheap (they range from $50 to $75 or more for a full day of heavy cleaning), but many families swear by them for a complete overhaul.

Transportation problems, the bugaboo of so many suburban mothers, can be solved by making a modest investment in outside help. Dancing lessons, math turoring, and Little League practice won't overwhelm you if the teenager you hire to supervise your kids and start dinner can double as a chauffeur. Make sure he or she has a valid driver's license, and go along for a practice ride to establish clear car decorum and safety rules.

Consider the possibility of transportation trade-offs: Mobilize any available parent for the Monday-to-Friday shift, while you handle weekend mornings. If you think she's getting the short end of the stick, hauling around a carful of kids in the afternoons, think of how grateful she'll be when you're behind the wheel for Saturday baseball practice and Sunday School and she can sleep until noon.

Taxi services are prohibitively expensive if your child rides alone. But when you combine forces with a few other working mothers, they are a quite affordable and dependable way of handling school transportation, doctor and dentist visits, and after-school activities.

Keeping Track

There may be such a thing as being overorganized (one woman was so organized that she delivered her children to school a day early!), but we have yet to discover a working mother who hasn't benefited from careful planning. Psychologists in fact have identified *advance planning* and *self-esteem* as the two crucial factors in a working mother's success. It is easy to see how these two are related. You're not likely to feel terrific about yourself if just as you're going into a meeting at the office you remember that there's nothing at home for dinner or that you forgot to tell the sitter to pick up your daughter at dancing school. Of course, we all suffer these mishaps; they only give us grief if they become a regular occurrence. Here are some ways to keep them to a minimum:

Write everything down. Efficient working mothers remember a thousand and one details because they're inveterate list-makers. Getting it down in black and white won't add hours to your day, but it can give you the feeling of control so many women complain they miss.

Jotting down appointments and "do" lists in an appointment calendar as we go along works for most of us (avoid easily lost slips of paper). If you need a firmer hold on your planning, follow the example of one enterprising woman who sits down with her husband every Sunday night and uses a large wall calendar to plan out the entire week: meals and shopping for the next seven days, after-school activities, birthday parties (with a reminder to buy a present a few days before), social plans for the adults. Taped to the refrigerator door, this plan lets everyone in the family keep track of activities at a glance.

Set up a communications center in your home. Station a bulletin board and pad of notepaper near the telephone. Your teenage daughter can leave word where she's going and with whom; you can post a shopping list for your sitter, along with a note telling her about your son's cold. This is also a good place to keep a running shopping list. For added efficiency, tie a string to a pen or pencil and hang it near the telephone.

Use a telephone-answering service to stay in touch when your youngsters are old enough to be in and out on their own. A real estate agent reports: "I check with the service between house showings in the afternoon. Before, my sons and I were always missing each other, and my small office staff resented taking messages for me. Now, with the service, the boys can always let me know where they are."

Housework and Other Necessary Evils

Neatness doesn't always count. No one but you is keeping score. Nowhere is it recorded that there are thirteen unmatched socks in your son's bureau drawer, that at least two cap guns and one headless doll are lurking behind the couch cushions. Although we don't suggest that you breeze off to the office letting the dishes and toys fall where they may, clinging to rigid standards can only be self-destructive.

With a little imagination and some common-sense strategies, you can have an efficiently run household without sacrificing your sanity. Here are some practical hints:

Own as many appliances as you can possibly afford. If you think a washer and dryer are beyond your means, add up what you spend at the Laundromat (be sure to include the dollar value of your own time) and compare costs. A dishwasher is a wonderful help, especially if you expect children to help with cleanups (even a six-year-old can load and empty a dishwasher). Buy a slow cooker or food processor and watch meal-preparation time shrink. A lightweight electric broom is easier to use than your vacuum cleaner and is ideal for quick cleanups (kids can handle these, too). A no-frost refrigerator and self-cleaning oven are labor-saving investments that will pay you back in short order. (See box below for more ideas.)

Streamline your home to cut down on housecleaning time. If you have very young children, consider replacing lamps with attractive ceiling track lights (a lot safer, too, with active youngsters). Store tabletop ornaments—ashtrays, bowls, empty vases—in a closet. Set out your favorites when company comes.

Next time you paint, try semigloss instead of flat paint throughout the house—dirt and finger marks will wipe off easily. You can also paint floors; three coats of brightly colored deck paint will give any room an easy-to-care-for new look. Try coating tabletops and desk surfaces with polyurethane finish (the same durable finish used on wood floors). Or spruce up an old piece with two coats of Varathane paint, a flexible plastic liquid available in an assortment of colors, which dries to a glossy, dirt-resistant hardness. When selecting wallpaper, stick to vinyls or one of the newer scrubbable coated papers.

TIMESAVING EQUIPMENT

• *Pressure cooker.* These are enjoying a new popularity now, and, happily, today's models have foolproof safety features.

- *Slow cooker.* Plunk meat, potatoes, vegetables, liquid into a slow cooker in the morning, and you'll have a delicious and nourishing hot stew for dinner. If you don't like stew, why not buy *two* cookers, one for vegetables, the other for meat.
- *Food processor.* This is the closest thing to a robot you can own. Marvelous for both plain and fancy food preparation, and indispensable if you aspire to any kind of gourmet cooking.
- *Seal-a-Meal.* With this special heat-sealing gadget and a roll of plastic pouches, you can freeze extra portions of everything you cook. Reheat them by immersing pouch in boiling water. You don't even have to wash the pot!
- *Microwave oven.* It's less expensive to remember to defrost something in the morning, but if you simply must own an oven that will bake a potato in three minutes, be prepared to spend at least $500. Be aware, though, that the high-frequency waves that permit food to be cooked so rapidly may carry danger in some models.
- *And a bunch of small helpers.* Electric can opener, toaster oven (great for reheating small portions), blender (handy if you don't own a processor), electric coffee pot (set it up the night before to save time in the morning), salad spinner (dries greens in 4 seconds), wok or electric frying pan (for quick stir-frying).

Coat wood floors with stain-resistant, high-gloss polyurethane (for best results, use three coats). Or use no-wax vinyl floors in kids' rooms and kitchen, easy-care industrial-grade carpeting in the rest of the house.

Part with possessions that don't earn their keep. Remember, the less you own, the less you have to clean, repair, and store. Have you worn that skirt in the last year? Does anyone fit into those ice skates? Go through your cabinets and closets at least twice a year; give away anything you don't use regularly. Or have a garage sale that the kids can run. (If you donate to a thrift shop or charity, be sure to ask for a tax-deduction statement.)

Make the most of storage facilities. You can get control of creeping clutter by finding new ways to store your possessions.

Some suggestions: Children's closets will hold twice as much if you use two rods, one hung above the other. Replace old box springs and mattresses with wooden storage beds (roomy drawers hold blankets, pillows, out-of-season clothing; practical on-the-floor design eliminates underbed dusting). Cooking utensils, cleaning equipment, even clothing will stay tidy hanging from pegboard on walls or inside closets. A full-length medicine cabinet attached to the inside of the door will make quick order out of the messiest bathroom. For last-minute cleanups, a pretty covered basket is a handy place to toss toys left on the living room floor.

Reorganize your children's rooms for easier cleanups. Don't spoil the time you spend with your children by forever nagging them to straighten up their quarters. Get rid of that oversize toy chest with its tangled jumble of odds and ends. Replace it with plastic shoe boxes, rubberized dishpans, old coffee cans (let the kids label and decorate them)—any convenient container that will store the hundreds of small items children love to collect.

Try baskets for marbles, crayons, stuffed animals; tuck yo-yos, puppets, and penknives into the pockets of a hanging shoe bag. Keep puzzles intact with the kind of rack schools use (order from the Childcraft Company, 20 Kilmer Road, Edison, N.J. 08818). Most kids hate using hangers. A row of hooks on the back of the bedroom door will keep your son's pajamas off the floor, your daughter's winter coat off the living room couch.

Are your kids too rushed to make their beds? Replace their top sheets and blankets with inexpensive indoor sleeping bags, which are lightweight, machine-washable, and available in cheerful patterns. Just zip them up in the morning for instantly neat beds. Carry the principle into the master bedroom by topping your own bed with a down-filled quilt that doubles as a bedspread.

Schedule an all-family, all-weekend major housecleaning every few months. As you do with your regular family schedules, assign tasks on the basis of preference. Draw lots for the ones nobody wants. Don't let yourself get trapped into always being the boss of the cleanup squad: Take turns with your husband or older children.

Little kids hate tidying up, but they love a real cleaning assignment. Let under-sixes shine mirrors, wash everyone's brush and comb, polish silver, strip beds. Older children can divide among themselves the remaining tasks: washing and waxing floors; polishing furniture; cleaning finger marks off walls; straightening out closets.

Take the drudgery out of doing laundry by following a few simple rules. Unless you find ironing relaxing, buy only permanent press and resist the impulse to "touch up" anything with a cool iron (touch-ups take as much time as the real thing). Solve the sock-sorting trauma by buying all one color for one child, another color for his brother. Finally, invest in large quantities of inexpensive children's underwear (try the dime-store variety), so that you can miss a week of laundry from time to time.

Make shopping stress-free. As soon as your kids are old enough to make decisions about their own clothing and other purchases, let them take over the shopping (an older sibling can go along with a younger one). If you worry about their handling money, open charge accounts with local merchants. Ask storekeepers to grant you return privileges.

If you're pressed for time buying your own clothes, try one of the shopping services that more and more department stores are offering at little or no cost. They're invaluable for helping you co-ordinate outfits.

Buying Christmas or Hanukkah presents will be a lot easier if you remember to do it all year long. Take along your gift list the next time you vacation in a place that has attractive shops. Put your store-browsing time to good use purchasing some of those pretty scarves or good-looking ceramics you admire.

You can take the same tack with the birthday parties your children are invited to. You'll never get caught running out on your lunch hour to buy a last-minute electronic game if you stockpile presents. You can always give the presents to your own children if you run out of parties.

PUTTING A PRICE TAG ON YOUR TIME

Anything that buys you time—your most precious luxury—is well worth the price. Here are seven gifts of time, one for each day of your busy week:

- *Taxis.* Take one home from the office on the day you're most tired.
- *Take-outs.* Order a full-course meal sent home on a night you have to work late. Check your Yellow Pages under "Catering."
- *Telephone.* Use it to order groceries (without impulse-buying you

may actually spend less), buy gifts, or even make big purchases (no problem if you stick to brand names).

- *Mail order.* Outfit your house, your kids, and yourself without leaving your living room. Send away for every free catalogue you see advertised (avoid the ones that charge a fee unless you're a super-devoted shop-by-mailer). *The International Catalogue of Catalogues*, by Maria Elena de La Iglesias (Harper & Row, 1982) will help you choose the right catalogues.
- *Postcards.* Use these to keep in touch with family and friends when you don't want to take the time for a visit or a phone call.
- *Doctors and dentists.* Don't cool your heels in their waiting rooms. If they insist on overscheduling, switch to a more understanding professional. Or try what one determined free-lance writer did. When she paid the pediatrician she enclosed a note explaining that she was deducting $30, her fee for the wait she had in his office.
- *Home hairdressers.* Save time and money by hiring a hairdresser who comes to your home and cuts the whole family's hair in one evening session. Ask a friend to recommend someone, or inquire discreetly at your beauty salon.

Chapter Seven

Feeding the Family

There are many ways to feed your family. One mother remembers: "I used to cook all weekend, and I'd freeze everything. My freezer looked like an aluminum mine." But she discovered that bending over a hot stove was not the way to her children's hearts. They were happier to eat simpler meals in exchange for seeing more of her.

Whether you throw together last-minute dinners or assemble a month of cook-aheads, here is a potpourri of nutritionally sound and easy-to-manage food ideas that will start you on your way to carefree meals for the whole family.

Basic Principles

Upgrade Your Kitchen Efficiency. Working smoothly in the kitchen cuts down on your time and makes chores pleasanter. Try doubling up on duties: Put the spaghetti water on to boil while you greet the kids, make the salad while your nine-year-old tells you about his day at school (or better, have him tear up the lettuce while you keep an eye on the meat sauce). *A word of warning*: Do not expect children to do several things at once in the kitchen. Anyone who's watched a child stop in his dishwashing tracks to carry on a conversation knows that youngsters do best when they focus on one thing at a time.

If your husband can't prepare a hamburger without setting fire to the pan, and your twelve-year-old doesn't know how to scramble an egg—if you yourself could use inspiration in the kitchen— consider cooking lessons. Kids love the sense of mastery they gain, and the whole family benefits from some fresh food ideas.

KIDS CAN COOK, TOO

Even an eight-year-old can handle these simple recipes—with a little help from an adult or an older sister or brother.

Julie's Kebab Dinner

Lamb on Skewers

Start marinating this dish right after school, and it'll be ready to eat at six-thirty. You'll need:

> 1 lb. boneless lamb, cut into 1-inch cubes
> 2 Tbs. lemon juice
> 2 Tbs. soy sauce
> 2 green peppers (cut into chunks)
> 12 cherry tomatoes
> 12 little mushrooms
> 4 skewers

Soak the meat in the lemon juice and soy sauce for three hours or overnight (if overnight, be sure to keep in fridge). String the meat on skewers alternating with the tomatoes, mushrooms, and peppers. Broil seven minutes on each side. Serves 4.

Fruit Kebabs

To serve 4 for dessert, or 8 as a snack, you need:

> 8 canned pineapple chunks
> 8 miniature marshmallows
> 8 seedless grapes
> 8 toothpicks

String one of each on toothpicks, and serve.

For more kids' recipes see *Young Children's Mix and Fix Cookbook* (Parents' Magazine Press, 1975; distributed by Scholastic, Inc.)—good for very young children—or *Super Heroes Super Healthy Cookbook* (Warner, 1981).

Encourage your husband and children to develop cooking specialties; each one can be responsible for one evening's meal, from marketing to cleanup. Try sharing the cooking with another family.

You'll need a few logistics—and a lot of goodwill—but you'll be rewarded when you come home to a chicken soup that you didn't make!

Plan in Advance.   Some women wouldn't think of leaving the house in the morning without setting the table for dinner; others shudder at the very thought. But everyone can gain from advance planning. Stay stocked with staples. Tuna fish, tomato sauce, and noodles in the cupboard will let you put together a last-minute meal anytime. Try to keep onions, lemons, and parsley in the fridge—they're terrific flavor enhancers.

Planning menus in advance helps you cut down on shopping time and encourages you to include at least one timesaving leftover meal in the week's plan. For the ultimate in simplified planning, make up a seven-day menu plan and repeat it every week. As appalling as this may sound to you, children usually don't mind it at all and are quite happy (and healthy) on a rotating schedule of pizza, hamburger, chicken, and spaghetti. Finally, save time and energy by using the Giant Shopping List on pages 114–116.

Simplify.   Tell yourself that those gorgeous platters in the women's magazine are the product of the retoucher's art, and stick to simply prepared one-dish or quick-cooking meals. You can still have the niceties of gracious living by adding touches of your own. Some possibilities: no-iron cloth napkins instead of paper, fresh flowers once in a while, wicker trays that hold an individual place setting and travel easily back and forth to the kitchen.

Simplifying doesn't have to mean pouring cream of mushroom soup over everything. For superb quick-and-easy recipes see *The New York Times 60-Minute Gourmet*, by Pierre Franey (Fawcett, 1981).

Make Your Freezer Work for You.   Stockpiling staples is only part of your freezer's work (see box, pages 110–111). For busy families, the freezer is a valuable storehouse for half of the casseroles, stews, or soups you prepare. Simply double or triple your best meat sauce and freeze it in two meal-size containers; for one hour's work you've got three meals. Instead of tieing up freezer-to-table casseroles, using them for freezer storage, line the casserole with aluminum foil, pour what you want to freeze into it, let it freeze, and then lift out the foil-wrapped portion and place it in the freezer. To reheat, just empty the contents into the original casserole.

Although store-bought frozen dinners are less economical and less nutritionally satisfying than your own concoctions, they can sometimes be the best answer to a tired mother's prayer. Be sure to experiment with brands; they differ widely in both price and quality.

Meals Made Easy

Dinners. These won't be a problem if you vary your approach. Try alternating *make-aheads* (here's where crock pots come in handy), *quickies* (don't overlook scrambled eggs for dinner), and *leftovers* (Sunday's turkey refurbished as Wednesday's Chinese dinner).

FREEZER DOS AND DON'TS*

To maintain the right degree of coldness, keep your freezer three-quarters full. Freeze quickly. Cool hot food in the refrigerator or in ice water, wrap in foil or freezer paper, label with contents and date of freezing.

Here are a few freezable items you may not have thought of:

- chopped nuts
- grated cheese (a money-saving way of using up ends of any hard cheese)
- chopped onions, grated lemon peel, grated hard-cooked egg yolks (next time you grate or chop make a double or triple supply)
- cooking stocks and sauces (keep in small containers, defrost as needed)
- pastry and cookie dough
- herb butters (small portions of butter mixed with fresh or dried herbs)
- milk and heavy cream

And never freeze:

- aspics or gelatins (they get rubbery)
- hard-cooked egg whites
- raw salad ingredients
- mayonnaise
- stuffings
- cooked potatoes (remember this when freezing a stew; it's easy enough to add the potatoes later)
- juicy fruits and vegetables (they turn soggy)

Thanks to Helen Barer for these suggestions.

For more delicious make-aheads, try perfecting a good meat sauce, which can go into two lasagnas or on top of two plates of pasta. To perk up a quickie meal of broiled fish or chicken, make and freeze a few food enhancers, like tomato butter, onion butter, and herb butter. Here's how to make tomato butter: cream together ¼ teaspoon unsalted butter, 1 teaspoon tomato paste, ½ teaspoon salt, ¼ teaspoon sugar. When the mixture is smooth, roll it in wax paper to make a one-inch-wide cylinder and freeze.

The trick with leftovers is to change the form of the original meal without adding much preparation time. If you have a sitter or a housekeeper at home (or even a responsible older child) have her cut and chop vegetables; when you get home, add these to leftover meat or poultry for a fast and inexpensive stir-fried meal. For an invaluable guide to leftover cookery, by a master chef, see *Michael Field's Culinary Classics and Improvisations* (Knopf, 1967).

Breakfast. Let your children invent new menus, and don't be shackled by convention. There's nothing wrong with soup or spaghetti for breakfast, and grilled cheese sandwiches are easy to make and can be eaten on the run. An apple and a piece of toast will pass in a pinch; so will a container of yogurt.

For the most nutrition in the least amount of time, nothing beats a do-it-yourself breakfast drink that you make ahead in the blender. Here's one recipe, which you can vary by adding berries or other fruits: To 2 cups of milk add 1 banana, 2 eggs, 1 tablespoon lecithin, 1 tablespoon vegetable oil, ¼ cup plain yogurt, ¼ cup soy flour, ¼ cup wheat germ, ½ cup frozen undiluted orange juice, 1 teaspoon vanilla. This pep-up drink is also good as an afternoon snack.

TWO QUICKIE MAIN COURSES YOU WON'T BE ASHAMED TO SERVE YOUR MOTHER-IN-LAW

Jo Ann's Marinated Flank Steak

Before you leave for work in the morning, place in a bowl flank steak and 1 cup of chopped or sliced onions. Pour over them ½ cup of prepared teriyaki sauce (enough to barely cover the meat). Cover with foil and refrigerate. When you get home, broil the meat quickly, about 5 minutes on each side, basting with the sauce. While the meat is cooking, let the onions simmer in about 4 tablespoons of the sauce in which they soaked. For a special touch, add sautéed fresh or canned mushrooms.

Note: Leftover flank steak makes a marvelous cold meat salad. Cube the meat and toss with a mixture of 1 part mayonnaise, 1 part mustard. Add some scallions if you happen to have them.

Helen Barer's Fish Fillets

Place any kind of fish fillets on a lightly greased baking pan. On each one, put 1 tablespoon of the following mixture (which you've kept in your freezer for just this occasion): butter, grated parmesan cheese, parsley. If you've got a bag of frozen shrimp in the freezer, boil a few for one minute, chop, and add to mixture. Roll fillets up, fasten with a toothpick, drizzle melted butter and/or lemon juice on them, and bake in a 400-degree oven for about 10 minutes or until fish flakes easily with a fork.

Lunch. The most important thing to remember about this meal is that you should not be making it. If your children are home for lunch, make sure you are well stocked with leftovers and standards like peanut butter and jelly, and let the sitter take responsibility for seeing that the kids are well fed. Filling the lunch boxes can be the work of any child over six. Some variations on the sandwich-and-fruit routine: chunks of cheese, celery, carrots; tuna or chicken salad

in a plastic container; ravioli, stew, or soup in a wide-necked ther-
mos (when using one of these for hot food, be sure to rinse it with
hot water before filling).

Snacks.   Your kids won't munch on junk food if you keep it out of
the house and if you lay in instead a good supply of raw vegetables,
fruits, nuts, raisins, and whole-grain crackers. For a hot snack try
individually frozen slices of pizza. Other possibilities: melon balls,
sesame sticks, granola bars, a bowl of yogurt as a dip for cut-up
apples and peaches, celery stalks stuffed with cottage cheese or
cream cheese. Keep everything within easy reach in store-and-serve
plastic containers. For more healthy snack ideas, see *The Taming of
the C.A.N.D.Y. Monster,* by Vicki Lansky (Meadowbrook Press,
1978).

Entertaining.   Working mothers report that having company is the
first ballast to go over the edge. But even though fancy sit-down
parties may be a thing of the past, there's no reason your life-style
can't include informal entertainment for friends and your own
family.
   Cooperative dinners are a lot of fun. Busy families learn that
asking dinner guests to contribute a salad or a dessert is a compli-
ment, not an insult, and they're able to enjoy company all year long
without wearing themselves out in the kitchen.

THREE THINGS TO COOK ON A WINTER SUNDAY AND EAT ALL WEEK

A Turkey Dinner

   . . . Because you'll never have time to make this meal during the
week, and because turkey is the quintessential leftover (remember to
clip recipes around Thanksgiving time). Be sure to save a few slices
plus gravy for small-portion freezing.

A Meat Loaf

   . . . Because it freezes well, and because it's wonderful the next day
at room temperature and can go to school in a lunch box or to the

GIANT ALL-TIME SHOPPING LIST

This list will help you devise one of your own. If someone else occasionally shops for you, be sure to include brand names and can sizes.

Dairy

___ American cheese
___ butter
___ cottage cheese
___ cream cheese
___ eggs
___ grated cheese
___ other cheese
___ skim milk
___ sour cream
___ Swiss cheese
___ whole milk
___ yogurt

Produce

___ apples
___ bananas
___ berries
___ carrots
___ celery
___ cherries
___ corn
___ cucumbers
___ grapefruit
___ grapes
___ herbs
___ lemons
___ lettuce
___ limes
___ melon
___ mushrooms
___ onions
___ oranges
___ parsley
___ peaches
___ pears
___ pineapple
___ plums
___ potatoes
___ radishes
___ scallions
___ spinach
___ string beans
___ tomatoes

Meat and Fish

___ chicken
___ chopped chuck
___ fish fillets
___ flank steak
___ frankfurters
___ lamb chops
___ leg of lamb
___ London broil
___ pork chops
___ pot roast
___ roast beef
___ shrimp
___ veal scallops

Drinks

___ apple juice
___ beer
___ cola
___ diet soda
___ ginger ale
___ grapefruit juice
___ orange juice
___ punch
___ tomato juice
___ tonic water

Frozen Foods

___ French fries   ___ orange juice   ___ waffles
___ lima beans   ___ pie crust

Drugs, Etc.

___ aspirin   ___ deodorant   ___ tissues
___ baby shampoo   ___ talcum powder   ___ toothpaste
___ Band-Aids   ___ tampons

Breads, Crackers, Cereals

___ bran cereal   ___ graham crackers   ___ rye bread
___ cookies   ___ pancake mix
___ crackers   ___ puffed rice

Staples

___ applesauce   ___ ketchup   ___ soy sauce
___ baby food   ___ macaroni   ___ spaghetti
___ beef consommé   ___ mayonnaise   ___ sugar
___ canned   ___ mustard   ___ tea bags
    mushrooms   ___ olive oil   ___ teriyaki sauce
___ chicken broth   ___ olives   ___ tomato paste
___ coffee   ___ peanut butter   ___ tomato sauce
___ cornstarch   ___ pet food   ___ tuna fish
___ flour   ___ raisins   ___ vegetable oil
___ herbs and spices   ___ rice   ___ whole tomatoes
    (jars)   ___ salad dressing   ___ wine vinegar
___ horseradish   ___ salmon   ___ Worcestershire
___ instant coffee   ___ salt   sauce
___ jelly   ___ sardines

Cleaning and Paper Supplies

___ aluminum foil   ___ dishwasher   ___ plastic bags
___ bulbs (100, 75, 60,   detergent   ___ soap
    3-way)   ___ furniture polish   ___ toilet paper
___ cleaner   ___ liquid cleaner   ___ trash bags
___ detergent   ___ paper napkins   ___ wax paper
              ___ paper towels

office in a brown bag tucked into your briefcase. The best meat loaves use a combination of ground beef, pork, veal, and lamb. A hard-cooked egg in the middle is a nice touch, but check with your children first. Kids tend to have funny ideas about what goes inside what.

A Stew

. . . Because you can put the whole family to work chopping vegetables. And because there's almost no end to the combinations you can concoct. Don't be afraid to make up your own recipes—and let the children add their flourishes. Keep in mind a few general principles: Brown the meat before adding liquid for a tastier dish; remove the part you're going to freeze a little before it's done, to allow for reheating time; make sure you're cooking enough for at least three meals (preferably more)—there's no point in doing all that work for one dinner.

Entertaining can also be a family affair. Let everyone help plan and prepare a big feast—a summer barbecue, a hearty cold-weather dinner, or maybe a small brunch—and invite another family as guests. Make sure the children participate, so that it's their party, too.

Chapter Eight

The Sharing Family

Even in the most liberated household, the daily job of keeping things running is no one's idea of fun. As sociologist Mary Jo Bane puts it: "Everyone's in favor of equal pay, but no one is in favor of doing the dishes." Yet dishes have to be done somehow, sheets and towels wear out, children have to be fed and clothed and cared for. With fewer than 16 percent of today's families fitting the tidy pattern of mother at home, father out working, there is a pressing need to restructure family life so that the responsibilities—and the joys—of parenthood can be shared more equally.

Social scientists have been probing beneath the surface of today's families to discover what happens when mothers and fathers share in raising children and managing households. What can we learn from them?

First, the good news. After decades of dismal statistics, we are seeing a slight upturn in men's participation in "family work," psychologist Joseph Pleck's term for the combination of housework and childcare. Husbands of working wives are likely to spend more time on domestic responsibilities than men whose wives are unemployed: about 1.8 more hours a week in housework and 2.7 more hours in childcare.

HAPPY SURPRISES ABOUT FATHERS

- *Fathers can "mother."* Psychologists who have observed men interacting with their infants have found them to be as responsive and caring as mothers.

- As pediatrician Mary Howell notes, "The childcare usually performed by mothers might just as well be carried out by fathers." Children who are cared for by their fathers alone know very well that fathers can "mother." One little boy put it well. When his teacher told him to bring his mother to school he replied, "My father is my mother."

- *Fathers are very important to their children.* Babies whose fathers are directly involved in caring for them and playing with them have scored higher on developmental tests and have been shown to be more flexible and relaxed, presumably because they've had to adjust to more than one caregiver.

- *Fathers' involvement with their children can begin at birth.* Fathers who are present at their babies' birth or soon after report that they feel extremely attached to the baby, that they can easily tell their babies' cry from that of others, and that the baby made them feel "elated" and good about themselves. These responses, which scientists have called "engrossment," suggest that fathers form close and loving attachments to their infants not unlike that of mothers.

- *Fathers and mothers relate differently to their children.* Fathers tend to interact more vigorously than mothers do, and they tend to play more actively and for longer time periods with boys than with girls. When a father has full-time care of an infant, his behavior becomes more like the mother's; for example, he may raise his voice higher when he talks to the baby and he is likely to smile more.

- *Fathers themselves gain a great deal from caring for their children.* Being directly responsible for another human being is both terrifying and exhilarating. But most of all, it is humanizing, for when people learn to take care of someone else's needs they learn to care for their own as well. Many fathers say they are grateful for the opportunity to get closer to their children, which they might not have had if their wives were at home all the time.

On the downside: Women still contribute more than twice as much time as their husbands. Many are still, in fact, what sociologist Arlie Hochschild calls "double-day wives," women who hold down two full-time jobs, one at work, one at home.

More interesting, though, than this scorekeeping, is a surprising piece of good news from Pleck and other researchers. For most men, family provides more satisfaction and involvement than work does:

Men say they perform their work for the sake of the family. It seems that earning the appreciation of their families for being the bread-winner gives men the dignity and self-esteem they need to keep going in jobs that are often less than satisfying.

Sharing: A New Look at Old Truths

If men are discovering the pleasures of parenthood, women, at the same time, are taking pride in their achievements outside their homes. These subtle shifts—in relationships and in roles—are help-ing to lay the groundwork for a kind of family life that promises rich rewards to fathers, mothers, and children. But creating a shar-ing family means taking a new look at some old truths. To learn how sharing can become a reality in your household, start by con-sidering these:

Men and women are raised differently. We are all brought up primarily by mothers, but only women are taught from childhood to "mother": girls in effect inherit their mothers' roles. As psy-chologist Diane Ehrensaft observes, for women parenting is *being*, for men it is *doing*. The tasks themselves are easily divided, she says; it's the psychological labor that is the problem: "There's the ques-tion, 'Who carries around in their head knowledge of diapers needing to be laundered, fingernails needing to be cut, new clothes needing to be bought?' Answer: Mother, because of years of sociali-zation to do so."

As a result, many of us, deeply invested in the feminine role of mother-homemaker, fear we will lose control and power if we give up some of our duties.

Norma, a full-time graduate student and the mother of two school-age children, reflects: "I loved being with the children. My husband wanted to be part of this. He entered my world; he wanted in, and I was afraid. One day I had a paper to write. I felt I would die if I didn't do it, and out of the blue he said he'd take the kids for the day. I was shocked and at first I was a little threatened." But as time went on, Norma managed to put aside her fears and let her husband take over some of her duties with the children. And there were no dire consequences; on the contrary, she gained more control over her life as she began to find more time to develop her career and to enjoy her hobbies. As Norma learned, letting go does not have to mean giving up.

Money Matters. Economics is a critical factor in the division of labor at home. In most households men still earn more than women, and there's a tacit agreement that the husband's time is worth more than the wife's. One woman remarked: "That's always the area that is going to suffer first, because he is making the money, number one . . . and number two, and number three."

When a husband and wife's incomes are nearly equal or when a woman earns more than her husband the man may participate more equally in family work. Psychologist Lydia O'Donnell found that "the more a woman's salary is depended upon to bolster the family income the more husbands are likely to increase their help around the house."

DR. SPOCK CHANGES HIS MIND

1946, 1st Edition of <u>Baby and Child Care</u>:

It doesn't make sense to let mothers go to work making dresses in a factory or tapping typewriters in an office, and have them pay other people to do a poorer job of bringing up their children. . . . The important thing for a mother to realize is that the younger the child, the more necessary it is for him to have a steady, loving person taking care of him. . . . If a mother realizes clearly how vital this kind of care is to a small child, it may make it easier for her to decide that the extra money she might earn, or the satisfaction she might receive from an outside job, is not important after all.

1971, <u>Newsweek</u> Magazine:

Women should have as much choice as men as to where their place will be. . . . If a mother wants an uninterrupted career, it is up to the two parents to decide, without prejudice, how to divide the child care or get part-time assistance from a grandmother or a suitable sitter. I admit my sexism in having presumably assumed that the mother would be the one who would limit her outside work at least to part-time until her children are three.

1976, Revised Edition of <u>Baby and Child Care:</u>

Parents who know that they need a career or a certain kind of work for fulfillment should not simply give it up for their children. . . . Both parents have an equal right to a career if they want one, it seems to me, and an equal obligation to share in the care of their child. . . .

If you make less money than your spouse, you can still strive for equality at home by reminding yourself—and your family—that the money you earn is an important part of the family's income, either for present expenses or longer term savings. Having your own checking account and taking regular responsibility for household expenses helps to balance the power at home. One woman who followed this advice comments: "Now that I pay the phone bills and the gas bills every single month—not just my own expenses like I used to—I see my money as real money, not play money. And little by little I'm finding I can ask more from my husband at home."

Time Counts. You probably don't split your household expenses fifty-fifty unless your incomes are nearly equal. Similarly, it makes sense to divide family commitments according to who has more time available. If you are a nine-to-fiver and your husband works from eight in the morning until eight at night, it may be impractical for him to dress your daughter for school or to cook the evening meal. Expecting him to do these things may be as unrealistic as is taking everything on yourself. You can still keep the spirit of sharing, though, if you are both involved in planning and problem-solving. Your husband may not be able to cook the meals, but he can make up menus or do the shopping. And if his paycheck is larger, it can help pay for household help that will buy more time for you.

Women who have been angry when their husbands contribute much less time at home told us that the more involved the husband became in the household problem-solving and decision-making, the less resentful they felt.

What if you're the one with the longer hours? Brenda is a self-proclaimed "macho mommy"; she earns more money and works longer hours than her husband. She describes a reaction familiar to many women like her: "I'd get home at eight and dinner would be on the table, and instead of feeling grateful I'd start to feel guilty that he was doing *my* job." Women like Brenda can rid themselves of these self-destructive attitudes by consciously reversing the roles in their minds. What man wouldn't be pleased to come home to a warm meal and a content wife? As Brenda came to realize, her husband was grateful to be freed of sole financial responsibility, and he saw nothing wrong in compensating for the extra hours she put in at the office.

Of course, in most families, time commitments are rarely one way for a lifetime. It's a little like riding a bicycle; for a while you're side by side, until first one, then the other, pulls ahead. But you're both heading for the same destination. Couples who are flexible enough to flow with these shifts have mastered the art of sharing.

Every Family Is Different.   We value the bonds forged by families that share. But at the same time we recognize that every family, every couple, is unique, and that families depend for their richness on a diversity of styles. Just as mothers must be free to choose whether or not they will work when their children are young, so they should not be bound by other people's ideologies.

Take Lila and Jerry, for example. Jerry is a loving father and husband, but he does not notice when the cupboard is bare, expects his laundry to appear folded in his drawers, and is all thumbs in the kitchen. When asked if Jerry shares, Lila laughs and says, "Sure, he shares himself." Sharing means something very different for Larry and Joan. They fill lunch boxes together at night, take turns delivering the children to the dentist, cook and clean on alternate weeks. Together they've built this life-style, which they see as the most nourishing for themselves and their children.

At the other end of the scale is Karen, a teacher whose husband, David, is on a fast track in a high-pressure field. It is David's salary that makes possible the expensive suburban house and the housekeeper, but David himself is not home very much. Karen has had to make hard decisions: to subordinate her career to her husband's, to recognize that although he loves her and the children, he will never be able to share the hands-on day-to-day parenting, that she must always deal with the little emergencies of family life: the lost library books, the foot sprained in the soccer game, the last-minute Christmas shopping.

Lila and Jerry's life-style will not work for everyone. Not all of us can be content with the trade-offs that Karen has made. If more sharing is what you want, here are some ways to begin moving family relationships in that direction.

Shared Parenting: The First Commitment

Children need both mothers and fathers, not so they can go fishing with Dad and bake cookies with Mom, but so they can experience tenderness and strength, guidance and affection, from two people who love them. Fathers can learn to wipe tears and soothe fevered brows as lovingly as mothers can. We even have a new word to describe this: "Kramerization," from the popular film *Kramer vs. Kramer*.

Shared parenting is the first leg on the journey toward sharing. Here are two important issues to consider:

Mothers Can Step Back. One way mothers can help fathers be more involved with their children is to stay out of the way some of the time and encourage them to be *primary parents*. Divorced fathers learn this the hard way, but, like the father in *Kramer vs. Kramer,* they are rewarded by the warm feelings that come from being wanted and needed by someone they love.

A man need not be separated from his wife to take full charge of his child some of the time—to serve meals and give baths, to arrange for sitters and go to school meetings without his wife coaching on the sidelines. A father whose wife went out of town for a few days remembers: "I sat in the park with my daughter; she was barely three months old. I gave her the bottle, and then I started to think about what I would do later. . . . I knew there was no one but me, that I was all she had right then. It was scary and wonderful. I felt like a *real* father for the first time."

Fathers Can Change. Fathers must learn to value their accomplishments at home as well as their achievements in the work world. Men must be willing to broaden and deepen their emotional commitments. James Levine, Director of the Fatherhood Project (see box below), says: "Men must deal with emotional vulnerability. To be sensitive and responsive to kids means to have to be in touch with your own feelings. It puts you on the line. Men have a hard time being in touch and expressing emotions." A lot of men, Levine adds, "have a yearning for closeness, but it's hard; sometimes the yearning is not enough to make you risk being vulnerable."

Some fathers have found that talking about these concerns and conflicts with other men helps them be comfortable with their own nurturing needs. If a man has attended childbirth classes with his wife, he can get together with other men from the group after the baby is born. Fathers told us that talking about the birth experience was the first step in breaking down vulnerability. And as time went on, the safe and accepting atmosphere of a group made it easier to share feelings about their family relationships and their conflicts about their male roles. Support groups can help liberate men—and women, too—from old-fashioned notions of masculinity.

Shared parenting means change, and change is never easy. But progress is slowly being made. Even industry is beginning to recognize that fathers as well as mothers care about their children: Major companies like Procter & Gamble, AT&T, and IBM offer paternity leave for fathers of newborns. Across the country courses are being developed to help fathers play a more active role in parenthood (see box pages 117–118). And families in which both parents "mother" are learning the pleasure of participatory parenthood and of marriages enriched by mutual sharing.

THE FATHERHOOD PROJECT

The goal of this path-breaking project, located at the Bank Street College of Education in New York City, is to "encourage the development of new options for male involvement in childrearing." The Project is shedding light on how fathers' increased participation affects: (1) child development; (2) women's opportunities for equality at home and at the workplace; and (3) the meaning of fatherhood in the lives of men themselves. Among the Project's activities:

• Research on innovative programs and policies all over the United States that support fathers' roles. Examples: The Cambridge, Massachusetts, Divorce Resource and Mediation Center, which helps set up postdivorce arrangements that allow both parents to raise their children; postpartum courses for men in hospitals and parenting centers; programs for teenage fathers to help them stay involved with their children.

- Creating model programs like the very popular "Oh, Boy, Babies!," an infant-care course for ten- to twelve-year-old boys; and "For Fathers Only," an educational support group for fathers of toddlers.
- Research on Sweden's model Parental Insurance Policy, whereby mothers *or fathers* can take up to nine months' leave after the birth of a child, at 90 percent of full salary. It is hoped that this innovative program will offer new options for American policy makers.
- Gathering and disseminating information on all aspects of fatherhood, including paternity leaves, childbirth education, nonsexist curricula, custody mediation, positive role models for boys, father's rights groups, and counseling aimed at strengthening the fathering role.

For more information write The Fatherhood Project, Bank Street College, 610 West 112th Street, New York, NY 10025.

Sharing: How to Do It

Sharing families take many forms, but at the core of every successful plan is the idea of *shared responsibility*. Here's how you can actualize it.

Look for participation, *not* help. People who view their domestic contributions as gifts are giving nothing to anyone. When you are the only one who notices that the bed is unmade or that the children need haircuts, you don't feel like a member of a sharing family, even if your husband and kids jump into action when you prod them. When "make pediatrician's appointment" appears in your datebook and never in your husband's, you're likely to feel you are carrying the heavier load. Sharing means taking into account both thinking about something ("Gee, we're out of milk") and doing something about it ("Hey, honey, can you pick up milk on the way home from work?"). Moving into this mode of thinking is not always easy, but it's worth the effort.

Make it official. It helps to have an official plan for both housework and childcare. The possibilities are endless. You can divide the responsibilities and let the person in charge assign the work. For example, if your husband is in charge of dental appointments, he might ask you to chauffeur a child, but the appointment will show up in his book. You can split up all the chores and take turns: he cooks, you wash dishes; next week you cook and get to sip coffee while he and the kids clean up. You can even split the chores on a permanent basis; there are happy families in which the man has never cleaned the bathroom and the woman has never made breakfast.

If you and your husband have about the same amount of time available, you can divide the week: he's responsible for everything from Monday to Wednesday; you take Thursday and Friday; and you each get one weekend day "off" (you switch each week to make up for the unequal number of days).

If you both have the same degree of intensity or indifference about household matters, you might get away with a casual ad hoc arrangement, but for most couples some kind of plan—whether in mind or on paper—eases tension and provides a basis for compromise and cooperation. As with any plan, be prepared for renegotiation and be flexible. One well-known writer still laughs about his year "on the plan." He remembers sitting lonely in his study while his wife snuggled the baby he couldn't play with because it wasn't "his" Wednesday.

Enlist your husband's cooperation. Communication, that old standby, is especially important in a sharing family. How we talk to each other can make all the difference. Try saying: "I'm having trouble getting the kids off to school in the morning. Can you take over the mornings a few days a week?" (Notice the absence of the word *help*.) Resist the temptation to say, "Why are you so selfish? Can't you see how hard I'm working?" Say, "How can we manage better?" and then show your good faith by accepting his solutions most of the time.

Encourage your husband to take over responsibilities—and then let him handle them his way. One woman reports: "Harry is the breakfast person in our house, and sometimes I want to scream, 'Cheerios again?!' But I don't, because I'm really glad that he's in charge." Remember, too, that kids like to see a parent willingly at the helm instead of one bossing the other around. Be sure, too, that you agree on what "in charge" means. If he's responsible for dinner on the night you work late, you don't want to come home to dishes in the sink and an empty pizza box on the table!

Support your husband's expertise. The more a father makes decisions at home, the more he becomes personally involved in family work. You can't expect your husband to hire a last-minute babysitter, for example, if he has to phone you for her number. In sharing families, fathers are used to deciding about everything from daycare to dinner plans.

Give up the role of administrator/perfectionist. If you insist on the cleanest house on the block or the kind of meals you prepared when you had all the time in the world, you are bound to be disappointed by your daughter's pasta surprise or your husband's once-over-lightly cleaning. Keep in mind that as long as you criticize their efforts, they have the perfect excuse for not doing household chores, since "you won't be pleased with the way I do it, anyway."

Sharing: A Learned Process

The path to sharing is rarely paved with enlightened family conferences shot through with insight, selfless performance of chores, and undivided desire to cooperate. What we have been describing does not happen overnight. Men, as we have seen, will gladly change the baby but rarely remember to buy the Pampers. Women, for their part, are sometimes too quick to fill the gap. And even the best of intentions don't always yield good results.

What, for example, does a woman do when she genuinely wants her husband to participate and he simply won't hold out that sharing hand? One solution is to back up your words with action. When her husband repeatedly refused to throw away dirty diapers after changing the baby, one irate woman left a diaper in the doorway where he would step on it. He quickly got the point. Another mother retreated to the bedroom and calmly sipped sherry until her husband and children tidied up the kitchen. Fathering expert James Levine, himself a sharing father, suggests you ask yourself two questions before you wage warfare:

1. *What have you communicated to your husband?* Don't be trapped thinking, "If he really loved me he'd know what I want." Sharing takes a lot of planning and a lot of very straight talk. Be sure you communicate what you want, not what you think he might be willing to give. Marilyn, a TV film producer, reports: "We have these summits—I would say every five or six months—I call them summit meetings because months slip by and I become more the one doing everything. Then I say, 'Hold it.' And I make a list of everything that I'm doing, and I say, as calmly as I can, 'Now, if you can add to that, please do.' And I try to be as honest and fair as I can."

   Marilyn was on the right track, but like many women she waited until the situation became unbearable before she called a meeting. If you discuss your feelings and your needs regularly before anger and resentment have a chance to escalate, you will save both of you a lot of anguish.

2. *What are you willing to risk?* This is the tougher question. Many women fear that they'll jeopardize their marriage if they ask too much. Comments psychologist Diane Ehrensaft: "Mom will be reluctant to shoo Dad away from the TV if the consequence is that he and his larger paycheck walk out the door, leaving her to support three kids on her own." You won't knock down this economic barricade overnight, but you will reach a higher level of understanding and cooperation if both you and your husband recognize that shared parenting is a positive right, not a negative responsibility.

Get the Kids into the Act

Having children take on tasks and develop the responsibility for carrying through on them is not only an old American tradition, it's also a centuries-old method for building character and confidence in a child. Children feel important when they are given appropriate chores to do at home, whether it's taking care of a younger brother or peeling potatoes for dinner. If they are assigned responsibilities from the time they are old enough to toddle around dusting the baseboards, they will grow up knowing that the work they do is meaningful.

Don't wait until your children are teenagers to ask them to chip in at home. Adolescents are not known for their willingness to change, and if they're not used to participating, they're more likely to retreat into the squalor of their own rooms than to cheerfully volunteer their labors.

Be careful, too, not to load too many responsibilities on your children. In *The Hurried Child,* psychologist David Elkind warns us: "It is not always easy for working parents to separate what is reasonable from what is not. If a child can start dinner, then why not have him or her prepare the whole meal? If the child can keep one room tidy, why not the whole house? The temptation to pile heavy domestic burdens on the child is strong for parents under stress. Helping parents is one thing; taking over their jobs and responsibilities is another."

Be sure to let children of all ages participate in planning shared household tasks. When children help decide how chores are to be parceled out, they are far less likely to balk at fulfilling their obligations. Here is how to go about getting the kids into the act:

1. *Have regular family meetings at which everyone helps set up household routines.* Make a list of all the necessary tasks and have each family member choose what he or she likes to do best; then plan to rotate the jobs no one wants. Be sure to make no assumptions about preferences—your ten-year-old son may actually prefer ironing to taking out the garbage, your daughter may find washing floors more satisfying than clearing the table. Schedule regular follow-up meetings, at which everyone can air beefs, renegotiate if necessary, or suggest improvements.

   Schedules work best when each member cares for his or her own personal belongings. Says one woman: "I'm the laundry person in our house, but I'm sure not going to be the one to fish my kids' underpants out from behind the beds: They've learned that if they don't put them in the hamper on laundry day, they'll just have to go to school with bathing suits under their jeans!"

2. *Once work assignments have been made, write them on a schedule.* Post the schedule where everyone can see it (taped to the side of the refrigerator is a good place).

Seeing that his or her chores are done should be up to each person, but some families allow switching around. One dismayed mother described how her three children, ages nine, eleven, and fourteen, had elevated the trading of household tasks to such a high art that much of the dinner-table conversation consisted of negotiating and bargaining. Amazingly, however, everything got done, and she admitted that these strategy sessions probably helped keep the kids' enthusiasm from flagging.

3. *Consider carefully each child's ability when tasks are being distributed.* Your four-year-old may be quite sincere when he offers to cook dinner while you clean his hamster cage. It takes tactful guidance to engage children in work they can handle themselves, but assigning chores that are appropriate to their ages will help them take the plan seriously and to sustain interest in it.

If a small child insists on doing something you think she's too young to handle, why not try helping her along? One eight-year-old became quite expert at removing wax from the kitchen floor (a chore no one else wanted) after a session of instructions from her father. And many an adolescent has graduated from sloppy joes to London broil after a few cooking lessons.

Most youngsters can be remarkably efficient and creative when it comes to housework and cooking. Let them take over as much as they are willing to do, and remember to offer generous praise and encouragement. Even very small children can take charge of keeping their own things neat, especially if you teach them from the beginning the basics like making beds and sorting out clothes and toys. ("Those little green pieces all go with the Monopoly set . . . see, that's where you keep shoes . . . here's the place for papers and crayons. . . .")

Children over the age of six can be expected to do such things as sort and fold laundry, set and clear the table, and empty and load the dishwasher. There are even ten-year-olds who can cook a credible Sunday dinner, eight-year-olds who can prepare breakfast for the family every morning, and at least one five-year-old we encountered who did a splendid job of vacuuming the family room rug.

For more no-nonsense advice, read the humorous *401 Ways to Get Your Kids to Work at Home,* by Bonnie Runyan McCullough and Susan Walker Monson (St. Martin's Press, 1981).

4. *Be realistic in your expectations.* If your job requires that you look perfectly groomed all the time, it may be best to send your shirts to the laundry rather than have your eleven-year-old iron them. But if you're willing to put up with an occasional burned pan or socks that turn up in the wrong dresser or a table that never got set because football practice ran late, you'll be rewarded many times over by the reduction in your own work load, and by the spirit of cooperation and caring that invariably comes when a whole family works together. As psychologist Lee Salk has said: "It's not the speed of setting the table that's important, but the joint participation, what you communicate in the inter-action, that's crucially important."

Should you pay children for the work they do? Some parents are adamant that children should be expected to help out at home without money changing hands; others feel that in a society that tends to reward work with money, children will perform better and feel more appreciated if they are paid for their efforts.

Most parents do agree, though, on the wisdom of giving a weekly allowance. A child's allowance should be scaled to his needs. As children get older and take on more of their own financial responsibilities—paying for movies, buying school supplies, purchasing hobby equipment—they are entitled to receive a larger weekly stipend. A good way of handling the payment problem is to supplement this allowance with additional money for chores beyond the routine ones. Older children or teenagers, for example, might receive money for work they would be paid for doing outside the home, such as baby-sitting, yard cleaning, and window washing.

Paying with added privileges or with tokens like gold stars is a good way of rewarding children for work especially well done. To some parents, letting a youngster stay up past her bedtime for a special TV program or allowing her to accumulate enough stars to purchase a new bike seems less like the bribery of cash payments.

If you do decide to pay your children for their chores, set up a strict schedule of values, and do not let yourself be persuaded to stray from it. If you and your five-year-old have agreed that folding laundry is worth a quarter, it is not fair of him to demand fifty cents two weeks later, just because his older sister explained inflation to him. Varying the dollar value of children's work capriciously can only undermine the seriousness of their efforts.

See box on page 133 for a practical system of paying children for work. And for sensible advice on family money management, including children's allowances, see *Your Money and Your Life,* by C. Colburn Hardy (AMACOM, 1980; it can be ordered from American Management Association, 135 W. 50th St., N.Y., NY 10020).

Kids sometimes need a little help. Children are not miniature adults: Even the most responsible among them sometimes dawdle infuriatingly over a job, forget notebooks, or lose their rubbers. Be patient. Children have a natural drive toward competence, and they'll get there if you give them your love and support, and an occasional helping hand. Here are a few tips passed on to us by working mothers:

- If your children dawdle in the morning or linger too long over some household chore, make them a present of an inexpensive kitchen timer and watch them try to "beat the clock."
- A note pasted on the inside of the front door won't win you any awards for interior decoration, but the simple message —"Do you have your keys, bus pass, lunch?"—will save you and your kids a lot of aggravation.
- Napkins, forks, and glasses will find their way to the right place at the dinner table if you post a simple "table-setting checklist" on your kitchen wall.
- From Eleanor Berman, the author of *The Cooperating Family* (Prentice-Hall, 1977), comes wise advice on handling a child who refuses to do his chores: "If tasks are continually neglected . . . let him see the consequences." If a person who's supposed to do the dishes lets them pile up in the sink, the

THE WINK PLAN

(Work INcentives for Kids)

A professor of mathematics, searching for a way to motivate his children to do chores at home, devised an ingenious scheme of monetary rewards. Here's how it works:

Each household task is given a value, ranging from 15¢ to 80¢. In order to earn a base allowance of, say, $5 a week, a child has to do $2-worth of tasks. If he does *less* than $2, he gets only the actual value of what he earns; if, for example, at the end of the week his chores add up to $1.75, that is what he earns. Only by hitting the jackpot of $2 can he earn the full $5—*and* he gets to keep every cent he earns beyond the $2 (if he earns $2.30, he actually gets $5.30). Here is how the system looks in practice:

Price List		Chores This Week	
Set table	15¢	3 times	= 45¢
Clear table	20¢	0 times	= 0
Take out garbage	15¢	2 times	= 30¢
Empty dishwasher	25¢	1 time	= 25¢
Empty laundry hampers	20¢	1 time	= 20¢
Do laundry (including folding)	80¢	1 time	= 80¢
		total	= $2.00

The system's only drawback, reports the professor, is that as the end of the week approaches there is a mad scramble for one more chore to fill the quota!

rest of the family can go out to dinner without him until he comes around.

A commitment to a job should not mean a pledge of servitude. Getting up at six to iron your daughter's dress or dashing home again at five-thirty to pop a perfectly seasoned casserole into the oven you scrubbed the night before may win you a ticket in the Supermom sweepstakes, but it will not give you the affection and respect that flourish when family responsibilities are shared.

The sharing family liberates not only mothers, but fathers and children as well. As mothers break through the constraints of exclusive mothering, fathers gain the pleasure of playing a pivotal part in their families' lives. And when family work is shared, children benefit from a larger emotional reservoir that helps them grow into confident and independent adults.

Chapter Nine

New Ways to Be Together

For the children of nonworking mothers, daily life means Life with Mother, a taken-for-granted reality. Children of job-holding mothers have a different reality. And how well they adapt to it depends a lot on how willing everyone in the family is to devise new ways of relating to one another.

You can make your working a positive experience for the entire family, but only if you are willing to restructure schedules, rethink priorities, let go of old prejudices. This may mean allowing young children to stay up till ten in the evening, substituting a giant Monopoly game and a living-room-floor picnic for a traditional Sunday dinner, or taking a week's vacation with your daughter while your husband stays home with your son.

Pay careful attention to your child to discover what his needs are. Don't make any assumptions based on someone else's experience. Try to find out what your own children care about.

If you aren't sure how your children would like you to spend time with them, try asking them directly. "Don't ask the experts," cautions a family counselor. "They don't know *your* kids. Ask the kids themselves. They'll tell you more than anyone else can. If you really listen to what your children have to say, you'll be able to learn what's bothering them and what they need."

Keeping in Touch

How do you keep in touch with your children when you are gone for up to ten hours each day? Most women answer with two words: "the telephone." "I call it my ten-cent umbilical," says Jennifer, a

West Coast legal secretary who emphasizes the importance of calling at a time the child is likely to have something he wants to talk about.

You'll get the most mileage from your phone call if you call right after school when your child is bursting with news or, if you're out in the evening, right before bedtime, when warm contact with you will help him feel less lonely.

Mothers of toddlers cared for at home wonder whether they should call every day. Although some children under three may be reassured by a call, many will find their mother's disembodied voice anxiety-producing. Lorraine, an executive secretary, had always made sure to call her ten-month-old son each day. "He was too young to answer back then," she recalled. But he certainly wasn't too young to cry. And that's what he did. "The sitter said he'd whimper and look sad after I called," says Lorraine. "Finally I decided that this need to call him was really my own ego trip. I think I was afraid he'd forget who I was."

Even older children can get unnerved by a parent's phone calls, especially if the parent is rushed or anxious. One woman described a common reaction: "Every time I called, Josh would say the same thing: 'When are you coming home?' He never seemed glad to hear from me, and I'd hang up feeling guilty and miserable." A good solution is to have your child call you or your husband, so that the contact is based on the child's need rather than yours. But regardless of who calls whom, try to make your phone contact as relaxed and friendly as you can. Avoid hanging up abruptly; let your child be the one to end the conversation.

If the phone never stops ringing on your desk, your child could be trying to communicate more than just a friendly hello. Constant phone calls may be his way of telling you he's lonely or needy. Says the mother of a twelve-year-old: "She calls if her pants shrink in the dryer, she calls if a comb gets tangled in her hair, she calls 'cause she's got a zit. If I put her on hold, I feel I'm rejecting her."

There are ways to handle this kind of problem. First, put a realistic limit on the number of times the two of you can talk during the day. Then, explain to your child that you miss her, too, but that you would rather save long conversations for the evening when both of you are less rushed. Try to help her find things to do when she's at home: have a friend over to visit; begin a special project you can work on together in the evening. Most important of all, take the time to find out what's troubling her, so that you can work together to find an appropriate solution. Don't let guilt prevent you from exploring what is really bothering your child.

Nights and Weekends

Mothers who are home all day are always available for their children's questions, for shared confidences that tell a child he is loved and cared about. When you are out of the house all day, you have only the weekends and evenings in which to establish this kind of open communication. But this is no reason you and your children can't build strong and enduring relationships with each other. Just remember that, like all relationships, these take work—and a bit of planning.

The Reentry Frenzies.   MOMMY'S HOME—EVERYBODY CRY, announced a headline in *Family Circle* magazine. And thousands of readers grimaced in recognition. For some women, the hardest thing about going to work is coming home.

Jacqueline, a Memphis personnel director and the mother of two boys, eight and nine, and a five-year-old girl, describes an all-too-familiar scene: "Everything would be quiet and calm, and I'd come home and suddenly everything would go crazy. Kids whining, screaming, hitting me. Once I literally took my coat and walked out."

Jacqueline used to feel as if her children were saying, "Who needs you? Why did you come home? All was settled until you came home." But she's come to understand the phenomenon better. Children need to let out all their feelings, to air their grievances and their triumphs many times during the day, but they learn to keep some of this emotion under control when they're with teachers and baby-sitters. A parent gives unconditional love. Your children know that no matter what they do, you will not reject them. And when Mommy walks in that front door, it is a signal to them to release the energy and passion they have been holding back.

Once you understand what the end-of-the-day frenzies are all about, it becomes easier to deal with them. As three pairs of sticky hands grab at your purse for the presents you promised to bring home, as your oldest asks you if he can sleep at his friend's house next Friday, your youngest tries to tell you how the plumber had to come because the toilet water came up over the seat and flooded the whole nursery school, and your sitter reminds you that she's taking tomorrow off, you try to sort out the voices from the cacophony and keep telling yourself that since you can't fight it, you might as well join it. Mothers who devote the first half-hour or so to their children—answering questions, running in to see what they built with their blocks, even getting down on the floor for a quick game —find the rest of the evening goes much more smoothly.

Other parents try to defer focusing their complete attention on their children until they can make a civilized reentry. Generally, the older—and fewer—the children, the easier this is. Still, one must admire the willpower of the divorced mother of three school-age girls who says: "I made an agreement with them that they'll leave me alone for the first hour. We say hello and then they go to their homework and I start dinner. By the time they're into the homework, the dinner's cooking and I'm ready to help or hear about their day." She adds that because she is so much more cheerful, they have learned to accept this "Mommy's hour."

Here are some tried-and-true strategies to help you make the most of your time with your children:

1. *Use travel time to be companionable with your child.* When you take a child to school or day care or pick him up at the end of the day (even if he's old enough to make the trip himself), you have a chance to talk more comfortably than at home, where there are all those household distractions.
2. *Be flexible about schedules.* Nothing traps a working mother more than a rigid attachment to set routines. Margaret, an advertising copywriter, was able to rearrange her nine-month-old son's nap and feeding times so that he would be awake during her at-home hours. If she had let the baby nap early in the day, he would have gone to sleep at seven-thirty, just as Margaret and her husband were gearing up to be with him.
3. *Reserve at least part of the evening just to be with your children.* Don't rush through the evenings. Be available to

your children—for your sake as well as theirs. "Bath time in our house used to sound like a speeded-up movie," admits Nina, the mother of a five-year-old boy. "I had so much to do at night, and I was frantic that I wouldn't get it finished, so I rushed and screamed at Andrew when he dawdled. When I read a story, it sounded like a *Reader's Digest* condensed book. I managed to reduce *Dumbo* to four minutes."

Nina, like many women juggling two roles, was obsessed about time—or the lack of it. But even as she was finding time for her chores, she was losing her child. "I may have suffered during that period more than he did," Nina told us. "He kind of adjusted; it was I who missed the bedtime stories, the friendly bath times. One day Andrew said casually, reminding me of a game we used to play with the boats in his bath, 'That was when you were my Mommy; now you're my Nina.' That did it. I decided then and there to give myself back to my son . . . and him to me. I've just stopped worrying about the wash or dinners. No one ever cared about all that stuff but me, anyway."

4. *Avoid phone calls or guests during the time you've set aside to be with your child.* Children's jealousy of the phone, especially when it's pressed to the ear of a parent they haven't seen all day, is nearly universal, and retribution is usually quick. "My three-year-old calmly flooded the kitchen floor while I was talking on the phone," recalls Deena, a good-humored midwesterner who works as a receptionist in a large manufacturing firm. "I was furious, but I understood . . . he hadn't seen me all day and he felt entitled to my attention. And he was right."

It helps to tell friends not to call during the hours you've reserved for your children, and to dismiss other callers with a polite "I'll call you back later or in the morning." If you are still plagued by interruptions, try taking the phone off the hook. Or use a telephone-answering service or machine.

5. *Be available to your children in a way that's comfortable for you.* If ice skating leaves you cold, find another way to build family togetherness. Don't just join your kids; choose activities you can enjoy together.

Fiona, the mother of three active youngsters, had a whole list of "shoulds" for the weekend hours. "I was convinced," she told us, "that if I didn't make a big Sunday dinner—a roast with all the trimmings—to make up for not cooking all week, I wasn't really a mother. That I was cheating my family. And so every Sunday I'd slave in the kitchen, and we'd all sit down to dinner, like a Norman Rockwell painting. And then my son would start fighting with my daughter. And my husband would scream at my son because he was talking with food in his mouth. None of the feelings I wanted to be at the table were there."

Fiona found a solution by varying the Sunday activities. There was much less tension when the whole family went to a movie or a horse show and then stopped for a quick bite at a Burger King or a Chinese restaurant. Fiona was able to preserve her dream of togetherness without assuming the control herself and thus putting strain on the entire family. And she found that their time spent together was now more likely to be "quality time."

What Is Quality Time?

What do we mean when we say "quality time," a phrase working mothers seem to use a great deal? Quality time is best defined by what it is not. The quality in time has nothing to do with ballet lessons or fancy summer camps or lavish parties. It may well be the two hours spent sitting next to your daughter at the hottest play in town, but it can just as easily be the twenty minutes you spend perched on the edge of the bathtub while your four-year-old is taking a bath.

Spending quality time with a child means simply *being with him, showing him that you care about him, that you are interested in what he is doing, in what he has to say*. It hardly matters what you are doing with the child, as long as your attention is given over to the relationship between you. Ellen Galinsky, of New York City's Bank Street College, also emphasizes the importance of quality in daily family life. Time that parents spend in problem-solving with their children—discussing the news at the dinner table, helping children handle their social life, making family plans—is time that leads to growth for both parents and children.

Can a busy working mother provide quality time in the limited hours she spends with her children? We believe she can, not only because she knows how important she is to her child—and so puts aside other activities to be with him—but also because she finds the time she spends with her child fulfilling. As one young woman commented, "Mothering makes you feel mothered."

Working parents spend just as much leisure time with their children as do families in which the mother doesn't work. Although nonemployed mothers usually have at their disposal a higher *quantity* of time to be with their children, the time is not necessarily of high *quality*. A lot depends on what a mother feels about what she is doing: Current research indicates that a dissatisfied, unhappy mother who would rather be working or a mother strapped by no money has much more difficulty establishing a healthy "quality" relationship with her children than the mother who is doing what she wants to be doing.

The debate is really less about quantity vs. quality and more about the true meaning of "quality." In fact, experts have decried the use of the word. Says psychologist Marcia W. Plunkett: *"The time a mother spends with her child should not be idealized this way. They need 'nonquality' time together, too—time spent in routine care and time to worry together. That's what real relationships are about."*

Here are some ways to think about quality time:

Look at the kind of time you spend with your children. Parent educator Carol Spero says: "When we speak of quality time we mean having the ability to transform the values of the adult world —the more disciplined, intellectual, self-controlled world—into the primitive world of children, tolerating the intensity of feeling, intensity of dependency, the intensity of primitive bodily needs." This transition from "civilized to primitive" means that you must have a "mind set that lets you be aware and prepared psychologically to *move into your child's world.*" Working parents face the difficult task of having to be both organized enough to create blocks of time with their children and flexible enough to pass comfortably between two worlds.

Recognize that your job as a parent demands skills and timing different from those of the work world. You can file a stack of papers while talking on the phone, but don't try these efficiency expert feats with your children. You'll cheat yourself and your baby if you prop a bottle instead of luxuriating in the pleasure you give each other; you'll get a big "nothing" if you wait for your kindergardener to respond on cue to "What did you do today?" Instead, stick around quietly and be amazed at the news he'll report!

Don't replace constancy with intensity. The mother who hired a helicopter to take her son and his playmates sightseeing on his fourth birthday would have spent her money more wisely by taking two days off and just hanging around the house. It is possible, in fact, to provide constancy without being constantly available. When you are actively involved in your child's daily routines—when you "choreograph his day," as one woman put it—you tell him that you care about him and that you are emotionally available.

The debate over quality time is far from over, and the emphasis is still shifting. As Betty Friedan writes in *The Second Stage* (Summit, 1982): " 'Quality, not quantity' is insufficient rhetoric; we must ask now how much parenting, when, how can it be best shared between parents, and with other substitutes for those aunts and grandmothers who no longer live down the block?"

Successful families in which both parents work have found new ways to spend time with their children.

One-on-One.   Quality time can mean simply one parent, one child, and no distractions. A family dinner, no matter how tasty or how long you've labored to prepare it, will be a lot less appealing to your nine-year-old than a date in a restaurant with just you and no other siblings. A three-year-old will delight in a trip with his father to a nearby ice-cream parlor.

One mother plans a night of Christmas shopping—in June, when the stores are not crowded and she and her daughter can browse happily while checking off their holiday purchases. Another mother makes a point of occasionally meeting her daughter for a school-day lunch date. Other possibilities: check your local museum for a night in the week they stay open; let your husband take one child to a basketball game while you escort the other to a movie. Resist the impulse to combine forces; remember, the point is to enjoy the intimacy of a night alone with one child.

Fun and Games.   Many of us are so busy we forget that playing games with our children is a valuable family experience. When you and your kids play games together, remember, once again, to be flexible. You'll never enjoy an all-family poker game if you try to convince your seven-year-old son not to pull to an inside straight!

Sara Friedman, author of *How Was School Today, Dear? (Fine, What's for Dinner)* (Reader's Digest Press, 1977) has this to say about the benefits of game playing:

"We play a lot of games in our family, in twos, threes, and all together. We argue a lot; some of us cheat; some of us are terrible losers. But we also find the experience a valuable means of communicating when we don't feel like talking. Playing games with our kids helps them channel their competitive and aggressive drives toward the world in general, toward each other, toward us in particular—not to mention ours toward them. Family games also help our kids work out growing pains and develop intellectual skills. They give our kids the chance to be on equal footing with us. And most important, they seem to give us all a chance to explore and work out naturally many of the complex family dynamics—both stressful and affectionate—that seem to smolder unheeded in so many families."

Homework.   Helping with schoolwork is an excellent way of relating to your child *if* you take some precautions. Resist becoming so invested that you cross the thin line between *helping* and *doing*; the hassles that will develop as responsibility shifts in your direction will make you sorry you ever peeked inside your daughter's notebook. Instead, use this opportunity for the two of you to share ideas, information, and maybe even a laugh or two.

A mother of a ninth-grader reported that reading *Julius Caesar* out loud to her son gave him a better grasp of Shakespeare as well as an hour of friendly dramatics every Saturday morning. Reading out loud for pleasure has in fact become a more and more popular pastime between parents and children, even teenagers. (*The Read Aloud Handbook*, Penguin Books, 1982, includes an excellent age-graded reading list.)

Your idea of homework-helping may not always be the same as your child's. Don't be offended if just as you launch into your most inspired speech on the Tigris and Euphrates valley your daughter dismisses you with an irritated "But, Mom, the teacher only wants three agricultural products." Remember, it's *her* homework; let her stay in control.

Kids' Time, Parents' Time. In our eagerness to spend as much time as possible with our children, some of us are tempted to let them join in all activities. Baking an apple pie together is quality time spent with your eleven-year-old. Allowing a five-year-old to fold the eggs into a noodle pudding is not. If you absolutely must get that porch railing fixed today, don't try to combine it with a pleasant visit with your toddler. Wait till she naps to do your hammering, and let her keep you company while you sort laundry instead.

"MOMMY WILL BE HOME IN A FEW DAYS . . ."

Travel Tips for Working Mothers

More and more women are traveling on business. While many of today's mothers (and fathers, too) limit travel when their children are very young, families are finding they can manage—and even thrive—when a parent takes a trip. Whether you travel regularly or only once in a while, here are proven strategies to keep you from turning a business trip into a guilt trip:

- Tell your child matter-of-factly about your trip in advance—where you're going, what you'll be doing, when you'll be back—and then tell him again just before you leave. Children need lots of reassurance that "Mommy will be home in a few days." Read younger children the quietly reassuring picture book *My Mom Travels a Lot*, by Caroline Feller Bauer (Warne, 1981).
- Make as few changes as you can in your child's routine. Small children are most secure in their own homes with the other parent, Grandma, or a trusted sitter in charge.
- Like E.T., working mothers need to "phone home." Avoid separation anxiety (your child's and yours) by calling when children are most receptive to conversation: dinnertime, bedtime, right after school. This may take a little advance planning, especially if you're phoning from a different time zone. Don't feel guilty about charging

your calls to your expense account; remember, Dad's "Hi, honey, how're the kids?" has traditionally gone on the company bill.

- Carry important phone numbers with you in case you have to negotiate a long-distance emergency. Leave at home the number of your hotel and places where you can be reached during the day.
- Little kids love getting postcards or letters on hotel stationery. Even if you're only gone overnight, try sending these instead of carting home expensive "guilt gifts." Limit obligatory gifts to trips of more than one week.
- Your grade-school son or daughter will feel very grown-up to go along with you on a short trip. If your job permits this, it is worth taking a child out of school for special time "alone with Mom." Make sure she is old enough to visit a museum or to use the hotel pool or game room while you're out at appointments; leave phone numbers where you can be reached, and warn your hosts that your child might call.
- Turn travel into a benefit by recharging your batteries while you're away. Even the solitude of a two-hour plane ride can be a shot in the arm. And a quiet dinner in your hotel room may be the most peaceful evening you've had in months. You can ease the stress of overeating and undersleeping by squeezing in a visit to your hotel's health club. Many large hotel chains are adding special facilities for traveling businesswomen, and in some cities you can get a guest pass to local health clubs or exercise classes.

Keeping in Touch With School

Many a confident working mother is turned into a sniveling wreck by none other than her child's teacher. ("I'm so sorry you won't be able to stay, Mrs. Green; Jennifer would so like you to watch her in the spelling bee.") Or by that formidable adversary, the school nurse. ("Jennifer's throat sounds a little scratchy, Mrs. Green, perhaps you'd better come and get her.") There are women who admit to shedding tears at the very sight of a note that begins with the familiar "Dear Parents: Tomorrow is the fourth-grade play. We very much hope. . . ."

"All the Mommies Were There But You." Writer Linda Bird Francke has said, "There is only one face that the school child who is the third violet from the left on stage, or has four alto recorder notes to blow in the recital is looking for in the audience. And that face belongs to the mother."

Not necessarily. In a modern family, those small eyes might just as well search out Daddy's face. Or Grandma's. Or even a favorite baby-sitter's. But certainly you want to be present for school events, not only because they are important to your child, but also because missing them is missing out on the joy of sharing in your child's life.

In the beginning of the school year, *inform the teacher that you are eager to attend all functions, but that you must have ample notice so that you can make arrangements.* Insist that you be notified about meetings, plays, and recitals with both a note and a reminder note (don't count on your child to tell you about these events). Giving the same information to the class will also help.

Encourage your husband or other relatives and friends to stand in for you when you cannot be in attendance. Knowing that the grown-ups in his life care about him in this way will help your child feel secure and loved, and will add an unexpected pleasure to the visiting adults' life as well.

Get involved in school affairs. If your time is very limited, leave the cake sales to less busy parents, but try to attend Parents' Association meetings or any other community events that affect school policy. Not only will this give you a needed say in what happens in your children's school, but it also reassures your children that you care deeply about an important aspect of their lives. "My kids always seem pleased when I tell them I'm going to a meeting at their school," comments one mother. "I think they see my going as a kind of involvement in their lives."

If you can't manage to bake the brownies or sell the raffles, support the parents who do. Offer your home for a special event; agree to chauffeur parents who don't have cars; donate money in lieu of your services.

Keep in touch with the teacher. Explain that you want to be kept informed about both progress and problems (if you're lucky, you'll then hear about Johnnie's star performance in the math test, not just about his abominable behavior in gym). Give the teacher your phone number, ask her for hers, and suggest that you and she confer on a regular basis.

Share with the teacher information about changes in your home life that might affect your child's performance in the classroom. A new baby, a divorce, moving to a new home, even a change in your husband's or your own job situation can have an impact on your child.

Hard Times—And How to Cope With Them

> *"My life is like a delicate well-built house of cards.*
> *One thing goes wrong and it all collapses."*
> *"I get so frantic when somebody gets sick that I've*
> *stopped taking temperatures."*
> *"Right after Thanksgiving I start worrying about*
> *Christmas vacation ... the closer it gets the more*
> *desperate I feel."*

Sound familiar? Juggling roles is difficult enough when everything is going well; when we are struck by circumstances beyond our control, the best of us have been known to falter. Even supermoms push the panic button when a child is sick. And there's hardly a working mother who has not agonized through the day-by-day planning of a school vacation. But the wisest working mothers have learned to cope with these hard times by constantly reminding themselves that: (1) their nonworking sisters are probably not managing any better than they are; they're just worrying about it less; and (2) mobilizing resources and tackling problems immediately is the best antidote to panic.

When a Child Is Ill. The glazed eyes of a feverish five-year-old, the croupy cough of an infant's bronchitis, hold special terror for the working mother. Says one: "Even as I'm shaking down the thermometer, all I can think of is which of us—my husband or me—will stay home tomorrow."

Not all of us can be as enterprising as the Baltimore judge whose daughter recovered from the chicken pox in her mother's chambers ("I granted every request for a recess for three days"). Or as lucky as the New York account executive whose boss thinks so much of her he pays for a sitter when her children are sick. But most working mothers do cope when their children are ill. Many feel perfectly comfortable leaving a child with the regular sitter, or with someone called upon for the occasion (experienced working mothers have long lists of emergency backup help). Many daycare centers have sick bays that can take care of children who don't have a serious or contagious illness. Some mothers even let a child who's feeling under the weather accompany them to the office for the day.

Many of us cherish memories of our own mothers sitting at our bedsides, faithfully spooning out medicines and helping us with our coloring books. But many children actually prefer to be left alone with a good book or a rare chance to watch TV for a whole day.

Children under the age of eight or so usually cannot stay at home alone. And even if you have a trusted person fill in for you, you may want to give your child some extra emotional support when she is sick. A good way to manage this is to stay home for a few hours: Your child gets the clear message that you care about him and are there to keep him company while he is feeling so miserable, and you are still able to fulfill your obligations at the office. If your child must be home for a few days, try to take turns caring for her with your husband.

If you do leave a child home alone in bed, be sure to call home periodically ("I let him stay in my bed, which is next to the phone, so he won't have to get up to answer it," says one mother) and have the foresight to leave a prepared lunch. Try to arrange for a neighbor to look in on him, and remember to leave plenty of reading material and other in-bed diversions.

Many a parent has found that not coddling the child with a cold or other minor ailment has actually helped him get better faster. Sensible advice along these lines comes from a New York City politician: "I handle it exactly the way my mother did. I remember it was extremely disappointing, but I also remember surviving it. The general message is, 'You're sick, but I'm not and I'm going to work, and you stay home and I will call you twice during the day, and you can have ice cream for your throat. And you'll be much happier and much less bored when you're back in school.'" She reports that, like herself as a child, her children tend to have few illnesses and to recover from them very quickly.

School Vacations.   Try trading off with a nonworking mother (you take her children on Saturday or Sunday) or teaming up with another working parent to hire a high-school student who can entertain your children for the day. If your children attend an after-school center, check their schedule; many centers offer a full-day program on days that schools are closed.

Keeping children happily occupied during the Christmas and Easter vacations presents more of a problem than do one-day holidays. An obvious solution, of course, is for the whole family to take their vacation at this time. Less obvious is for one parent to take a vacation with the children during Christmas, the other during Easter week.

Older children present a special problem for working parents, since they may be too young to amuse themselves or to find jobs easily and too old for traditional camp experiences.

Here are some possibilities:

Volunteering. Hospitals, nursing homes, and childcare agencies welcome aides. Youngsters can tutor children, help in arts-and-crafts programs, assist in laboratories—while gaining valuable work experience.

Summer school. Not as grim as it sounds. Here's a chance for your child to catch up on problem subjects, or to study computer programming, photography, typing, ceramics, dance, or other subjects she wouldn't ordinarily encounter.

Part-time work. Mowing lawns, delivering groceries, and baby-sitting give youngsters a chance to earn money and practice independence.

STRATEGIES FOR SCHOOL VACATIONS

Plan ahead. Avoid the panic of last-minute preparations by taking the time well in advance to schedule entertainment, hire helpers, make arrangements. Don't get caught short by an unexpected one-day holiday: Post your child's school calendar in a place you can always see it.

Do your homework. Look into community services—YMCAs often have inexpensive Christmas and summer programs; churches and synagogues operate sleep-away and day camps. Check the classified section of your local paper for parent cooperatives, or try forming one of your own.

Combine forces or trade off with another family. You take Christmas, they take Easter. Sharing a summer rental or taking turns vacationing with a brood of kids is a good way to give your children new experiences—and to save money at the same time.

Hire a mother's helper. This can make the difference between a boring vacation for your children (plus guilt and aggravation for you) and a fun-filled week of activities. You'll need an older student (preferably one who drives) for longer vacations, but even a twelve-year-old can manage to sustain enough interest and assume enough responsibility to entertain small children for a few days.

===

Succeeding With Teenagers

*"[They] have to establish themselves as separate people who can make some decisions, live with some freedom, and exercise some control over other people . . . learning to balance feelings of independence and needing to be cared for, on the one hand, and the need to be independent or separate, on the other. People around [the developing person] usually experience this upheaval . . . with almost as much unpleasantness as the person feels."** *

It sounds like the perfect description of your teenage daughter. One minute she's pulling you in, the next she's pushing you away. But, surprise! The writer is not talking about teenagers at all. In fact, this is a description of toddlers. That it fits equally well our adolescent sons and daughters tells us something important about this brief, but intense, period of human development.

Like the two- or three-year-old, the teenager is involved in a fierce struggle between autonomy and dependence, and, like that earlier struggle, this one is necessary and normal. The adolescent's task is to separate, to move away from us, while at the same time keeping a watchful eye out to make sure we don't forsake him.

Much has been said about the adolescent's contrariness, his drive

* From Robert Lurie and Roger Neugebauer, eds. *Caring for Infants and Toddlers.* Vol. II. Child Care Information Exchange, Copyright 1982, page 17.

to be his own person. But it is the other side of the push-pull that working parents need to pay special attention to. The toddler stamps her foot "no," runs away, dashes back to the safe berth of our lap. The teenager's course is less direct, but the message is no less clear: "I need you; I care what you think of me; I want you to care about me."

Liberated from bottles and diapers, we sometimes forget how much teenagers do need us. When your 5' 10" hulk calmly informs you that he knows more than you do about cooking, cars, and most of western civilization, it may be hard to remember his neediness. But if you listen carefully, the message will come through, and you will be able to respond helpfully.

Fifteen-year-old Jeff, whose mother works two nights a week, complains that no one is around to serve him dinner, even though he's perfectly capable of doing this himself. His mother reminds him of his competence, but she also acknowledges his need for nurturance: "Jeff, I know you don't like eating alone; let's see how we can solve this problem." Reassured that his feelings are taken seriously, Jeff says, "Well, I guess it's not that bad . . . and maybe we can eat together on Thursday." A solution will be found. Sixteen-year-old Janice announces that she's tired of "cold food," frozen dinners that she must prepare herself. An alert parent hears a plea for family warmth, not merely for hot food.

Jeff and Janice remind us of the crucial importance of touching base, which often centers around dinnertime. Overburdened working parents and overscheduled teenagers make it all too easy to let this part of family life slip through the cracks. Even if it's chaotic— and many dinners are—the evening meal is a natural time for sharing experiences and ideas. You can use this opportunity to talk about your own work experiences, to help teens sort out their own career options. Some parents, in fact, make a point of inviting friends to dinner who have a variety of jobs and provide additional role models for their youngsters.

If you have only recently returned to work, dinner-table conversation may explode with you and your teenager clashing in the identity-seeking arena. In the beginning, be especially sensitive to this potential conflict by putting your child's needs before your own. Resist the impulse to chatter about your job. Be available to hear about your son or daughter's plans and aspirations.

It's important to be available to teenagers on their terms and within their time frame. For working mothers, gone for most of the day, this may mean rearranging your schedule—canceling an evening appointment or sticking around on Sunday morning instead of going off jogging—so that you can give your youngster your emotional energy and time. The mother of a thirteen-year-old comments: "He's the kind of kid that if you spend X amount of time you will find out what's happening. You just have to be willing to take the time."

What of the other side of adolescence, the push toward autonomy? If we see opposition—messy rooms, loud music, long hair—as normal expressions of the separation process, we won't get so involved in a battle that has no winner. Here the working mother has an edge. A nonworking mother has this to say: "Every fight we had was about control. I tried to remember that she was not just trying to destroy me, but still we fought constantly." The mother who works is more involved with her own life, less inclined to identify with her children's every move, and more able to gain perspective.

Communicating respectfully with teenagers, acknowledging their feelings but setting firm limits on their behavior—above all, keeping your sense of humor—will lead you to what psychologist Sandra Scarr has called "peace with honor." Here are some markers to guide you along the way:

Take Them Seriously. This is not always easy, since teenagers live in a state of urgency that often defies reason. In your sixteen-year-old's eyes, the report you have to type by tomorrow pales in significance to the pimple that has just erupted on his chin. As Carol Eisen Rinzler reminds us in her hilarious and unfailingly true *Your Adolescent: An Owner's Manual* (Atheneum, 1981), "Time moves oddly for your adolescent—in the space of twenty-four hours it can have its life ruined forever by wearing the wrong belt, and experience euphoria by receiving two invitations to go out on Saturday night." Remember, though, that these roller-coaster moods are very real to a teenager—and, what's more, he somehow expects us to share the intensity of his feelings. A loving parent does her best. Ask any mother who's jeopardized her career dashing out of the office at three-thirty to search for the exact right map for the social studies paper due tomorrow.

Communicate Without Evaluating.   At no time in your career as a parent is this more important. New York City parent educator Nancy Samalin, following the teachings of psychologist Haim Ginott, has helped hundreds of mothers and fathers talk to their children in ways that make the most of their limited time together. Samalin says: "If your teenager promises he's going to do the dishes and you've come home after a long day and you're tired and you see all the dishes in the sink, you can say, 'You rotten slob. You're going to turn out just like your uncle Si, and he's a pig, you know that.' Chances are you'll have the kid either telling you you're a slob yourself and the dishes'll still be in the sink, and you'll end up doing them with a lot of rage. Or you can talk about yourself rather than telling him what a slob he is. You can say, 'Johnny, I'm very upset to walk in and see a sink full of dishes. I expect them to be taken care of now.' And then, if you're smart, *you'll walk out of the room, because he'll save face; he'll have a chance to do it.* And when he does it, it's important to say, 'Thank you, I appreciate it,' not, 'Well, it's about time.' "

Don't Nag and Don't Argue.   "Adolescents are notoriously mother-deaf and father-deaf," says Samalin. "They expect us to criticize or chastize them, so they simply turn us off." Write short notes instead of nagging: "Dear Johnny, I was upset to find the new typewriter half off the edge of the desk. This situation needs a solution. Love, Mom." Nice notes are important, too. Saying, "I was so appreciative to come home exhausted and find the dishes put into the dishwasher," will make your teenager feel, as one youngster expressed it, that you're on his side, not on his back.

Don't despair if your youngster complains about what you ask him to do—as long as he does it. Jo Ann and fifteen-year-old Mike have gotten this message. Here's a typical dinnertime scene:

JO ANN: Mike, please cut the bottoms off these artichokes and put them in the pot.

MIKE: I'm not cutting no bottoms off no artichokes. *(as he deftly does just that)*

JO ANN: *(thinking: At his age I'd have been thrilled to eat an artichoke—and where did he get that grammar?)* I heard the funniest story at the office this morning.

MIKE: *(interested enough to be polite.)* Yeah? What d'you want me to do with this cucumber?

JO ANN: Just slice it and put it on the table. Well, this man said—

MIKE: I'm not slicing no cucumbers. *(as he does so, expertly)*

JO ANN: Thanks, Mike . . . so this man started to tell us . . .

Jo Ann's story continues, and so do Mike's remarks, as mother and son amiably prepare and eat dinner.

Give Rules, not Advice.   Teenagers do not want to hear how much harder life was for you when you were their age or how they should be grateful for the opportunities you give them. Preoccupied as they are with their social and sexual yearnings, they pay scant attention to our efforts to socialize them. What they can't ignore, however, are our rules, especially if these are presented unambivalently. "When a mother says 'no,' and she really means 'maybe,' says Samalin, "the child hears only 'maybe.'" (Be prepared, though, to negotiate curfews and privileges as your children get older.)

Firm rules about drug and alcohol use, sexual behavior, and car safety are very important. No evidence suggests that children of working mothers are any more prone to delinquency, addiction, or sexual promiscuity than those whose parents are around all the time, but there is little doubt that they have much less daytime supervision. Some parents feel a terrible lack of control: A Houston mother announces quite earnestly that she plans to stop working when her oldest child reaches seventh grade. This may be an extreme solution, but with drug and alcohol use reaching epidemic proportions even among preteens—latest estimates suggest that nearly 95 percent of teenagers have experimented with drinking or marijuana—rules will reassure both you and your teenager.

You may want to prohibit after-school visitors, insist that your teenager call you every afternoon to report where he is and what he's doing. You'll probably want him to check in by six o'clock. Remember, setting limits tells your child that you care about him and also paves the way for honest communication about your values and expectations.

Don't underestimate how much your opinion counts. One mother reported that simply saying the following to her thirteen-year-old helped keep him out of trouble: "You're too young and inexperienced to use this drug; I believe it is harmful, and I'm definitely against your using it. I don't care what other kids are doing. Marijuana is illegal, and I can't condone or protect you from the consequences of doing something that is against the law."

Give Them Privacy. Teenagers need connection and communication, but they also need privacy. Don't hound them with questions; instead, try to be available when they choose to confide in you. Knock before you go into their rooms; respect their separateness. One mother resolved the conflict between privacy and safety by having her seventeen-year-old daughter leave in a sealed envelope a note where she was going in the evening. The mother agreed not to open the envelope unless there was an emergency.

As we have seen, the teenage years are a time of both change and continuity. Adolescents seek to establish their own identities separate from ours, yet based on our role models. Even as your daughter dismisses your job as "gross and boring" she may be planning to follow right along in your footsteps (studies show that adolescent daughters of working mothers are most likely to name mother as the person they most admire).

Like their preschool counterparts, adolescents are a mass of contradictions, but if we steer clear of the crossfire, sharing our lives with teenagers can even be rewarding. One mother told of finally being awarded a Ph.D. after nearly a decade of hard work. After all those years of feeling guilty and enduring her children's resentment, it's no wonder that she was stunned—and more than a little pleased —when her son introduced her at a party, saying, "I'd like you to meet my mother, Dr. Daniels."

The Bottom Line

As we develop new kinds of relationships with our families and discover new ways of being together, we learn that the road to work is not the road to ruin for our children. We find out that children are resilient; they are far more adaptable than many of us realize. They do not need our constant attention to grow into self-reliant, self-respecting adults. They do need our love and the devotion and protection of other adults in their world. And this we can give them whether or not we hold jobs outside our homes.

But we can also give them something else: models of ourselves as creative, satisfied women, models that will help them make intelligent choices for their own futures. We can, by our own example, show them men and women breaking away from old patterns, so that they can ultimately enrich their own lives and the lives of their children. We can give them the space to experience loneliness, to suffer some of life's disappointments, and to learn and gain strength from these experiences.

And, finally, because we must demand their cooperation, we can teach them to take pride in their own efforts as well as the group endeavors of their families. These are valuable lessons.

Part Two

Your Career

Verbal Irony

Chapter Ten

Succeeding on the Job

By sheer numbers working mothers may be a revolutionary force in the American labor market. But we've certainly not revolutionized the work place yet. Thanks to legislation of the past few years, pregnancy is no longer a cause for dismissing a woman employee, and maternity leave is becoming a standard benefit (though only about 40 percent of working women are now offered maternity leave). But succeeding on the job as a working mother is still like running an obstacle course. Here are some of the hurdles you may encounter and ways of handling them.

Demonstrating Your Commitment to the Job. Often you may feel you can't give as much to your job as is expected. Conflicts will arise. You may not be able to work late every time your boss asks. You may have to say no to special assignments or travel. Or take time off from the office to take your son to the dentist. It's especially important then for your colleagues and supervisor to know you care deeply about your job. As most of us have learned, a manager often judges a worker not on the basis of how she does the job, but on a complex of subtle factors that are sometimes summed up as "attitude."

Your commitment may be conveyed by simply telling your boss how much the job means to you and that it's not just a place you go every day. Or you can take extra care to abide by customs of your company. If long lunch hours are frowned on, don't stretch yours out. If your boss likes a certain style of report, be sure yours follows it.

Occasionally your commitment may be demonstrated when you

go to great inconvenience to join in special events or help out during pressured times of the year. You may join your co-workers for a weekend think tank, despite the extra arrangements and sitters' fees it costs you. Or take work home for a week if you can't stay late while your co-workers are putting in overtime.

You may sacrifice some of your personal satisfaction for the greater good. "I *never* miss a deadline," says a writer for a small neighborhood paper. "I would love to have more time to polish my stories at the last minute, but it's more important to everybody else on the staff that I simply get things in on time. So even if I want a little more time to make it read perfectly, I make that my sacred rule—don't miss a deadline."

Try to figure out the most important single requirement of your job and deliver it. It's easier than trying to achieve every one of the many goals that a job entails. And if you've demonstrated your basic commitment, you're much more likely to meet understanding when you have to come in late, leave early, or otherwise alter your job conditions.

Finding the Right Atmosphere.   Different jobs offer different kinds of pluses for the working mother—and different kinds of strain. Having a profession, like medicine or law, may eventually mean having more freedom in your schedule, but for years before reaching that, you'll have a hard apprenticeship with long daily hours. For some women, the solution is to select a specialty, such as pediatrics for a doctor, or nontrial work for a lawyer, that offers a more regular schedule.

If you work for a large corporation, you'll probably enjoy the prospect of greater job mobility—more departments, more different kinds of jobs that you can aspire to. You'll probably also enjoy good benefits—better medical insurance, disability, and dental plans—and since financial security for your family is a big reason why you're likely to be working, these are important pluses. Both these advantages compensate the corporate woman for some of the rigidity in office hours, job descriptions, and generally bureaucratized systems that a large organization requires.

Working in a small office, on the other hand, where management and co-workers know you well, may allow you to set more of your own working conditions. Jennifer, who works at a real estate busi-

ness with four other agents, found she could bring her five-year-old
son to the office for the two afternoons a week her sitter was un-
available, but only because she insisted. "All the people I work with
are childless, either divorced fathers who see very little of their
children or women who've never had any. So when I brought Jerry
to the office, they just didn't know what to make of it. There were
some complaints, until I subtly reminded them that I'd put up with
all their problems. One woman had a drinking problem we all
tolerated, and one of the men was tied up in a messy affair for a
long time. We just looked on these as human problems that we had
to cope with. If I've been able to accommodate to them, they can
accommodate to me."

If you own your own business, you may discover it takes more
time than working for someone else. You won't necessarily have the
freedom to come and go, close the shop for emergencies, that you
imagined. Still, if you have a talent that you can package in your
own business, and if you can take financial risk without undue
nervousness, being an independent can be the best way of life for
you.

Make a list of the drawbacks and benefits of your own work
atmosphere. Try to find ways to relieve the strains and maximize
the benefits. Or, if the negatives seriously outweigh the positives,
you may need to think of changing jobs.

Conflicts Between Work and Parenting Responsibilities. What do
you do when your child is sick? The first impulse is to reach for
the phone and call in sick yourself. "The whole office," says Sara, an
associate in a law firm, "thought I had flu when my son was the one
who actually had it. Then when I got it myself, I struggled through
and missed only one day from work."

Whether they're assembly-line workers or account executives,
mothers fear that staying home with a child is an unacceptable
excuse to call in with. Yet the sick-child conflict has probably caused
more worry by managers and by mothers themselves than it actually
merits. "Absentee rates of mothers are just the same as other workers," says one personnel director. And a Public Health Survey found
no statistically significant differences in illness and injury time between men and women, with men averaging 5.2 days a year off and
women averaging 5.6.

If you must stay home with a sick child, present some alternatives to your employer for getting your work done during your absence. You can:

- offer to work at home (maybe this is a good time to catch up on a disagreeable job you've been putting off)
- offer to work extra when you return
- have a clearcut backup plan at work for emergencies

Just as with your childcare system, having a work backup plan for crises is so basic you should devote time to developing it. Diane, an executive secretary with two young boys, works closely with her boss in a job that is a team effort. Unlike a pool typist, she can't easily be replaced. So Diane defied one of the alleged rules of business (*make yourself indispensable*) by organizing her files so carefully a temp could retrieve whatever her boss needed. For her boss's reassurance, she also prepared a slim index detailing every subject he might need—"1984 Sales Budget," "Regional Sales Reports," "Client Followups"—with numbered directions showing where to find the information ("File Cabinet 2, Folder 29"). Not only did Diane feel less pressured when her children needed her to stay home, she and her boss found her meticulous organization helped them perform better when she was there.

Organize your files, records, or working materials so that co-workers can find key papers or follow your guidance by phone. Careful record keeping takes time, but you'll feel easier when your daughter is throwing up at seven A.M. and you're trying to decide if you should stay home.

Another backup plan is to adopt a work buddy. Acquaint yourselves with each other's jobs and be prepared to fill in for each other. It's easier to call in that you'll be out if you can say in the same breath that "John will look out for my phone and call me if anything major pops up."

Overtime and Special Arrangements.   One of the two daily trials in a working mother's life is getting to work on time. The second is leaving on time. Do you often get last-minute assignments or problems at the end of the day that make you end up racing to your daycare center, and paying the five dollars or more that many centers charge for late pickups?

Laura, a medical technician who works at a clinic run by six doctors, was distressed that several times a week, a scant half-hour before she was to leave, she would be deluged with samples that the doctors wanted tests started on. "Of course, they all want their results the next day so they can phone Mrs. So-and-So." Laura fumed for months until she finally totaled up the late charges she was paying to her daycare center. She spoke to her employers and showed what they were costing her by asking for only ten or fifteen minutes of extra time.

As a compromise, Laura suggested that she be notified two hours in advance when appointments were running late, so that she could arrange for her husband to pick up their child. The doctor agreed, and even volunteered that in cases where he couldn't let her know in advance, the clinic would foot the late charge.

What if *you* need to make a change in your workday? Usually the best solution is a trade-off with your employer. An accountant who worked largely on her own decided that it was extremely important that she accompany her daughter for several months every Wednesday at four-thirty for a speech therapy session. Instead of sneaking out on those days, she told her employer that she felt it was vital to her daughter that she go with her to therapy and that in return for leaving early she would take a half-hour lunch break on Wednesdays. She took the same occasion to tell him about a new system she was developing to speed work flow in her department. She left him feeling that he could count on her loyalty and commitment despite a little irregularity in her hour of leaving.

Socializing.   Do many of your co-workers spend afterhours socializing with clients, each other, or superiors? Do you feel they're accomplishing an important part of their job through these off-the-job contacts?

Establishing good relations with others throughout your company, not just within your own department, can be important to your progress. But that needn't mean gathering with the gang everytime they have an after-work drink. Compensate by having lunch with people in your company or through shorter exchanges during the workday. Make up your mind that, whatever the gains you imagine your co-workers to be making from extracurricular friendships, your life simply doesn't permit it. And the advantage they're getting may be slighter than you think.

When you do join in, pick your occasions carefully. For example, you might choose to skip the farewell drinks for a co-worker (perhaps arrange for lunch instead), but decide to hire an extra sitter so you can go to a company baseball game where you'll have the chance to talk to key executives.

Seeking Promotions.   If you want to move ahead but can't possibly find time and energy to handle the next job up, see if you can figure out a way to do a part of it. Job categories aren't necessarily graven in stone. An assistant store buyer who felt she couldn't handle all the extra travel involved in covering trade shows for an entire women's sportswear department suggested that she take on just the junior sportswear lines. She was able to keep growing—and get a good raise based on her expanded responsibilities.

Accepting Promotions.   Sometimes a golden opportunity comes your way just when you're least prepared to take advantage of it. Leslie, a technical writer for a computer firm, had arranged to take six months off after having her baby. Two weeks after the baby came, her boss unexpectedly took another job across the country, and Leslie was offered his position as head of the writing section. Because turnover in her company was so low, and she was happily settled in the city where her job was located, Leslie decided to make the sacrifice and come back. She did arrange to work a nine-hour a day, four-day week for the first year, leaving her Fridays free. Looking back three years later, Leslie remembers how hard that first year was, but she's sure she made a wise decision.

On the other hand, don't assume that this is the only promotion offer you'll ever get. Opportunity doesn't come knocking only once.

What If You're Passed Over?   You and a man are up for the same job. He gets it, and you have the feeling that your parental responsibilities were the reason. What can you do? Since it's illegal to discriminate against a woman because she's a mother, no one in authority is likely to come out and tell you it's so. But a careful talk with whoever made the decision *is* in order. Find out if you're being passed over for this job because: (1) this was a one-time decision based on your employer's judgment about who was right for this particular job; or (2) it reflects a basic decision about either your capabilities or the ability of any mother to perform positions of greater responsibility within the company. If it seems you're not likely to be chosen for the next opening, it's time to go job-hunting.

If you have overt evidence that you were passed over only because of your being a parent, you may file a complaint with your state human rights division or with the federal EEOC offices. Complaints must be filed within ninety days.

Childcare: How Can Your Employer Help?

Childcare absorbs about 10 percent of most family budgets. Daycare expert Dana Friedman points out that childcare is the fourth largest expenditure in most families, ranking right after food, housing, and taxes. Some employers are beginning to see this major expense as a possible perk or optional benefit. Spurred on by new government tax incentives, more employers—about 500 as of 1983— are providing some form of childcare support. Possibly your employer would be willing to help if acquainted with these progressive new possibilities.

"Cafeteria" benefits. One way of providing benefits for employers with children is through a flexible plan, where workers choose the benefits that suit them (as though from a cafeteria selection). A young father, for example, might elect to take childcare benefits rather than the pension plan. Employers may actually reduce their expenditures on benefits by offering a flexible plan. And since benefits are not taxable as income, you may enjoy more real compensation from receiving childcare payments than from a higher salary.

Information and Referral Services (I & R's). One of the most direct services an employer can provide to working parents is a referral service to childcare facilities in the area, including daycare centers, sitters available for overtime use, and even length of waiting lists at centers. The I & R may be operated directly by the company (usually by the personnel department). Or if your company doesn't feel it has the expertise to maintain the service, it may contract with a nonprofit or other reliable group. Several companies may join to sponsor an I & R for all their employees.

General Mills, Polaroid, and Honeywell (Honeywell appropriately has a computerized childcare information network) are corporations that offer an I & R service.

On-site or Near-site Daycare. Many mothers dream of being able to work upstairs in the office while, downstairs, Johnny plays happily in his play group. Imagine the hours saved in hassled travel to his daycare center before coming to work! Imagine the comfort of being close in case of an emergency! Dr. Lester Rothman, a New York general practitioner who numbers many working mothers among his patients, says that the extra stress of getting a child across town to daycare is one stress too many. He thinks "on-site childcare in all our big skyscraper complexes should be required."

While on-site daycare would seem the ideal solution, Dana Friedman notes that there are few studies available to prove to corporations that this service would positively reduce absenteeism, tardiness, and turnover. And the legal, financial, and organizational complexities have made many companies shy away. Fewer than 100 on-site childcare facilities are in operation in the United States. The leader, often cited in discussions of the subject, is still the daycare center run by Stride-Rite in Boston, Massachusetts. Employees pay 10 percent of their salaries for childcare on the premises, and the rest of the cost is financed by Stride-Rite and the Massachusetts Department of Welfare.

But companies need not establish swings and nurseries within their own plants. They may be equally helpful by sponsoring a *nearby* childcare center where parents can quickly drop their children on their route to work. The corporation may help in several ways: by donating land, food, cleaning services, or a cash grant to a center nearby. Such benefits can be tax deductible for the corporation.

Vendor and Vendor-Voucher Systems. Only a few years ago it was impossible to imagine, but some companies are providing parents with a *voucher* to help defray the cost of childcare. The employee is then free to pick and choose the childcare that fits his and his child's needs best.

The company may fund the voucher by simply making an outright grant to the parent: Ford, for example, pays up to 50 percent of childcare expenses directly to families earning less than $25,000. Or the company may buy slots in existing centers at a discount rate and then pass the savings on to employee-parents. Or a company may join with other companies in a consortium that sponsors a group of daycare homes for employees' children.

Experience shows that corporate help works out best when the services are tailored to a particular community's needs. If the community already has a wide range of childcare choices, an on-site care may be redundant and fail to attract enough participants. If few options exist, the corporation might find other ways of encouraging more to come into being: either through grants to employees; grants to qualified daycare proprietors; or other noncash grants.

You can get more information on employer involvement in childcare by writing to the National Employer Supported Child Care Project, P.O. Box 40653, Pasadena, CA 91104-7652. Or order the useful booklet, "Child Care and the Working Parent: First Steps Toward Employer Involvement in Child Care" from Children at Work, Inc., a private consultation service at 569 Lexington Avenue, New York, NY 10022.

Besides childcare aid, corporations can provide other help for working parents, such as:

- Parenting seminars. Some corporations are hiring parenting counselors to address their employees on the problems of working parenthood and ways to handle them. Indeed, the parenting seminar has become a mini-boom, as corporations like Exxon, Citicorp, Philip Morris, and the United Energies Company offer this service.

  Even without a professional leader, a regular rap group with you and other parents over lunch in the cafeteria can be equally useful. Your company may donate a meeting room for your group, or provide coffee and refreshments.
- Sick days that can be used for children's illnesses.
- Bus pools that help speed parents to work and children to childcare. In Houston, for example, where transportation is

often hectic, Southern Bell and its next-door neighbor, the Houston Independent District School, collaborate on a much-valued van service that picks up parent and child simultaneously and deposits each at work and school.

Perhaps your employer will be responsive to helping parents. There are many tax deductible ways a company can help, ranging from those that cost no money to major investments.

Searching for the Flexible Schedule: Flexitime, Part-time, and Other Solutions

A job that will let you work fewer hours one week, more the next . . . a job that only makes you work thirty hours a week but pays regular benefits . . . a job not tied to the nine to five schedule—these may still only be fantasies that play in your mind as you sit drumming your fingers in the eight-thirty A.M. traffic jam or sink exhausted on the couch on a Friday, wishing you could only put three days together at home.

True, over 80 percent of all full-time jobs in America are rigidly programmed into the forty-hour, nine to five, five-day week. No major change has occurred in the American work week since the late 1930s, when the forty-hour standard was mandated by the Fair Labor Practices Act of 1938, a New–Deal-inspired reform that limits a nonmanagerial worker's week to forty hours and requires overtime pay for longer hours. While workers' benefits in salary, insurance, vacations, and other job conditions have escalated in the years since, the hours spent working haven't changed one whit.

Meanwhile, about half of all part-time workers are women between ages 20 and 44, and most of these hold jobs with medium to low wages as clerical workers, retail sales clerks, bookkeepers, receptionists, teachers aides, childcare workers, beauticians, nurses, teachers, or real estate agents. Yet the Bureau of Labor Statistics points out that between 1970 and 1978 the number of women working part-time in professional and technical jobs increased 36 percent, to over 1,000,000 women. The number of women working part-time in managerial and administrative jobs increased nearly 60 percent in the same period. More and more mothers are yearning for serious work with less than a rigid forty-hour week. While it's hard to arrange, corporations are beginning to explore alternative work patterns.

If you are running yourself ragged or need more time at home, here are some of the recognized new styles of flexible schedules to explore:

Job-sharing. Two people share a full-time job, usually splitting the hours in half. You and your partner might split days in half, with you on in the morning, your partner in the afternoon. Or you might alternate days. Or you could split 75–25.

Teachers, nurses, and bank officers are all among job-sharers. Two New York vocational teachers took their sharing even further and shared childcare. When one was teaching, the other kept both children.

The advantage of job-sharing is that you have a part-time job, but with full-time commitment and prestige. The disadvantage is your half-salary, and the possible loss of full fringe benefits, since few employers have proved willing to pay two sets of benefits for two half-timers.

Essential to the success of a job-sharing arrangement is a great deal of trust and likemindedness between you and your partner. And you should both be flexible about sitting down and evaluating problems and procedures as your experience together grows. For more information on how to present a job-sharing proposal to your company and other problems, write *New Ways to Work* (475 Kingsley Avenue, Palo Alto, CA 94301).

Compressed Work Week. The 4/40 compressed week allows you to put in ten hours or more of work in four days instead of five, leaving a stretch of three days off for your home activities. The advantage of having this span of time is great for some mothers, who say the three days off relaxes the grip of office tension and lets them have better, more relaxed time with their children. But others find ten hours daily, coupled with transportation time, much too long to be away from their children.

Flexitime. Maybe one of the most welcome of solutions, this system has been widely heralded and experimented with. You work forty hours a week but are only required to be in your office during a "core time"—usually ten A.M. to three P.M. Depending on your personal needs, you can come in early or late, and leave when your eight-hour day is done. The advantage is that you gain far greater flexibility at the beginning and end of the day—two of the crisis points in the working mother's life.

Part-time.   Part-time work can occupy you anywhere from a few hours a week to thirty, which is nearly a full work week. (Less than thirty hours a week, and an employer may not be required to give benefits.) You may work part-time on a free-lance basis or via a regular employee relationship with a firm. You may develop your talent into a free-lance business, negotiate a contract with a former employer, or take up a part-time occupation, such as being a home-based salesperson. Remember, part-time takes determination. To find out about likeminded part-timers, write the Association of Part-time Professionals, P.O. Box 3632, Alexandria ,VA 22302.

Your Own Flexible Schedule.   You may work out all sorts of varia-tions on a flexible schedule, depending on your employer's needs and yours. Amy, an editor, works three days a week from two P.M. to twelve midnight for a small weekly newspaper that closes on the third night of her schedule. Sue-Ellen works thirty-eight hours a week as an insurance salesperson, but she works six hours of each day as she wishes, depending on when potential customers can see her. Mary works at home mornings and afternoons at her office. What works for you and your employer may follow no one else's pattern.

Whatever you opt for, follow these rules to negotiate for your own flexible schedule—either to work *fewer hours* a week or to allow you more choice in the *times you work*.

1. *Negotiate as a known quantity.* Whether you want to job-share, arrange to take off Fridays, or otherwise create a schedule more suited to your home responsibilities, you'll probably have to start as an employee with a recognized value to the company. Marie had been with her accounting firm for six years when she proposed that her work could be compressed into four nine-hour days. Because she had

proved herself over the years as a committed employee, the partners of the firm were willing to believe her when she said she could organize herself to do the work in that span of time. (She also agreed not to expect a raise for two years, one of the many financial traps that the woman in search of a flexible schedule can fall into.)

2. *Look for a situation that can benefit not only you but your company.* A data processing firm had two small firms it was servicing. The two firms' needs did not require a full-time person on staff, but they did require someone who could respond immediately when a system broke down and needed an on-site visit. Helen persuaded her firm to let her work half-time but to make herself available *full-time* when emergencies arose. While it's seldom realized, many businesses have tasks that require less than a full-time employee but demand high-level skills. Look around your company for such opportunities and you may have the perfect proposal for a part-time job that will still pay well. Janet, a lawyer, works mornings serving five small clients. Her employer is happy to have Janet's skills, and at half-time, her salary is right for the fees the smaller clients pay.

3. *Develop a workable plan, complete with your financial compensation.* Be ready to demonstrate exactly how your work load would be handled. If you're looking to go part-time, or job-share, propose how your fringe benefits would be justified in full or altered.

4. *Suggest a trial period.* Even with the best plan in the world, and the most trusted employee, an employer is bound to be leery of work schedules that potentially could disrupt the office. She or he will probably protest that other co-workers will resent your "easier" schedule, or that no one will know what's going on unless you're on the premises at the same time as everyone else. A good proposal to suggest is that you try it for three months and evaluate the results; agree to look at the situation again in six months, and again at the end of the year. If it's not working, agree to come back on the old regular schedule. Even if the experiment doesn't work out, you'll learn something about your own needs by

having at least three months of an alternate working pattern.

5. *Don't underestimate your worth.* While you are asking for something special, remind your employer that the quality of your work is going to be the same. If you're working fewer hours but still producing the same volume of work, you deserve the same salary. And if you plan your alternative workstyle to be only temporary—a year or two until your child goes off to nursery school—remind your employer that you'll be back on the job before long. He'll avoid the risk of hiring an unknown person and the worry of training your replacement.

6. *Don't forget that small changes can be helpful.* You know you can't job-share. The kind of work you do demands that you be in place at the same hours as everyone else. You can't afford to go part-time. Is there any help? Don't overlook small adjustments in your schedule that could be godsends. For example, Kathleen, manager of a restaurant, managed to arrange her schedule so that she had a half-day off each two weeks. The four hours seem inconsequential, but they enable her to "have my hair done, go to the dentist, and sometimes take my two kids out for a special treat—all the things I could never do under my old schedule."

Can you do work at home occasionally? If you do establish a pattern of working regularly at home during normal office hours, your at-home efficiency may be confirmed and the practice can become accepted informally. This may be the icebreaker that can lead you to arranging a formal flexible schedule down the road.

We hope that the growing presence of women in the work place will bring change, will make the world of work more compatible with our responsibilities as parents. But experience tells us that changes always come hard. They will come only through the spirit and energy of women who realize their worth and find ways to persuade their companies to accommodate human needs. Whether you're making big waves or small ones in your company, chances are you're one of those women of spirit and energy.

WORKING AT HOME

For many mothers torn by doubts about leaving their home scene, the perfect answer may seem obvious: Work at home.

Maybe. While it's true that you can more easily sneak away for an afternoon of shopping when your "office" is the attic, you may find that it's not so easy to wear two hats under one roof. The number of career options you can pursue is limited, and the financial rewards are uncertain (remember, too, that you will forego medical insurance and other benefits). You may miss the companionship of an office, the sense of being part of a work team. Most important, unless you happen to be one of the rare at-home mothers who earn a lot of money, both you and your family may have trouble according your work the same respect that you would a job. In any case, you'll probably have trouble separating your working time from your mothering time. A Mommy-behind-closed-doors can be more confusing to small children than one who leaves the house each morning. And, as Cornell University psychologist Urie Bronfenbrenner notes, mothers who are on the premises all day are less likely than office workers to benefit from their husbands' shared participation in childcare and housework.

Despite these disadvantages, it is possible to make working at home work out well. Whether you are a graduate student or an artist, a free-lance writer or the proprietor of a mail-order business, you and other home-based career mothers face strikingly similar problems. Here are some tested solutions that will help you succeed:

- Set aside a work area that's yours and yours alone. Declare this space off limits to the family, and as a boost to your privacy, install a lock on the door.
- Invest in a separate phone and phone number and discourage other family members from answering your phone. Instead, install an answering device that will record calls while you are away from home or when you want to work without interruption.
- Decide what your working hours will be and then discipline yourself not to waver from them. Follow the lead of novelist Norma Klein, who applies makeup and gets dressed each morning as if she were going to an office. Or adopt the example of countless at-homers who rise at six A.M., dash through minimal morning chores, and settle down at their desks by eight-thirty A.M. as soon as their husbands and children leave for the day. Not interrupting your work

to walk the dog or stir the soup can make the difference between a satisfying career and unproductive busywork.

- Let teachers, other parents, even your friends know that you are not available for conferences, car pools, or chitchat during the hours you are working.
- Schedule all house service people—the exterminator, plumber, appliance repairman—on the same day. Don't arrange to have packages delivered at home just because you'll be around. Manage deliveries just as you would if you were working away from home.
- Combat the isolation of working at home by scheduling carefully planned breaks in the middle or at the end of your workday. Try to combine out-of-house chores with social visits. If your work is sedentary, use your breaks for exercise (try jogging to the corner for the newspaper instead of driving or having the paper delivered).
- Since few children really understand the meaning of "Mommy's working," don't try to work when they're around, unless you have nerves of steel. If your children are not in school, hire a sitter to entertain them during your working hours.

INSURANCE BASICS

Remember that you are a source of income to your family, and you should protect them from the potential loss of that income by adequate insurance. Be sure you understand what your company offers in both life and disability plans and how much coverage you're getting.

Life Insurance

What is life insurance? It's a plan by which you pay monthly sums to guarantee that your beneficiaries will receive a certain sum upon your death.

What kinds are there? Two basic kinds of insurance exist: term and cash value (also known as whole life, ordinary life, twenty-pay life, thirty-pay life). Term insurance offers the most coverage for the least money. It can be bought for any term up to ninety-nine years, and benefits are paid only in the event of your death. Cash-valued insurance is a mixture of life insurance and a savings account. As time goes on, the policy accrues in value and you can cash it in should you need the money. Payments are naturally higher for cash-valued insurance, and if you are disciplined enough to save on your own, you'll earn higher interest on your money in an ordinary savings account.

How much insurance should you carry? One rule of thumb is that you should carry an amount equal to your annual income. Another equally quoted rule is that a family should be insured for four or five times its annual income. But your decision will depend on how many other people your children could count on in the event of your death and how much you realistically can afford. Don't let an insurance agent pressure you into something you can't afford.

What's the best buy? Assess your personal needs and then shop around. Usually your best bet is to take out insurance through your employer, since group rates are cheaper. If you have substantial debts, you may want to take out extra insurance.

What traps do you look for? Be sure to read your contract, which, by law, must be in understandable English. Two points to check: be sure your policy is *renewable* (can be renewed after five years at higher rates agreed upon at the time of your original contract) and *convertible* (allowing you to change to another form of insurance should you choose to).

Disability Insurance

This kind of policy insures you in case you are disabled temporarily or permanently and unable to work. If your employer doesn't furnish disability, look for a policy with these features:

- It should pay when you are partially unable to work, so that you don't have to be totally disabled to collect.
- The best policy protects you in the work you do; it doesn't force you to take another kind of job in order to maintain disability benefits.
- When buying a policy be sure: (1) it can't be cancelled as long as premiums are paid; (2) benefits can't be reduced; and (3) premiums can't be increased.

Chapter Eleven

Pacing Your Career

Success as a working mother doesn't necessarily mean unbroken years of work. There may come periods when you need to think about taking time off, going on hold on the job, changing to a less taxing occupation, or even quitting. Will you feel a few pangs of jealousy during these times—when you see your old colleagues, your husband, or friends landing an exciting promotion, moving on to new job challenges? Yes, occasionally. But then pacing your career requires a good deal of courage about not following the pack.

Certainly there can be little sense of worth in working without a commitment on your part. But that does not have to mean a career with no breaks, a rise to success patterned after and paced to a man's. It *does* mean that you may have to be more energetic, flexible, and risk-taking than others.

Fortunately, a mother's duty to children is widely accepted, you will enjoy a few time options that men don't. "When a man comes in with five years blank on his resumé," says a veteran executive recruiter, "my guard immediately goes up. I may understand perfectly well why he took time out to travel, try out a creative endeavor, or just find himself. But my corporate clients don't always share my understanding. They're worried that he might be too individualistic, unstable. But with a woman, it's no problem to explain, 'She took time off when her children were young.' Sometimes it's even a plus. The employer regards her as settled in life, with family responsibilities."

Kathleen McDonald, a personnel executive at Exxon, adds that women also benefit from their ability to separate their images of themselves from work. "One of the advantages of being a woman," she says, "is that our status isn't measured totally from work success. If we don't succeed in the established ways at the established companies, it's not going to affect our egos in the same way it would for a white male chemical engineer who's been raised to believe he had to rise in a recognized company every year. If a woman chooses to take time off, or go and work for a lower-paying, but more satisfying, job in the public sector, that's not going to have significant impact on her status as a woman—at least not *yet*. Who knows what it will be like in ten years? For the present, it means we haven't locked ourselves in the way men have. We have more options to set our own goals and shape our careers."

You as a working mother may well achieve a more humane and balanced work life. Having another strong commitment besides your job forces you to wrestle with your deeper needs and make choices that childless women and men aren't forced to confront until it's too late. The magnets of success and ambition are powerful in our competitive, individualistic society, and few of us question the work ethic or the price of job achievement.

Pursuing such goals single-mindedly for the first twenty years of their careers, American men typically suffer a crisis of doubt about their work in their late thirties. Many working mothers long before that have thrashed out their personal balance between ambition and fulfillment with family and have avoided being pressed into an over-investment in career success, to the exclusion of other human needs. Says the powerful woman head of a publishing house: "Having the children tempered my ambition in a useful way. I haven't pursued success with the same anxiety I would have otherwise. Maybe I'd be president of the company by now if I hadn't had children, but I think what I do now gives me more pleasure."

One good question to ask yourself along the way: Are you following deep impulses within yourself that require fulfillment in work —or driving yourself in a need to "perform" for the world? In school, we, far more than men, tend to perform as "good students" for teachers—studying for tests, giving the "right" answers we know are expected, hinging our self-worth on teachers' approval. When we work, many of us continue right along in that path of passive performing, exchanging teachers for bosses as judges of our work. A hard-driving magazine editor who's pushed to the top of her field surprisingly confesses herself a victim of this hang-up: "Even if I think I've put out a terrific issue, I never *really* think so until my male editor-in-chief pats me on the back and says 'terrific.' I still perform for his approval."

Bosses certainly have to approve of us; work must certainly be done according to our boss's needs; but a woman who always depends on her superiors to set goals and tell her how good she is isn't likely to ever have the independence to take control of her own career. Deciding how much energy you want to put into work just now . . . whether that new title and raise are really what you want (and whether you're willing to pay the price of having less time for your family) . . . deciding whether the lockstep achievements your profession prescribes can be shortened or omitted—these are the gut issues you have to wrestle with. In the struggle, you just may discover that you can defer some of the demands of your career without feeling guilty about cheating yourself or achieving less than you've been educated for.

No one says it will be easy to make choices, but one thing is certain: Decisions about your career ambitions are not something you can tuck behind you until next year, as the childless can. Elizabeth, a brilliant, divorced, thirty-five-year-old law professor who's managed to publish several important articles, win a landmark case in her state, and hold down a full-time teaching job while raising her three sons alone, told us, "When you're forced to make daily decisions about how you're spending your time—you either are going to the PTA tonight or you're staying home to work on a professional article—you have to stop a minute and say, 'Look, is my career important to me because I *want* to be working so hard at it right now? . . . or is it because everybody else says I ought to be working so hard at it right now?' "

An intense, fragile-boned woman who's never without her leather briefcase bulging with such miscellanea as a Little League sponsor pin, an hour-by-hour schedule book, and a sheaf of papers from a law casebook, Elizabeth formed a small rap group with other teaching mothers to confront their common problems. She is convinced that professional women have the clout to make their careers more flexible and less consuming. "I think there are real deficiencies in the male model of successful work, and women have got to feel strong enough to put their families first when it's important.

"We don't need," Elizabeth says angrily, "to feel defensive about wanting to be with our kids at important times as they grow up. I am good at my job, and I think it's fair to say they're lucky I'm working for them, but my family right now comes first for me. That doesn't mean that my profession isn't important, but it's going to have to give in some ways for the time being."

Because Elizabeth has managed to be highly successful while staving off many career pressures, she is often called upon to advise other women who are reluctant to sacrifice their personal lives and time with their children for getting ahead. "Sometimes," she says, "women just need someone to say it really is okay, your personal life is more important than your professional." Or, we hasten to add, that you *can* space your commitments, you won't necessarily destroy your professional investment with unorthodox decisions or gaps. Working mothers are developing new strategies for working without sacrificing their families.

Career Planning

One of the most effective precautions you can take in planning your work life is to find out how the job market will develop in coming years. Despite bows to career counseling in high school and beyond, this simple act is one many women neglect. If you're taking time off or doing double duties as mother/worker, you don't want to face the added hurdle of a tight job market with two job openings and two hundred candidates. It is essential to assess where your field—or one you could be interested in—is going in the next five to ten years.

Where will the jobs be? We're living in a time of rapid occupational upheaval. Technology—particularly the expanded use of the computer in all phases of business—is creating a burst of growth in many occupations. Meanwhile, as the United States moves from heavy reliance on goods-producing industries, like steel, cars, heavy machinery, to businesses dealing with information and technology, many industrial-related jobs are declining or at a standstill.

Getting a college degree—once the ticket to jobs and upward mobility—will no longer guarantee that a perfect position awaits you. For as the number of graduates rises, the possibility of a graduate finding a job suitable for his education is lessening. One large

TEN HOT JOBS FOR THE 1980s

Job	Current estimated number in field	Current average income	Prospects from now to 1990
Computer programmer	228,000	$17,000–$26,000	Excellent, as computer usage expands. Best opportunities in accounting, business management, data processing services.
Computer console and peripheral equipment operator	558,000	$14,300	Expansion of computer applications will cause much faster than average growth. One exception: *keypunch operators* will decline in number as direct data entry techniques become more efficient.
Computer service technician	83,000	$20,000	Very strong demand.
Dental hygienist	36,000	$10,000	Excellent for full-time and part-time.
Physical therapist	34,000	$21,600	Much faster growth as support for disabled and aging increases.
Occupational therapist	19,000	$21,000	Very good with increasing support for rehabilitation.
Physician	424,000	$74,500	Little difficulty for new physicians in most areas. Highest demand in rural areas and certain specialties.

Job	Current estimated number in field	Current average income	Prospects from now to 1990
Respiratory therapy worker	50,000	$18,000	Very fast growth.
Secretary	2,500,000	$13,000–$15,000	Large number of jobs and regular turnover will create many openings. Excellent prospects for full-time and part-time. Only demand for *stenographers* will decline as companies use electronic communications.
Systems analyst	205,000	$22,000–$26,000	Very hot, with opportunities in computer service firms, accounting, research and development, and in design of software packages.

GOOD JOBS FOR THE 1980s AND BEYOND

Job	Current Number Employed	Average Salary	Prospects
Accountants and auditors	900,000	$15,000–$30,000	Very good. Experience important.
Auto mechanics	845,000	$20,000	Plentiful opportunities.
Bank clerks and tellers	1,000,000 plus	$8,000–$10,000	Many openings.

GOOD JOBS FOR THE 1980s AND BEYOND (continued)

Job	Current Number Employed	Average Salary	Prospects
Bookkeepers and accounting clerks	1,700,000	$11,500–$13,500	Good outlook.
Bricklayers	150,000	$23,000	Good prospects.
Cashier	1,600,000	$9,000–$17,500	Many job openings.
Claims representative	210,000	$15,000	Good.
Corrections officer	103,000	$10,600–$13,000	Good.
Dental assistant	140,000	$9,000–$11,000	Excellent. Part-time jobs also available.
Dentist	126,000	$55,000	Good outlook.
Dietician	44,000	$21,500	Good.
Drafters	322,000	$11,700–$17,200	Good prospects.
Geologist	44,000	$30,000	Good.
Hotel managers	84,000	$20,000–$80,000	Favorable.
Health services administrator	220,000	$35,000–$50,000	Favorable for those with degrees.
Licensed practical nurse	550,000	$12,500	Very good.
Medical technologists, technicians, and assistants	205,000	$15,800–$20,600 (technologists) $16,000 (technicians)	Good, especially for technicians and assistants as new automated laboratory test equipment allows them to perform more tests previously requiring a technologist.

Job	Current Number Employed	Average Salary	Prospects
Medical assistant	90,000	$10,000	Excellent.
Market research analyst	29,000	$27,000	Good, though subject to swings of the economy.
Radiologic (X-ray) technologist	106,000	$17,400	Very good.
Receptionist	635,000	$10,000	Good.
Registered nurse	1,105,000	$17,000–$20,000	Good for full-time and part-time jobs.
Securities sales workers	63,000	$40,000–$88,000	Good outlook.

JOBS FACING COMPETITION IN THE 1980s

Job	Current Number Employed	Average Salary	Prospects
Air traffic controller	29,000	$29,900	Jobs will increase, but competition will be keen as the number of qualified candidates increases.
Architects	79,500	$30,000–40,000+	Architecture schools will turn out more graduates than jobs. Outlook depends on construction trends—luckily a rise in non-residential building is anticipated, but this could be affected by general economic conditions.

JOBS FACING COMPETITION IN THE 1980s (continued)

Job	Current Number Employed	Average Salary	Prospects
Buyers	150,000	$19,000–$28,000	Competition will be keen, since merchandising attracts many college students.
College and university teachers	691,000	$30,700 (for full professors)	Enrollments in colleges will decline, and competition for shrinking faculty jobs will be keen in most areas (exceptions: engineering, law, computer science, business administration).
Economists	44,000	$20,500–$27,600	Competition heavy in academic areas, but many persons trained in economics will be able to find jobs in industry, business, or consulting firms. Those with strong backgrounds in marketing and finance have best prospects in business.
Flight attendants	56,000	$19,000	Competition for jobs as more career-minded people enter the field, causing less turnover.
Keypunch operator	200,000	$10,000	Increased use of direct data techniques will reduce need for keypunch operators. However, because of

Job	Current Number Employed	Average Salary	Prospects
			high turnover, openings will occur. Many operators should get more advanced training.
Lawyers	425,000	$35,000–$60,000+	High number of graduates will flood market. Geographical mobility and experience will be important in getting a job.
Librarian	135,000	$21,000	Job market stagnant, but declining number of library science graduates is expected to ease tight job prospects in late '80s.
Mail carriers and postal clerks	515,000	$19,000	Number will decline as more automation is used. However, no full-time postal carrier or clerk now working is expected to be laid off.
Photographer	91,000	Varied	Competition keen for portrait and commercial photographers; better prospects for law-enforcement and scientific positions.
Psychologists	106,000	$26,000–$36,000	Declining academic positions will force more psychologists to look for jobs in business. Persons with

JOBS FACING COMPETITION IN THE 1980s (continued)

Job	Current Number Employed	Average Salary	Prospects
			only a master's degree will face severe competition.
Secondary school teachers	1,237,000	$17,725	Shrinking public-school enrollments will lead to decline. Best opportunities for teachers of special education, vocational subjects, math, natural and physical sciences.
Real estate agents and brokers	580,000	$29,000 (brokers)	Demand will rise, but field is highly competitive.
Social workers	345,000	$20,000	Competition keen in established areas. Best opportunities in growing areas, such as the Sunbelt, and for workers with advanced degrees.
Stenographers	280,000	$15,000	Decline will continue as dictating machines and electronic communication increase. Court reporters are the exception.
Telephone operator	340,000	$10,000	Technological advances will slow need for operators.

shrinking occupation is teaching, the very profession that currently accounts *for over 75 percent of all women in professions.* Historically, becoming a teacher has been a way for women to achieve a respected, professional position. But the slowing birth rate has cut enrollments and caused many schools to close or consolidate, and left this avenue less promising. (Take heart, kindergarten and elementary school teachers can look to enrollments rising again in the late eighties as more women reach child-bearing age. And the secondary-school teacher who specializes in science, math, or special education will be in demand.)

Yet changes in the national economy can mean not a setback for you but new opportunity. You may consider a different occupation from what you'd have expected five or ten years ago. And you may also find some of the doors to traditionally male occupations have eased open a bit. It's heartening that the years between 1971 to 1980 showed sizeable increases of women working in jobs previously marked male. For example, women for the first time became a majority in such jobs as psychologists, assemblers, insurance adjusters, real-estate agents, and bill and account collectors. And the number of women accountants jumped from 21 percent of all accountants to 46 percent, women bartenders moved from 24 percent to 43 percent; postal workers from 29 to 35 percent; pharmacists from 15 to 27 percent.

Where is the growth? Three general areas of jobs are expected to show sharp growth in the immediate future. First, the rapid spread of computers in business and homes will explode the need for systems analysts, programmers, console and peripheral equipment operators, and computer service technicians (someone has to be on call to keep those computers running!). The only job in the computer field that will decline is that of keypunch operator, as data entry systems become more efficient.

A second area of growth is the health field, which appeals to many women. As the population shifts to a larger percentage of aging citizens, and as more support and technological breakthroughs foster better rehabilitation efforts, the need for physicians, nurses, LPN's, administrators, and assisting personnel such as medical assistants, physical therapists, lab workers, and dental hygienists will rise. However, many of the ancillary jobs in health pay modest salaries.

Financial and credit services will expand, fostering a good job market for credit managers, securities salespersons, bank tellers, cashiers, accountants, bookkeepers, and bank clerks.

Now let's look at the future by the eleven job categories used by the Bureau of Labor Statistics (BLS). *Professional and technical workers*—which includes many highly trained workers, such as scientists, engineers, medical practitioners, pilots, writers, and teachers —will grow by 20 percent or more from about 16 million workers to 20 million. Scientists, engineers, and technicians will enjoy strong demand. So will computer professionals, like systems analysts. Though medical professionals will continue to be in demand in most areas, lawyers, architects and many other professionals will face rising competition as schools turn out more graduates.

College and university faculty will decline, as enrollments level off.

Managers and administrators will increase as a group by 13 to 21 percent from about 9.5 million to 11 million. The number of self-employed managers will decline, because corporations are dominating more business, but bank officers, buyers, credit managers, and many corporate managers will grow in numbers.

Clerical workers will continue both as the largest occupational group and the group that will offer the most job openings of any group in the years to 1990.

Clerical jobs include bank tellers, bookkeepers and accounting clerks, cashiers, secretaries, and typists. Clerical jobs will grow by 20 percent or more by 1990, swelling from 19 million to 23 million. High turnover in the jobs will assure constant openings. However, some clerical jobs will decline, including stenographers (companies will turn to more electronic communications) and airline and reservations and ticket agents, who will be partially displaced by improved technology.

Sales workers will grow by 20 percent or more, and their ranks will expand from seven million to eight million or more. Inner cities are declining as centers for shopping, and more suburban and mall stores will provide good opportunity for full- and part-time salespeople.

Craft workers include a wide variety of skilled workers, like carpenters, tool-and-die makers, all-round machinists, electricians, and automobile mechanics. This group will rise by about 20 percent and grow from 12.4 million to about 15 million. But opportunities will vary according to trends in different industries. Construction crafts workers will probably rise, while railroad workers will shrink.

Operatives except transport. This BLS title denotes production workers that include assemblers (now an occupation with a majority of women), production painters, and welders. Here as with crafts workers, job prospects vary by industry with some going up, others declining. Textile operatives, for example, will decline as more machinery is used.

Workers who drive buses, trucks, taxis and other vehicles (*transportation operatives*) will grow at the average rate of all occupations. *Private household service workers,* which includes housekeepers, childcare workers, and maids, will remain about the same, numbering nearly 1,000,000 workers.

Finally, if you work in what the BLS calls the *services occupations,* as a beautician, fire fighter, bartender, chef, police officer, or waitress, you're in the fastest-growing occupational group. Growth is expected to be from 24 to 32 percent, rising from about 14.5 million to 19 million. Service workers will enjoy a strong job market as people go out to eat more, have the income to buy more services, from beauty treatments to lawn care.

Farmworkers and *laborers* will decline in our increasingly technological society.

Where Is the Money? You're probably not just looking for a job; you're looking for a job that will pay you well. The direction? If it's not in technology, it will probably be in a field that has been male-dominated. Consider this statistic: The median income of women in 1980 was $10,600, compared to the male median income of $16,700. In other words, *women take home only 63 percent of what male workers do.* There is a marked correlation between occupations in which women predominate (teaching, social work, library science, clerical work, bank teller) and low wages. "Women's work"—even if it's in the office—is consistently paid less than male-dominated occupations.

Finance, insurance, and banking are potentially well-paying areas, already have a predominantly female work force at the lower levels, and all three areas are growing, offering a good market for the woman who can work her way above the lower levels.

Law, medicine, engineering, and dentistry are admitting more female graduates. Women in the law went from 4 to 13 percent from 1971 to 1980, engineers from 1 to 4 percent, physicians from 9 to 13 percent.

A final rule of thumb for a woman who wants to earn high wages: Don't get stuck in the woman's side of your field; if you're interested in getting as much pay as a man, don't sell dresses, sell *cars*. Don't aim to manage the secretarial pool, aim to manage the *factory*. Don't file the insurance policies, *sell* them. Don't remain at the social-worker level, move on to the *administrative* job above.

Where Is the Information?　If you want guidance in your field, contact the professional organization or labor union that represents your group. If you'd like to explore the future of your occupation or other possibilities on your own, the best single source is *The Occupational Outlook Handbook*, a huge, but readable tome (once you understand the organization) of job information published every two years by the U.S. Bureau of Labor and available in most libraries. If you can't locate a library copy, order one for $9 from the Superintendent of Documents, Government Printing Office, Washington, D.C. 20402.

If you want individual counseling, first seek out free services, from your Y, local state college, or other community sources. If you then wish to seek professional career counseling, be sure you understand in advance what fees will be charged and what services will be rendered. A counselor may be able to match your interests and aptitudes to an occupation you don't yet know about. But don't be buffaloed by batteries of tests or expert advice. While knowledgeable counselors are invaluable, you're still the final authority on what job will be right for you.

Long-Range Strategies

Pacing your career is a mixture of attitude and specific ploys. Here's what the women who are managing have discovered.

Establish Yourself. The tried-and-true plan for combining a career and family is to establish yourself first. Get a good basic training and several years of work experience, and you'll have a firm foundation for returning to work if you take time off to have a child. Or, if you plan to work through your child's infancy, you'll have more clout as an experienced employee to tailor your job a bit while you're putting in heavy energy at home.

Whether you're a telephone operator or a TV reporter, having a few years of job experience before you take on family responsibilities that will last for eighteen or more years gives you an important chance to test yourself in the work world and absorb its rules and dynamics. Experimenting in several fields or with different companies can teach you more about yourself than the best planning or training.

But don't assume this means you must deny yourself children for years. Establishing yourself doesn't have to mean fifty-hour weeks.

Avoid Either/Or Thinking. Janet, a bright, hard-working M.B.A., joined a Chicago conglomerate after graduation, and moved up the ranks. On her way up, Janet married, bore twin boys, and went right on rising, winning an assistant vice-presidency on the twins' fourth birthday. When her boys were six and in public school, her company president offered Janet a plum: developing a new branch of the company in Atlanta. The job was one Janet was logically working up to in her company, and turning down this spectacular offer seemed unthinkable. Refusal would tarnish Janet's winner's image in the company she had worked for during her ten years since school.

Janet was torn. "Our community was ideal for raising kids, and our boys had the same housekeeper they'd always known. My husband was very settled in his job, and we felt very happy in our surroundings. I really went through agony for a week. Accepting the promotion would have meant one of those long-distance marriages you read about, or else taking months or years for Jim to find a job in the South. It was very painful. I had to rethink my values." In the end, Janet turned down her promotion.

Within six months, Janet accepted an offer with a smaller local firm that offered her a wider range of responsibilities. "I don't think most men would have had the guts to turn down something they'd worked toward so long. But when I really got down to what means the most to me, my family happiness does. I know over the long range of my work life, I'll move up. And as it's turned out, this crisis forced me into a good move. I had my sights too narrowly focused staying with the same company."

Janet's experience is instructive for other mothers who are torn by an attractive offer that interferes with their commitment to their families. Does the job offer seem so fantastic you'll never get another chance like it? Perhaps so. But the statistical chances are that an equally attractive offer will come your way again. A woman long experienced in women's career management muses about a young woman with two small children who recently was offered—and accepted—a heady job as college president. "I think probably she made a mistake," says the career guidance official. "If she's really got the stuff, she'll be even riper and will succeed on the next round when she's older. And if she doesn't, then she won't succeed now either."

She offers reassurance to other business women: "You're really not likely to get only one great offer in a career. Usually the offer you get is commensurate with your particular worth. Moreover, you learn an awful lot between the ages of thirty and fifty. Whatever makes you attractive to an employer now will make you even more attractive in five or ten years."

When you feel ambivalent over a difficult career choice, avoid the bleak, short-range either/or view. "Either I take this promotion, or I'll never move up." "Either I push myself to do this, or I won't be taken seriously."

Establish That Your Years of Limited Work Responsibilities Are Limited. No employer is going to automatically look favorably on a woman employee who is reluctant to take on wider responsibilities. How can you avoid being disregarded—or stuck in a dead-end job or at the same salary? Tell your employer frankly that you'll be ready for greater responsibility in a few years. That you're continuing to perform dependably in the job you have, but that you definitely don't plan to vegetate. When your children go to school (or to high school or whatever milestone you're looking toward), you'll be ready and eager to move up and out. Many working mothers are amazed to discover how simply reassuring their bosses of their long-range ambition produces a different attitude toward them. "My boss is very tight," says a secretary who plans to move into a more demanding sales job as soon as her three-year-old son goes to school, "and he loves having an overqualified secretary who can analyze sales reports and knows the products so well he doesn't have to spell out everything when he dictates. But I've let him know that I expect to be rewarded when my time comes to move on. Right now we both feel we're getting something we want."

Making a deal with your boss to hold your place in the promotion line can be tricky. Veteran career analyst and Catalyst president Felice Schwartz warns, "You can't expect an employer looking for his return on investment to settle for less from you than he would from a man. However, you *can* make a deal by saying, 'Listen, I'm a high-potential person who's willing to work in a lower-potential job for the next two or three years. But let me stay abreast of what's happening during these three years so that later I can maybe make a quantum leap.' "

Peaks and Valleys in Work Life. Recognize that there may be periods when you'll ease back from work, perhaps take a couple of years off. Once you've proved that you can make it in the business world, you'll feel less anxious about pulling back when your children demand more time. Consider how Jean de Boskey, a successful Colorado lawyer in her mid-thirties, is pacing her career.

Jean spent her first pregnancy campaigning all over her state for a reform candidate for attorney general. Her man won, and Jean was appointed to the number-two position of assistant attorney general. While in the last stages of pregnancy, she set up her office staff, and then, with the help of a cooperative husband and a dedicated sitter, made it neatly through the next two years, balancing her pressured job with the needs of a young baby. But then Jean had a second child. She's resigned her job to stay home with both babies for several years. Does she regret sacrificing the momentum of her career, a withdrawal that startled her colleagues?

"Not really," says Jean. "If you want a balanced life, you have to plan for it. Women more than men. That's all right. Maybe I won't zoom ahead as fast as I might. But I can go back in two years. Meanwhile, I plan to do a lot of professional catching up on my reading and studying. Right now, my son needs to know more about his mommy, whom he's only seen at night and on weekends."

Take Time Off When It's Meaningful to You.   As part of your independent attitude, take time off from working when *you* think it's right. We generally assume that the time to stop working is when your baby is born. Not so for everyone. Ellen, an assistant buyer for a West Coast fashion house, worked straight through the babyhood of her two girls. But when the elder reached three, Ellen quit to stay home for the next three years. "I feel that's the age when you really instill values in your children, when they're able to talk and learn about the world. That's when I want to be with them, to take them to zoos and play with them and read books and answer all their questions myself. I don't think they would have gained anything from *me* as an individual during those first years, when they just needed someone to change the diapers and feed them." Set your own pace and timetable.

Late Bloomers' Energy.   One of the secret weapons you have in pacing your career is the extra burst of creativity and energy that many women experience in their late thirties and forties. A fascinating cross-cultural study by University of Michigan psychologist D. L. Gutman revealed that as women age, they become less passive and assume more active, dominant roles in their societies. And women past child-bearing age seem more comfortable about expressing aggressive impulses. Perhaps biologically based, this outward turning of a woman's energies seems to erupt when her physiological childbearing functions are ending. Of course, her mothering function is also usually less demanding, and her new energies could come simply from having more time for herself. Men at forty, on the other hand, are often worn down by years of work and restive to shed job pressures.

Whatever the reason for this phenomenon, this sudden energy and confidence transforms too many women not to believe it's a common pattern. A woman novelist who's puttered around finishing her long-overdue second novel suddenly hits her creative stride . . . a thirty-eight-year-old woman who's drifted from one career to another opens her own boutique and finds a vocation . . . a forty-five-year-old woman stuck in office managing suddenly gets a chance to join the executive ranks and discovers she loves it. . . . Your late thirties, forties, and even fifties can be the beginning of a whole new work life. If you're forced to hold back at work during some part of your children's growing-up years, you can still look forward to being a successful late bloomer.

A Well-Paced Career

One of the women most successful at career pacing whom we talked with was Elizabeth. Her career as law student and now as law professor demonstrates several pacing principles.

Elizabeth's first hard choice came when she discovered that top-flight law schools refuse to allow part-time study. She still gets angry remembering how her family-law class was always inconveniently scheduled at four in the afternoon: "Here I was supposed to be studying family law just when I needed to be getting home to my family." But because her choice of a school would determine her career future, she decided "it was going to be hard enough being a woman in law. I didn't want to face the double disadvantage of being a woman and not having gone to the best school possible. So, although it took a lot of sacrifice from my family, I went full-time."

As Elizabeth's children grew older, the strain eased (even though she was divorced in her last year of school), and on graduation, she was offered the biggest plum: a coveted clerkship with a U.S. Supreme Court Justice. Elizabeth put in ninety-hour weeks at her Washington job (with the help of a carefully chosen live-in baby-sitter), but won "the kind of insight into the judicial process that you get *nowhere else* in American law."

Once her two years in Washington ended, she made a dramatic switch, not derailing her career but not taking the next obvious step up the ladder either. "I was hot property then and happily I had job offers from lots of good schools." The most tempting bid came from a major urban university set in a ghetto area. Elizabeth would have had to establish her children miles away in the suburbs—and spend a minimum of an hour commuting each way. Demonstrating unusual self-awareness, Elizabeth simply refused to go to the interview. "I knew my ego would get involved and I wouldn't be able to turn it down."

Instead, Elizabeth job-shopped carefully, finally accepting an assistant professorship at a West Coast university located in a small town. This relaxed, child-centered setting puts her next door to her work. "I can bicycle to work in ten minutes, which also means I can get back in ten minutes if I need to. It was important to me, since I am divorced, to have an atmosphere where the kids can get around on their own safely and know our neighbors. We have a house and small-town friendliness. But we also enjoy the culture that exists in a college town."

After her intense involvement in Washington, Elizabeth is delaying some obvious professional moves she could be making—but with full confidence that she can recover the ground when her children need her less. "I'm good and I'm well trained, and nothing's going to hold me back." In fact, she stunned her college superiors recently by asking them to delay reviewing her record with tenure in mind. She explained that her family responsibilities as a single mother prevented her from researching and publishing as she'd like, and asked the committee to let her proceed at her own pace. She won her request—and has been besieged ever since with admiring inquiries from women and men colleagues who'd like to do the same thing.

As a result, Elizabeth can spend a good part of her weekends not holed up in the library, but cheering on the Little League where her middle son plays shortstop, baking a birthday cake for her youngest, and embroiled in the other activities of a child-centered town. She's confident that her priorities are in the right place.

Elizabeth has acted on our basic principles of pacing a career. She established herself, and when she needed to take a step essential to her career—attending school full-time to get a prestigious degree— she asked her family to accommodate. Now, secure with a degree and professional credentials, she has the flexibility to take time off from her career when it's important to her. And she's avoided the grim either/or route, instead forging her own unique way that's sacrificing neither her motherhood nor her professional talents.

How to Drop Out—But Keep Your Hand In

If you do decide to drop out of work for a while, don't expect the world to stand still waiting for your return. Take out insurance that you'll be able to reenter with a minimum of strain. As a start, be sure to collect a letter of recommendation from your boss, who'll most likely have moved up or away when you return.

Keep Your Hand In Part-Time. Most people prefer to hire a proven quantity, someone they already know, and for this reason, you'll be wise to work part-time in your field. A Texas accountant kept up her career by working part-time during the overflow tax season, not only for her former employer but for several other firms. When she was ready to resume full-time work, she had her pick of jobs in six firms, all of which knew, firsthand, her competence. "If I'd just dropped out," she says, "I would never have gotten back in at the salary I did. And I probably would have been scared to death to even try."

Contacts with people in the work world are also priceless when you're reentering. A kind of law of conservatism seems to work in most job markets, where an inner circle of people who know each other hire and get hired. Having contacts with those who are working assures that you'll learn about new jobs when they occur and have valuable sponsors.

Look Ahead. Don't wait for the morning your child walks off to first grade to start searching the newspaper want ads. Use your years at home to prepare. If you can't spare time for evening classes, you can take correspondence courses in your home, in almost any field from basic accounting to designing, business writing to shorthand and typing. ("The smartest thing I ever did," says a TV producer who finished Wellesley with honors and won a Woodrow Wilson scholarship, "was learn shorthand and typing." Whatever your training, learn how to type; it's a basic business skill.)

If you can't afford tuition, take advantage of free classes offered in your community. Check at your local Y, church groups, and publicly funded colleges.

Bone up on job fields that are growing (see pages 180-186). Now's the time to get career counseling. An expert can be particularly helpful in guiding you to areas that will be most rewarding to you—and then helping you lay out a program to prepare.

A cost-saving word on career counseling: At least for your first try, scout around for one of the many helpful *free* career-counseling services being offered by Ys, university women's centers, and other groups. Remember that the value and quality of career counseling need not bear a relation to the size of the fee charged. And, of course, when you use a counselor, be *sure* you know beforehand what it's going to cost you.

Keep Up.   Maintain your membership in any business associations you've joined, whether it's your city-wide accounting group or the women's baseball team of Union Amalgamated. Lunch with old friends from work occasionally. Many a job has been heard of and won over a martini.

Develop a Specialty.   One of the best techniques for insuring your profitable return to the job market is to develop a skill that's in short supply. Dottie, a lawyer with four children, worked three afternoons a week when her children were small, "at a job no man wanted—state bankruptcy official. It paid very little and had no prestige." Now that Dottie's children are in school, she's in the enviable position of being one of three top bankruptcy experts in her state and has her pick of offers from a number of large law firms who need her specialty.

Teachers might use their time at home to prepare for a specialty insulated from the academic slowdown, such as special education or guidance. Professional women can use their freedom from the job to complete research projects that will add to their credits.

Volunteer.   Unpaid volunteer work is much maligned these days as exploitative and time wasting. But many a mother unsure of her abilities can benefit from well-chosen volunteer work. Performing any job well will give her a good dose of confidence, and she may also get a chance to demonstrate high-level managerial abilities that will be impressive on her resume when she decides to reenter the business world.

Evelyn, a forty-one-year-old mother of two boys, married to a psychiatrist, hadn't worked for fifteen years when she volunteered to help the local fund-raising campaign for the public television station. Her energy, imagination, and organizational skill propelled her to take charge of the entire campaign, supervising a staff of thirty-five solicitors, cajoling local merchants to donate prizes, and devising a new marathon appeal. One of her volunteer phone solicitors was a newspaper owner who was looking for a bright advertising manager to revamp his chain of small neighborhood newspapers. He offered Evelyn the job, based on the showcase of talent her volunteer work had provided.

Reentry. If you plan well and are determined, a return to rewarding work is possible. And don't give up too soon: Finding your way back into a good job after absence from the job market can be a disheartening, arduous, and lengthy process. Smooth your search with one of these tactics.

Pick a job that requires maturity. Employers are increasingly aware that the experience of women in mid-life equips them to perform some jobs more effectively than a younger woman. Catalyst president Felice Schwartz, who's turning her organization's efforts to searching out jobs where mid-life women are welcome, cites two opportunities. One unexpected one: managing a McDonald's restaurant. "McDonald's does *not* want someone just out of college," explains Ms. Schwartz. "They want a thirty-five-year-old woman who has the authority and presence to manage the average McDonald's staff of sixty-five kids. Someone who appreciates a good career opportunity but doesn't mind the tough work. Their favorite candidate is a thirty-five-year-old divorced woman with kids, who was a teacher!"

"Insurance sales is another excellent area," continues Ms. Schwartz. A mature woman can be far more effective in selling a product, like life insurance, that requires authority and responsibility.

Taking the time to master basic skills before you reenter is essential. "My advice," says dynamic film producer Linda Gottlieb, "is to learn to type and take shorthand so that there's something you can do that people can pay you to do. Get over the ridiculous attitude that it's beneath you. Once your foot is in the door, you can absorb what goes on and advance to bigger and better things."

Another suggestion for women trying to break in: *Offer to do a job without pay*. Linda has helped ambitious women get nonpaying jobs on films because any sort of experience there is valuable in the long run. But she adds this caution: Even though you're working for free, do so with a sense of your own worth. Communicate that you're convinced you have something to offer and that you'll prove it on the job.

If part of your reentry strategy has been to go back to school, start working at getting a job *before* you graduate. In her useful *Put Your Degree to Work* (Norton 1979), Marcia Fox advises students to attend conventions in their field to pick up contacts as well as to school themselves in the "style" of their professions. She also counsels you to develop your regular work—term papers, special projects —into a dossier of your abilities to show employers.

Does Being a Mother Help You on the Job?

No look at your long-term career plans can be complete without thought about one deep issue that unites your personal and work life—how being a mother may eventually help your career. Many women who sacrifice getting ahead in the short term discover it well worth their while in the long run. For they discover that being a mother can help them uncover new talents or impel them to greater accomplishments in work.

We gain confidence when we have children because childbirth, the ability to produce life, confirms our womanhood, putting to rest the fears we all have about performing inadequately in our sexual roles, whether we're male or female. Having fulfilled these personal goals, many of us then become more outwardly motivated toward career achievements. Harder to summarize is the emotional widening that motherhood can confer, leading a woman to deeper understanding of people and human relations. And from this widened knowledge comes the confidence to pursue work of her own.

What do women take from their mothering that helps them in their careers? And why do the very women who seem most taxed— running a job at the office, another at home—often prove the most efficient workers?

A high-school teacher: "Maybe what makes us such good workers is that we learn to juggle so many things, to grab opportunities to make time for ourselves, so we become proficient at handling many things at once, to switching gears all the time . . . and that makes us extra versatile and adaptable at work."

A professional writer: "I have more energy, more drive. I'm even writing a book besides my regular job."

An actress: "I always thought I was good at my job, but I found the depth and scope of my work has improved enormously."

A former editor, now managing her own bookstore: "Having a child made me reexamine my whole career and why I was unhappy with it. There's nothing like a little kid to make you grow up fast. All the old identity problems come to the fore and you have to face them honestly. It gave me the courage to take the risk and try something new that was better for me."

A college history teacher: "Being a mother has made my teaching far more human. I had had a rather cold, intellectual vision of history. Now I'm concerned with the human emotions behind the events—I can communicate that excitement and force to my students, not just the treaties and the politics and the economic changes."

A thirty-seven-year-old school-board member who's just won a city-wide election: "I would never have dreamed of going into politics unless I'd mothered three children. Probably I would have ended up with a technical job, like a city planner, because I'm interested in social action. But the experience of being intensely involved with —*responsible*—for three little human beings made me realize I could help people grow. I was a person able to do something constructive for myself and others as well."

Some of the benefits to your work come simply from the personal growth that parenting can bring. Perhaps one of the most affecting spin-offs of being a mother is that you're thrust back to your own childhood. Linda Blachman, a social worker with the Parenting After 30 workshops in San Francisco, points out that being with your baby, you rediscover playfulness, learn to regain a spontaneity, an openness that you've lost. You're put in touch with a different rhythm from that which exists out in the workaday world.

And as you confront your child's problems of growing up and try to handle them, you may be thrust back into some of your own childhood problems that have yet to be resolved. Viewing them— whether they were feelings of inferiority, or of being stifled, or of not being loved—with yourself now in the parent's role can afford you the chance to relive and relieve old anxieties. Ms. Blachman sees this as one of the most profound—as well as one of the most disturbing things—about having a child. "It really brings you against your innermost self."

You will reexamine the values you want to give your child, perhaps deepening your own in the process. Many women report a coming to terms with their own mothers as well that brings great peace and a sense of acceptance. A hard-driving career woman says, "I learned to accept my own mother, who stayed home and whom I've never wanted to be like. I appreciate her strengths now and what she gave me as a mother, although I'm not like her. It's helped us end years of quarreling."

Moreover, the joy of nurturing another person, of helping your child grow and expand in the world, is an experience not comparable to any other. It fulfills deep needs for generativity, as Erik Erikson labeled our drive to extend ourselves through younger people, to pass on our knowledge and experience.

Invariably, being a mother enlarges our perspectives and makes us look at our own lives with new authority. Zane Kotker, novelist and working mother, says, "Parenthood is the great watershed of life, the great changer and transformer. It's as though you used to see through the glass darkly and then all of a sudden you see it all from the other point of view. It makes you a different, fuller person."

When a woman can draw from her experience of mothering, feelings that overflow and make her a more confident worker, and when her work feeds back into her mothering, she realizes a dream that all of us have: to unite the worlds of love and work; to join seamlessly the purely individual needs that each of us carries throughout life along with the needs of our family; to balance our powerful complex of demands so that neither robs the other and we can better enjoy both halves of the fully human person—caring and achieving. An elusive marriage, but one well worth working and fighting for.

Chapter Twelve

Having a Baby

With so many women at an all-time high of good health and fitness, pregnancy need not hamper your contribution at work. And the oddity of the pregnant businesswoman is fast fading. Pregnant women argue cases in court, type letters, make sales presentations, and generally carry on with their normal work.

Announcing Your Pregnancy.   Once you know you're pregnant and have some idea of whether you want to take standard maternity leave or a more extended stay, tell your boss before he discovers your pregnancy on his own. Managers resent having important information concealed from them, and hearing the news directly from you rather than secondhand from office gossip will put your supervisor in a better frame of mind for dealing with your temporary absence and making arrangements for your return.

Unless you have a warm, personal relationship with the person you work for, you may experience some anxiety announcing it. "The man I work for is well known throughout the company as a toughie," reports Ursula, an insurance claims adjuster, "a guy who sees the people who work for him as numbers, and heaven help you if you don't perform according to his quotas, so I really dreaded telling him I was going to do something so messy and dislocating as having a baby. But after putting it off for weeks, I knew he'd hear the news if I didn't break it. I was really surprised; he patted my hand and said how wonderful it was and not to worry. It was the first time I'd ever seen him act human." Few people can resist feeling at least a little excitement and awe over the creation of a human life.

Planning Maternity Leave. If possible before telling your boss, check up on your company's maternity leave policy. (See box, page 206.) If you'd like a longer leave than your disability entitles you to, find out if your employer will guarantee you a position equal to your present job. The rule of thumb to remember about what's due you is that pregnancy must be treated the same way your company treats any temporary disability, be it an operation or a dislocated back. That means you must get the same amount of leave, sick pay, or other benefit as would any sick person in your company.

In your planning, remember that six weeks is a minimum, according to Dr. Marcia Storch, New York obstetrician and gynecologist. If you must return sooner, try to work out a part-time arrangement. For longer stays at home, you may be able to add your vacation to maternity leave.

Armed with the information about what's possible in your company, you still may not be sure of exactly what your plans are. If so, tell your boss you don't quite know your plans now, but you'll inform her as soon as possible. It may be helpful to discuss the options and arrive at a mutually satisfactory plan. Don't expect your boss to come up with all the suggestions for covering your work in your absence.

Keeping Your Professional Cool. With so many of us working through our pregnancies, you'd think stores would be rushing to provide businesslike clothes with expandable waistlines. Not so; many women complain that maternity-clothes designers still continue to put out nothing but coy costumes with Peter Pan collars. For a catalog of stylish business clothes, send $3 to *Mother's Work*, Box 625, Weston, MA 02193, a company started by a computer executive who became pregnant and couldn't find any clothes suitable for making her sales presentations. By shopping carefully, you can find wonderful variations on the skirt suit, classic dresses, crisp blouses adapted for maternity use, and even bathing suits in designs that manage to be both pretty and dignified.

Don't buy your whole wardrobe early in one fell swoop. You can't tell how you'll carry the baby or how big you'll grow; what looks flattering and feels comfortable now may not in your later months.

So save something in your budget for a new outfit or two in the seventh or eighth month.

Don't be surprised if co-workers—perhaps from primitive fear, envy or social uneasiness—handle their uncertainty by teasing. It may be hard to smile when you hear the same tired joke from the sixth person. One office worker found her forbearance tested when office-mates kept teasing whenever she went to the Xerox machine— "Be careful, you'll have twins." Understand that teasing simply may be a response to not knowing how to express good wishes. But if the office chat becomes upsetting, put a stop to it.

Most of the women we interviewed experienced little of the morning sickness that is part of the popular lore. "Morning sickness is really not that much of a problem for that many women beyond the first twelve weeks," says Dr. Storch.

Fatigue will be noticeable in the early weeks and last period of your pregnancy. "I felt more tired than I ever did in my whole life," said an energetic programmer. Luckily in midterm you're likely to feel energized, perhaps even more so than usual. It's a good time to prepare for the baby's needs and get your office in good shape, too.

Cut back on your social life to get more rest. And much as you'll want your work to go as always, recognize your limits. Jean, a sales manager, exceeded hers in her last weeks of pregnancy when she went to lunch with her company president and a client. "First, the client was delayed by forty-five minutes," she recalls, "and I didn't have enough sense to grab a snack. By the time we sat down and they each proceeded to have two drinks, I was starved, but I didn't want to spoil the atmosphere by hurrying them. When I finally got my food, I wolfed it down and suddenly got dizzy. My doctor later said he thought I'd cut off a vein supply in my stomach for an instant. Anyway, the next thing I knew I was lying flat with my face on the table—I'd fainted dead away. The waiter was waving smelling salts under my nose and furious that all his customers were alarmed by this fainting lady."

During Your Maternity Leave. If you take more than six weeks off, think about ways to maintain your presence in the office. If you work in a competitive atmosphere where visibility is important, find ways to stay in touch. A lawyer who took twelve weeks' leave arranged to come to the office at least once a week after the first month: "I checked my mail, made myself available for colleagues who were handling my cases while I was gone. I made sure I said hello to senior partners."

You may make yourself available to handle questions by phone or even take on *short* work assignments. One last tip: Bring the baby into the office only once for friends to see. After that, return to your usual image as worker.

FIND OUT ABOUT YOUR MATERNITY BENEFITS

Most companies' health-insurance plans include maternity coverage. Now's the time to find out how much you'll receive. If your company employs fifteen or more people, federal law requires the firm to provide you with the same insurance and disability benefits as they would for any worker with a nonwork-related sickness. But the amount of leave and the other benefits provided differ widely from company to company. Visit your personnel office and find out:

- If and how much coverage your company health insurance provides for your hospital stay and physician.
- Normal number of weeks' leave granted by your company. Six to eight weeks is usually accepted as the time you will be physically unable to work after childbirth—and thus eligible for disability pay. Some firms require your doctor or a doctor designated by the company to certify you as disabled. If you experience further complications and are unable to work beyond the six- to eight-week leave, a doctor's statement is usually required.
- Use of vacation time. You may be able to tack on saved-up vacation to your disability leave and extend your paid time off work.
- Will you be guaranteed the same job or an equal job when you return from a normal leave? Will this guarantee change if you decide to stay out longer without pay?
- What forms and procedures are needed to arrange for leave and insurance coverage? When must you notify your employer about your plans for returning?

Having a Baby in Mid-Career

Only 20 years ago, doctors considered age twenty-seven or twenty-eight "late" for bearing a first child. Now thirty-five seems to be the new dividing age on the biological clock. Having a baby after you're already established in a career, which usually means you're anywhere from your early thirties to forties, is a growing trend. Between 1970 and 1980 the number of first-time mothers in their thirties *more than doubled*. And Census Bureau surveys report the rate of women bearing a first child in their early thirties is still rising sharply, while the birth rate in women in their early twenties is actually declining. In New York City—where the pursuit of careers is probably more intense than any other American city—the birth rate is at an all-time high, higher even than during the postwar baby boom.

Clearly the mid-career mother represents a new pattern of mothering. She's in the first generation of women who have had the option to conceive or not conceive, thanks to the widespread availability and acceptability of birth control. She's taken longer to get around to motherhood. But not necessarily without great uncertainty and even agony.

Laurie, a thirty-two-year-old lawyer, says about her own indecision about having a child, "It's like having a gun against your head, and you don't know which way to move. Some days I worry that having a baby will make me unable to carry on my law practice that I've worked years to build. Other days I worry that I'll end up bitter and childless and worn out from work by the time I'm forty. *Then* I worry that if I wait one more month I'll be unable to conceive. I've never been pregnant, unlike most of my friends who've had at least one abortion. And then I lie awake and worry that if I do conceive I'll have a deformed baby, because I waited too long and my eggs are getting old. It's the hardest decision I've ever faced, and I can't seem to grapple with it because it's such a *final* decision."

Why Wait for Motherhood? From a career standpoint, there's not much doubt. Waiting is better. Many occupations in our society today demand long training and a consuming apprenticeship. A woman is more likely to move ahead in most fields if she's childless during these critical years and can devote the same energy to her job as males do.

As a childless person, without extra financial responsibilities, you can also be mobile, experiment with different companies, even different careers in your twenties. "I think your twenties should be a time to test out your dreams," says a head nurse, who tried several different specialties, signed on with the Peace Corps, and worked in such various places as Paris and a woman's health care center in Washington before she had her son at age thirty-one.

Money has never been known to improve anyone's moral stature, sex life, or basic happiness, but it can go a long way to reducing the stress of being a working mother. In your second decade of earning life, you're better able to pay for superior childcare and other extras. Not having to worry about the cost of a visit to the doctor with a feverish baby or overtime pay for a sitter when you must work late can turn parenting from a highly stressful experience into a challenging but exhilarating passage of life.

Among mid-career mothers we interviewed, the most important reason for waiting, however, was that the woman didn't feel emotionally ready.

"When I was in my twenties," said a science writer, "I didn't know who I was. Until I lived long enough with myself to find that out, I couldn't have been a decent mother. I didn't have values of my own."

"My husband and I were very close," says another new mother of thirty-seven. "We shared a lot of activities and loved being able to travel and do as we pleased. We didn't want to sacrifice our intimacy. It was only a year or so ago that we both began to think we needed a child to complete our family."

"If I'd had a child and felt tied down," says a social worker who's gone to part-time work since she had two girls, "I think I would have visited that frustration on the child. Waiting until I was really ready and longing for my daughters means I can be a less ambivalent parent. And I have more judgment, so much more balance and trust in myself by now, that I feel up to the strains of being a parent. I would have been a terrible mother five years ago. I couldn't have made a child suffer for my growing up."

This conviction was repeated again and again by the mid-career woman. Being more mature when she had a child enabled her to be far more loving and consistent as a parent. While little research exists on the effect of parent's age on children, one pediatrician told us that in her experience younger mothers are far more likely to blame the baby when it cries of acting from revenge or meanness. More mature mothers, who possess greater understanding of human motivation, realize the baby can't possibly be acting from such vengeful motives and can deal with problems with less anger.

Reporting from the child's viewpoint in *Sooner or Later* (Norton, 1982), an in-depth study, Pamela Daniels and Kathy Weingarten concluded, "Many children of early timing parents seriously wondered in retrospect whether their parents had been ready for them and for parenthood in their early twenties." And they go on to report that children of older parents in their study did not feel their parents had been "too old" to be effective parents.

Husbands of mid-career women generally seemed more relaxed about being fathers as well. They are more likely to be better established in their careers as well, and this may give them the freedom to be more involved parents. When Louise, thirty-five, and her husband Alex, thirty-seven, adopted a child, Alex took two weeks off from work so he and Louise could start out as parents together. (She arranged a three-month leave of absence.) As a couple they struggled with giving the baby his first bath—something neither had ever done in their lives—and worked out the routine of caring for the baby without his having to rush off to work. "He was even the one who got up the first night to be sure the baby was still breathing. It strengthened our own bond to be sharing the experience together, and we're better parents for having started it right together."

JANET'S STORY—A WOMAN WHO WAITED FOR MOTHERHOOD

"I came of age during the first flush of women's liberation, and I was determined to work and be independent. I was determined *not* to be like my mother, who raised four children and stayed home in suburbia and never did a thing besides be a mother. I knew I didn't want that.

"And I was raised to think I could achieve things. I won a scholarship to college and I was elected to several class offices. So, going to work was something I always expected to do, and not just as a stopgap to finding a husband. I wouldn't have known what to do with myself if I hadn't been in the big world of work, trying to prove myself and always looking forward to challenges.

"Somewhere after twenty-five I began to think occasionally maybe I would like to have a baby. But I was just getting really established in work. And I hadn't met anyone I wanted to spend my life with. Focusing my energy on work was the right thing for me to do then. It was my whole life, and every time I got promoted it felt really good, wholly satisfying. I got more confidence every time. . . . All through my twenties I kept moving up and spreading my wings. I thought if I was doing the same thing next year that I was doing this year I was dropping behind. I changed companies twice because I felt bottlenecked. And then—I don't remember exactly when, but it must have been a few months before I approached the dreaded age of thirty—I began to feel twinges about this biological clock that we've all been told is inevitable. You know, have a baby before you're thirty-five or that's it. You won't be able to conceive, or you'll have a deformed child, and you'll wonder why you thought work was your only priority while you let the human side go.

"I began to question my work a bit. Especially those nights when we'd work till the wee hours to get a presentation right for the client at ten the next morning. Two of my peers in the office—both my age —got pregnant, and one of them quit and the other one made an arrangement so she'd stay at her job but not be expected to put in late hours. I felt funny watching them bring their babies in for us to see— sort of envious. I've always prided myself on being someone who sets her own course in life. So, I didn't want to be influenced by them.

"But I think my own internal needs were speaking to me. I settled down with the man I was seeing, we bought furniture together, started building our nest. I was still driven at work, still loved feeling competent, in control. But when I got my vice-presidency, it was like I finally felt I could take some time for the other side of me.

"There were practical reasons for that. First, I was finally at the salary level where I felt I could afford to have a baby and have the kind of help that would enable me to go on working. And second, I felt important enough at the office to make some of my own demands. And last, but not least, I was ready to get married. I won't say Alan and I didn't waffle a lot, but about a year after we were married, we decided to stop birth control, and she came the day after my thirty-fifth birthday. I think I waited until just the right time, too."

What Are the Risks?   Health care and expanded life expectancy being what they are these days, most women can look forward to motherhood in their thirties or early forties with a sense of the odds being on their side. Dr. Storch says, "The health of the infant is really dependent on the health of the mother, and in this society, most people who are thirty-five or forty are perfectly healthy. I don't think there's much difference between a healthy twenty-three-year-old and a healthy thirty-three-year-old," she says, but goes on to enumerate the areas where a twenty-three-year-old has the advantage.

Fertility.   Present knowledge suggests that a woman's prime for conceiving is around age twenty-four. A slow decline in fertility follows over the years, but conception is possible up until menopause in a woman's late forties or early fifties. (Age of *father* appears to play a less vital role in fertility than age of mother.) Babies have been born to women in their late fifties. For good or ill, the magic figure of thirty-five has become the cut-off age in many women's minds, around which they plan. But women feeling secure about delaying recently were alarmed by a widely publicized French study concluding that female fertility declines noticeably after age thirty rather than thirty-five. Yet many older mothers get pregnant on their first try. And the rising birth rates among thirty-plus women will undoubtedly lead to even more effective infertility treatments.

Increase of chromosomal disorders is the risk factor most worried about by older mothers. The most common is Down's Syndrome (mongolism). Incidence rises from about 1 baby in 1,500 among mothers under thirty, to 1 in 350 at thirty-five, 1 in 100 at forty, and 1 in 40 at age forty-four. Fortunately, a medical test, amniocentesis, has evolved in the past few years into a virtually foolproof detector of Down's Syndrome (some 500 other disorders can also be tested). Performed at 14–16 weeks, the test, which involves drawing fluid from the womb via a needle inserted in the abdomen, is 99.9%

accurate. The occasional mistakes from the test come in predicting the sex of the baby, a fact that some parents prefer not to know in advance, anyway.

Amniocentesis is usually recommended for any pregnant woman of thirty-five or over. Women over thirty or those with a history of abnormality in their families may also wish to undergo the procedure to relieve anxiety. Dr. Storch stresses that amniocentesis has become an "extremely safe procedure," and ultrasound equipment today allows the physician to visualize the fetus in the womb and thus withdraw fluid without any danger of accidentally harming the child.

Delivery. Statistically, mothers over thirty are more likely than younger women to have their babies delivered by Caesarean. One reason is that both doctor and mother view the baby as possibly being the only one she will have, and the physician is more likely to intervene if any difficulties in labor occur. Like amniocentesis, the Caesarean has become safer and safer in recent years. Recovery time will be longer after surgery, however, and a woman may have to extend her maternity leave after a Caesarean to regain her strength.

One thing older mothers don't have to worry about, generally, is risk to themselves. "Our maternal risk is so low today that you can't really talk about risk for the mother per se," says Dr. Storch, pointing out that among middle-class women maternal mortality in the past fifty years has dramatically dropped from 600 per 100,000 to about 2 per 100,000 live births.

Whatever her age, the individual health of a woman is an important determinant of the health of her baby. Risk factors that any woman *can* control include smoking, drug and alcohol use, and general physical health. You can go a long way toward preparing yourself for pregnancy by a conscientious regimen to improve your general health habits.

How to Decide? The continuing expansion of life span, then, and more sophisticated detection and delivery methods have made postponing motherhood a more viable option. Only a couple of generations ago, age forty marked the beginning of old age for a woman. Today a forty-year-old woman looks forward to her most productive work years. As a result, work life for many women covers a longer span than active mothering. It's natural to try to plan your time of mothering so that work life can also be satisfying and progressive.

What signals you that you're ready to have a baby? While time is a pressure, no woman should have a baby simply to accommodate prime conception years. Late mothers we talked to were motivated by complex emotional stirrings.

"Once I felt I had arrived in life, somewhat proved myself in the world," said Janet, "I really began to think: Is this all? I want to feel something larger than my own ambition and accomplishments in work. I can't believe that all life's satisfactions come from work."

A basic drive in humankind is "generativity"—the desire to pass on our own experiences and values to the young. Laura, an office manager, had experienced these feelings and the pleasures of expressing them with younger women in her office. "I enjoyed teaching them and seeing them grow. When I realized I really did have something to pass on and give, I started wanting my own flesh and blood."

"Having a baby is really a deep expression of being a woman," said a thoughtful co-owner of a bakery. "I think we all go through our youth trying to prove ourselves in our sexual role of woman. And having a baby is kind of the ultimate proof. But I had to get to the point where that was the next step for me as a woman. I wasn't so dependent on men and on just feeling attractive to them."

Deciding to wait does involve some risk. But so does having a baby in your twenties, when you may find it hard to support a child or question your own stability. Whatever you choose, you gain support from the fact that women today are doing it according to both patterns—late and early—and being good mothers and workers whichever they choose. Lucy Scott, a San Francisco psychologist who pioneered Parenting After 30 workshops, concludes "there is no one right time to have a baby." You yourself have this "horrible, powerful, wonderful choice."

What Will Happen to Me?

Even if you become pregnant by choice, don't be surprised if you feel a sense of loss despite good feelings about the baby. Taking on the tremendous responsibility of a baby means a major redirection of your energy and attention. Some of your ambitions for yourself—however unrealistic, like becoming a concert pianist or an astronaut—may have to be laid aside forever. One woman saw a young girl and boy walking down the street and wept at the fact she would never be that young and carefree again.

It's natural to feel some grief at leaving behind this self you've known for some thirty years. Dr. Scott explains, "It's because you're saying good-bye, letting go, feeling some sadness and mourning for that self that you so carefully constructed for such a long time and that you'll never be again. It's predictable, and almost coincides with what some women experience as postbirth depression." She advises women to acknowledge this "shadow side" of becoming a parent, in order to turn next to the possibilities for great personal growth that can come with motherhood.

Most women awaiting the first baby worry that the child will take over their lives, even end their desire to work. *Don't make the mistake of armoring yourself against this fear by making extra commitments to work.* Unwise as it seems, a number of women discover too late they have unconsciously tied themselves into fail-safe work commitments. On discovering she was pregnant, Mary, a personnel officer, signed up to complete a research study for a local university with a delivery date in fifteen months. "It was terrible that first year with my daughter," she recalls, "and so unnecessary. I was jumping up all night to nurse her, working all day and desperately sandwiching in this research on weekends and late at night. Somewhere along the way, I realized I had overextended myself because I was afraid of being subsumed by this baby on the way."

Another woman who ran her real estate business from home took no chances she might be lured into slowing down. Four months before the baby was due, she hired a housekeeper and moved her business to a separate office that required commuting. "Somehow, somewhere, I had made this deal with myself that if I went to the expense of an office, there was no chance I'd want to sit around and turn into mush at home with the baby. It was foolish and very expensive. And it took me a year to move my business back home."

The Birth Experience. Since they've waited and since this may well be their only baby, later mothers look on the birth of their first child as a once-in-a-lifetime event. Typically they train for childbirth as though they're entering the Olympics. They gather all the information they can get their hands on (a fine idea) and attend childbirth classes (especially important to prepare you for labor that may be more difficult than for a younger woman). But don't harbor overly romantic expectations. It is also important not to assume your experience will be as glorious or even similar to someone else's.

Marcia, a new mother of thirty-one, remembers that another woman, forty-one, at her office "was having her first baby and delivered a week before me. She called me the very next morning after the birth and said, 'Oh, it was wonderful, the most glorious thing that's ever happened to me, I loved her from the second I saw her head pop out.' Well, I didn't love it. I had to have a Caesarean and when I woke up and they were shoving this baby at me all I could think was leave me alone, I'm sleepy. And the next morning they wanted me to nurse and all I could think was I hurt, I can't. And I was so ashamed of myself, already a bad mother."

Needless disappointment with the childbirth itself can inspire unwarranted misgivings in a woman about her mothering ability. Remember that you can't control the experience. "Childbirth is determined by a lot of factors you can't control," Dr. Storch reminds us, "factors that determine whether you're going to have a functional, progressive labor, or a dysfunctional labor where intervention must take place. Size of baby makes a difference, for example. If you're a little woman with a big baby, over eight pounds, you're more likely to have a long, hard labor than if you're a big woman with a little baby."

Ease of delivery has nothing to do with how good a woman you are or how good a mother you will be. Nor should you worry if you experience no mystical feelings on first seeing your child or an instant "bonding" between you. Childbirth theorists until recently heavily stressed the first hours after childbirth as a particularly critical period for mother and child to form their love bond. Many hospitals reorganized to allow mother and baby to be in contact during this first twenty-four hours to facilitate bonding. Mothers who miss out on this period because of Caesarean delivery or other complications often worry that they are already scarred in their relations with their child. New studies fail to show that this period is more important than any other. You have plenty of time to form a good relationship with your baby. Don't be alarmed if your first contacts are tentative.

Expect life to be unpredictable.   As a woman who's been in charge of her life for years and is accustomed to managing your time, be warned that a whole different mind set will be called for now. Realize that no matter how good a manager you are, babies are unpredictable.

Joanna, for example, quit her job as an editor shortly before her first son arrived, but she planned to handle regular free-lance assignments at home. Her son developed a routine of napping from one to three in the afternoon, and Joanna was confident she could complete her work in that neat time period. But no sooner did she take on a number of assignments than her son decided to give up his nap. She became angry at him and desolate over her lost work time. A more experienced mother would have realized that such lost plans are par. Don't blame the baby for not heeding your needs.

You can't predict when a baby is going to be hungry, or going to cry or laugh, when he's going to feel like sleeping through the night. Schedules are more often broken than kept. Make a rule for yourself that the value in motherhood is not always in controlling but in responding. You are the one who has to give.

Nor should you apply the same success-equals-results measures that work in business. Denise, an assistant interior designer, notes, "At work, you're used to planning your day. You expect to get x, y, z done. But with my daughter, sometimes the goal for the next fifteen minutes may be just to get her to put her sweater on so we can leave nursery school." Priscilla, a productivity expert, comments: "All day my job is to analyze and refine efficiency. But when I come home, productivity is sitting down with my son for an hour and playing a game that has no clear point. It's hard to make the switch."

New mothers who've polished their planning and efficiency skills over the years can feel unskilled at the kind of patient, repetitive nongoal activity that's involved in playing a hiding game with an eighteen-month-old. You'll get better at it if you recognize it doesn't run by office rules.

Older mothers are more likely than younger women to have limited contacts with other mothers—the so-called park bench exchange of useful information about child behavior, sitters, and services. Make a special effort to tap into a formal or informal network of parents. Jessica stayed in touch with the older mothers in her childbirth classes. "As each of us gave birth, we exchanged help over the phone: how to handle your mother-in-law who's staying too long; the feeding problems; the sleeping problems. Who could know that just learning to feed your baby could make you feel so uncertain? Having someone to discuss it with made it all go easier. And later we joined forces and scoured the city for good daycare. Together we covered every place in a short time, and we found the best one. All of us send our children there now."

Falling in love with the baby. Women we interviewed were invariably surprised by the power of feelings for the baby that overwhelmed them. "It's like falling in love," said one. "I've always been a controlled sort of person, and I've never felt like this toward anyone. I love just watching him. When he smiles, it's like a miracle. It's corny, but it's real."

STAYING CLOSE TO YOUR BABY

With days spent away from their babies, many mothers worry they'll lose touch. Try these ways to keep a warm contact between you and your baby.

1. *Take responsibility for your baby's day.* By providing the best possible substitute arrangement—and then staying in close touch with the people who care for your baby—you become the orchestrator of her day. The more involved you are, the more secure both you and your baby will feel.
2. *Pay special attention to transition times.* Babies need to experience a "continuous world." Linger for a moment at the daycare center or with the sitter to review the baby's day; take the time to talk to your caregiver about the baby's mood, his behavior, even your own feelings. Show interest in her. If you and she are a team, she'll take better care of the baby.
3. *Find your own way to reconnect in the evening.* Settling in for a

private session of nursing, just cuddling in a chair, enjoying the evening bath—whatever you do, make sure your choice seems natural to you. Your baby's sense of security comes from feelings that grow between you, not from care that's imposed as a duty. Feel free to change his schedule to suit yours. Pediatrician T. Berry Brazelton recommends that babies be allowed to nap longer during the day so that they can stay up with their working parents.

4. *Recognize your own need to be with the baby.* Psychiatrist Stanley Greenspan points out that "choosing or needing to work does not eliminate a mother's strong desire to be home caring for her baby." Some mothers defend against these feelings by staying aloof from the baby. Others overcompensate by playing too vigorously with their infant. Overstimulation can make a baby cranky and tense and cause him to withdraw. Avoid these disruptions by deferring evening chores, setting aside relaxed time to tune into your baby's needs—and yours.

5. *Be prepared for your baby's developmental changes.* The tiny infant that snuggled contentedly in your arms at three months may suddenly push you away a few months later. Don't let this "rejection" send you on a guilt trip. Dr. Greenspan suggests instead that you take the time to "gently woo baby back into a loving and satisfying sense of relatedness." Both the baby and you need to know that comfort is available.

———————————————————————

"I've always loved going to my office," said another, "and I couldn't believe the actual physical wrench it was to leave my son. Even now that he's two, I often feel this loss, this desire to run back when I get on the bus. These are such fleeting, precious times, and before long he'll be off at school and have his own activities."

Don't be afraid of your feelings, which can be one of the most enlarging experiences of your life. Looking back, one thirty-one-year-old mother regrets, "I was so busy being so intensely efficient—doing the breast feeding and finding good childcare and rushing back to my job—that I cheated myself. I should have taken more time to luxuriate in this new feeling of being a mother and loving my son."

Expect to Suffer the Overload Syndrome at Work. You may be troubled to discover you can't jump right back into your old work efficiency. Perhaps nature seeks to draw the mother's full attention on the baby during its first year of life, but many women during the first year complain they can't concentrate as well, or focus on details. "I haven't read the paper in months," says one mother, "and staying informed is part of my job. But all I can manage now is a light magazine."

A corporate treasurer says, "I used to be a person who could meet somebody once and meet them ten years later and not forget the name. Now I have this memory problem, so I have to write everything down. But still these mistakes upset me. Will I always be like this?"

Remember that you now have a whole separate world of information to keep in your head, along with information from the office. They're bound to get confused sometimes. An editor says, "I find things coming out of my mouth that obviously are a combination of worrying about something at home and work. I told the copy editor the other day, 'Check in the crib,' when, of course, I meant to say, 'Check in the manuscript.' It's embarrassing." A secretary was also embarrassed to be discovered by her boss rocking the files.

As you adjust to your new routine, you'll regain your old form. Meanwhile, all the tried-and-true memory devices will keep the essentials at home and work from getting lost. Keep a meticulous office calendar and review the coming week each Friday so you can gather files, do homework, or otherwise prepare for next week's work.

You'll also discover you can tolerate more fragmentation than you thought—at home and at work. Motherhood has been described as a period in which a woman never finishes a sentence. No sooner does she handle one problem than another appears. Oddly enough, newly promoted executives feel the same fragmentation, the disjointedness of not being able to complete anything. As managers become responsible for larger operations and more people, they often find themselves having to learn the ability of interrupting their thoughts, switching emotional and mental gears rapidly to turn from one task to another many times during the day.

WORKING MOTHERS <u>CAN</u> NURSE THEIR BABIES

While it may call for careful logistics, nursing can actually make your return to work easier for both yourself and your child. The warmth and intimacy of the nursing relationship helps the baby tolerate your absence and usually makes him more content and less demanding when you are home.

When you nurse your baby, you and he quickly establish the deep psychological and physical bond so important for both of you. "When I come home," says Shirley, a midwestern teacher who's nursed her daughter for the first year of her life, "I immediately nurse her and we're in touch again instantly." Another benefit for the working mother: the relaxation and serenity that come after a hard day at work. "I sink into a comfortable chair, with her in my arms," says Shirley, "and we feel at one with each other after not seeing each other for six hours."

Here are some pointers for successful breast-feeding:

As soon as possible after the baby's birth, learn how to express milk from your breasts and to store it in the refrigerator or freezer (a nurse in the hospital or another nursing mother can show you how). Accustom your baby to a relief bottle as soon as possible after birth. This may be a formula feeding (prefilled bottles that don't require refrigeration are now widely available) or a bottle of breast milk.

If possible, rearrange your schedule to accommodate the nursing relationship. One woman leaves her baby with a sitter only five minutes away from the factory at which she works. She's arranged with her employer to combine her lunch hour and two fifteen-minute breaks into two forty-five-minute breaks during the day. With five minutes to the sitter's house and five minutes back, she has thirty-five minutes to nurse her baby twice a day.

Take especially good care of your own health during the nursing period. Try to get as much rest as possible (avoid social engagements and other obligations during this time). Make sure your diet is well balanced, and for extra energy, try a supernutritious drink of fruit juice and brewer's yeast.

La Leche League, the worldwide organization dedicated to helping nursing mothers and their families, offers support and reassurance in the form of educational pamphlets, workshops, lectures, and personal counseling. If you live in a large metropolitan area, you can find the address of your local La Leche representative in the phone book. Or contact La Leche International, Inc., 961 Minneapolis Avenue, Franklin Park, IL 60131.

For more information on nursing, read *Nursing Your Baby* (Pocket Books, 1976) or *The Womanly Art of Breast Feeding*, (Plume, 1983) or available by mail from La Leche International.

How to Work It All Out for You and Your Baby

It sounds trite, but it's the most basic advice we can give to women eager to be good mothers yet not abandon their love of work: *You will have to adapt, sacrifice, demand according to your own deep feelings and the unique responses of your baby*. One woman may sail right ahead in her career without pause. Another rethinks her career goals.

Some mid-career mothers switch to less demanding jobs. One thirty-two-year-old teacher changed, after her daughter was born, from an emotionally involving job teaching handicapped children to an administrative position. Her new post is not "a heartthrob job—something I get up in the morning all excited about. But it leaves me with energy and emotions for Karen, and she's all the excitement I need right now."

Or the new expansion that motherhood brings you may make it tolerable for you simply to stay in place for a few years. Anne knew her field of teaching English was shrinking and was seeking a career change. Instead she became pregnant and now, the mother of a toddler and sure she wants to have a second child soon, she's decided to just "hold on careerwise. Occasionally I resent that and worry that I'll be too old to make a switch. But then I think I don't want to wake up at forty and ask why didn't I have this second child? Just because of my work?" Anne has learned that just as having a career involves many sacrifices, so having a child—and a second child—demands giving up some things.

One sacrifice every career mother has to make is the pleasure of doing everything to the peak of perfection. A successful lawyer who recently had her third child confides that while she writes her briefs with the same accuracy, she no longer enjoys "the luxury of doing every last bit of research or writing as perfectly as I can." If your job has involved a great deal of overtime, or if you've developed the habit over the years of bringing work home, you'll probably have to develop a new workstyle.

The wisest thing you can do is to place fewer demands on yourself on the job. You may not invest the same single-minded devotion on your work as before, but you'll get the job done. Again and again, mothers told us, "I've had to accept that I'm not always as good a mother as I wish I could be, and I'm not as good at my job as I wish I could be, but it's all I can do. And even though I often feel I'm compromising, it's better that I'm both."

The two women's stories that follow illustrate that different values and lifestyles can still lead to the same outcome: being a good mother.

Limited Career Investment. Libby, the mother of two girls and a boy, is a lawyer specializing in estates in a large Midwestern law firm. She went to law school "because I wasn't sure what to do with my liberal arts degree, and my father encouraged me. He thought whatever I ended up doing, training in law would be useful."

Libby always planned to have children, though she planned to have a career, too, unlike her mother, who'd devoted herself entirely to Libby and her two brothers. Libby fell in love with a fellow law student and, after their graduation and marriage, accompanied him to Washington where he clerked for a Supreme Court Justice. His total concentration on his demanding job led Libby to realize she didn't want that same career involvement for herself and her husband. When they returned to the Midwest, and her husband threw himself into his new job, Libby joined a large firm and asked to be trained in the trusts and estates division. "It's the one part of a law firm where you can count on going home at five without feeling you're welching," she says. "Of course, I do have demanding spells, like just before tax time, when I work all hours, but it's rare and pretty predictable."

Libby pursued her career with pleasure but without a sense of long-term commitment. "I often thought, there's got to be a better way to make a living than this, and I assumed I'd quit when I got pregnant."

To her surprise, after she became pregnant at thirty-one, Libby began to feel comfortable in her job and realized she was very happy practicing it. She now believes that being pregnant made her feel generally less pressured. And having a strong interest in the baby, which made her happy, helped her adjust to the daily routine of work.

Still, she wanted time to be with the baby, and she put on paper for her boss a pioneering plan at her firm proposing she work three days a week. He counterproposed a five-day week, but with shorter hours, from eleven-twenty to five-thirty, with a reduced salary. Libby thought this would give her valuable time in the morning to be with the baby. Instead, she discovered that transportation was slow in nonrush hours, and she wasted an extra half-hour commuting. And while she could still "walk out at five-thirty holding my head high because I knew I was being paid less, the work piled up and I was in fact doing it at home on my own time."

Libby decided to come back full-time. Since then she's had two more children, but she's continued working. "I've thought about quitting, but it keeps coming back to me that the way we've arranged it works well." In the morning she has three hours with the children, and when she gets home at six-thirty, she devotes a couple of hours to playing and being with them. A live-in housekeeper helps her manage, but Libby emphasizes that her husband is an involved parent, too. Even when he comes in late, he reads a story to the children in a nighttime ritual.

Like many women, Libby cites her family's need for her second income as a strong reason why she continues. "One of the advantages of a career-type job is that you make enough money to pay for the housekeeper and extras and still come out far ahead." If she were home, Libby points out, she'd have to give up her help and devote herself to housework and she wouldn't have any more real time for the children than now. "I'm not a driven careerist, but I feel good about my work. And when the children are off to school in just a few years, I won't be left high and dry."

Demanding Career. Cathron also has three children and is a lawyer, but her family arrangements and energy devoted to career reflect a different set of priorities. She is a busy trial lawyer with a West Coast firm, who routinely works to seven or eight and sometimes she must travel out of town for a week or more.

Cathron discovered her vocation after a series of jobs when she landed in the contracts department of a corporation and discovered she had a mind for legal detail. She went to law school and landed an associate's job in a prestigious firm. "I took to it like a duck to water. Every week I learn something new, whether it's from watching one of the firm's lawyers execute a great deposition or from a new case that comes in."

Cathron's husband, Ron, is a free-lance producer of background music for commercials, and works from their home. He is a devoted parent who devotes several hours during the middle of the day to looking after their children, all under the age of six. Cathron says he is incredibly supportive and the only reason their life works. "He really mothers us all and is a magical father. He loves being with the kids; it's not a burden." This is very important to both Cathron and Ron, for unlike Libby, they do not feel comfortable with leaving their children with another person for the entire day.

Cathron didn't come to their sharing arrangement by design. Their first child, born when she was in the fourth year of her eight-year apprenticeship as associate, didn't change their lives. But when she became pregnant again, they wondered, could they manage two?

The factor that influenced their decision was that Cathron was coming up for partner. If she left before that, it would carry a stigma, suggesting forever after that she'd not made the grade. Ron encouraged her not to throw away her investment in work and at least give full-time working a try. He volunteered to cut back on his own free-lance work whenever Cathron worked overtime in twelve-hour days. If it became too much, they agreed they'd find another solution.

She made partner, and when her second son was only six weeks old, took him and his sitter along for a two-week stay in another state so she could breast-feed him while she argued a case. Her basic strategy for managing her job is to "let my partners know I'll be there when they need me." She spares neither herself nor any expense to perform as best she can. She's been known to bundle her children out at seven A.M. to a substitute sitter so she can make an eight o'clock hearing. And she often works after midnight polishing her briefs after the children have gone to sleep. "I never use the children as an excuse for not making an appointment or getting something done on time."

On the other hand, Cathron doesn't work the 200% she used to, maybe "only 125% . . . and none of this would be possible without Ron there. I couldn't leave my children a whole day with a stranger, no matter how loving or kind. We both feel being a parent means teaching your children about life, and he takes them to the gym to learn to swim, teaches them songs and about dinosaurs. As much as I love my work, I know and Ron knows and the kids know that they're my number-one priority. If my work ever really made them suffer, I'd drop it in a minute."

Many Ways. There is no one right way to have children and continue a career. *But there probably is a best way for you.* Becoming a parent offers tremendous possibilities for testing yourself and growing as a person. Fortunately some of the spin-offs from that growth can benefit you at work. For example, the confidence of working through the problems of parenting may make you more assertive. Carla learned "that you can't take garbage. I learned for the first time as a mother that you have to say what you'll do and won't."

The strain also has a way of stripping things down to size, showing trivial things to be just that. "It used to be," says a newspaper reporter, "that I was so driven, every interruption bothered me. I would get into a traffic jam in a taxi and I would almost have a heart attack. Now if I get in a traffic jam—well, I live in New York City, what did I expect?"

Another thirty-four-year-old nurse finds a new serenity. "I just don't worry as much about work things. It used to be I would take things home—rehashing decisions, worrying over disputes. Now there's just no time, and everything goes better that way." Another woman told us that her new serenity took the form of believing now in "muddling through." "Nothing scares me now the way it used to. No matter what problem I'm presented with, I don't fall apart. I know somehow I will get through this day and it will be okay."

For some women, a surprising side effect of motherhood is that they are more popular on the job. "People like me more now that I'm a mother," says a vice-president of sales for a cosmetics firm. "At the office you really don't have much to talk to people about except business. But now there's the children. Women here who looked on me as cold are now reassured because we can talk about our children." Another corporate woman—the lone female in her department—finds that talking about children is the one common ground between her and her male colleagues. "The fact that we both worry about our children's educations and values makes them see me as one of them. It makes up for not playing golf together or discussing the American League scores."

Changing Values. As a woman who's already established in a field, with proven value to an employer, you'll have more clout if you try to change some of the givens of your work life. Without losing status, you may be able to work part-time during your baby's infancy, or arrange to travel less, or cut back from the fifty-hour week that many career people work to forty hours. Customs and ideas about "how we have to do business" are more likely to alter if women with your value manage to make them and still do the job.

At the same time, established women may have such ingrained ideas themselves of what a "serious worker" in their field is expected to do or accomplish that they themselves are reluctant to ask for changes. Or if they do, they suffer a diminished view of themselves as professionals. A psychotherapist cut sharply back on her practice after her daughter was born and was surprised to discover that she saw herself in a lesser light professionally. "I feel like a dabbler. I feel apologetic to myself because I'm not dedicating as much energy to my patients. I keep watching to see if I'm less sharp with my remaining patients, because there was a kind of flow that developed when I worked with more people and spent many consecutive hours working with patients."

Her reaction is not unusual. It's clear that not only corporations and professions need to redefine their expectations of employees. What we all think of as "being a professional" will also have to be reexamined.

And yet, even though you may often feel like a pioneer, hacking a new trail, not knowing yourself for sure where you're going, your example in the work place is important. Even if you make no changes in your work schedule and carry on your job exactly as before, your co-workers and superiors are bound to get a new view of what a successful worker can be. The fact that you continue to produce and contribute to the business, while being a good and devoted mother, will help overturn stereotypes based on the way things have been done in the past and demonstrate that a woman (or a man) can be more than one thing at once.

Adding up the pluses against the hardships of bringing a baby into their lives, most women told us the pluses came out much higher. Mostly they found the universal, yet always unique, experience of being a mother added more depth to their lives than all that had gone before. Business, after all, tends to be a horizontal experience. The kinds of skills and emotional strengths you develop on the job may vary in level but not in type. Self-regulation, discipline, deferred rewards, relations with others on a business level— these tend to be the qualities that are valued at work and are sharpened when you gain work experience. As you move up in the work world, the characters change, your company and job change, but the basic tactics of working remain the same. Parenting, on the other hand, tests your capacity for loving, nurturing, and even forces you to reopen your childhood, perhaps finish unfinished business from your younger years.

Sums up one career woman, the mother of a five-year-old, "After you've done a great sale or you've been promoted, it's sort of over with. But having a child is always still here. It's not the most intelligent thing anyone could say they've done because anybody can do it. But there's something so miraculous and rewarding that *you've* done it. Sometimes I look at her and think, *I'm somebody's mother.* You are totally responsible for this person. It's the best thing I ever did for myself."

Part Three

Yourself

Chapter Thirteen

Succeeding with Yourself

Scratch a working mother and what will you find festering right under the skin?

Guilt.

With more and more mothers employed—today the *typical* schoolchild has a mother who works—guilt has begun to loosen its hold. But for some it still gnaws quietly, occasionally flaming into consciousness.

A young woman, Beth, smiles at her eleven-week-old son nestled in her arms. She will be returning to work in another week, she tells us. Her friendly look turns guarded when we ask how she feels about the maternity leave ending. "Well," she says, drawing the baby closer to her, "I love him so, but I need my job . . . I *like* my job." She is almost apologetic. We assure her we approve of her choice, but she doesn't seem to notice. In a rush of words she sets out to convince us—and herself?—that what she's doing is fine. She ends with ". . . and, anyway, we need my income . . . I have no choice."

Another mother, Janet, ponders our question, "What makes you feel guilty?" Finally she answers. "He tugs at my heartstrings," she says, pointing to her three-year-old son playing with blocks in the corner of the room. "When he was a baby it was easier somehow; he couldn't tell me what was bothering him, and he didn't seem bothered. Now he says things like, 'Mommy, stay with me today.' I know I'm doing a good job as a parent . . . still, there are times I worry. It's always a conflict."

Are Beth and Janet guilty mothers? Perhaps. But more likely

what they are experiencing is normal conflict and a natural sense of *loss*, of missing something. Occasional feelings of loss are common for mothers of young children who leave them for much of the day. And every mother experiences conflicts between her own needs and her child's. But guilt—the feeling we have when we are ashamed of something we do—is by no means inevitable.

When a woman's job is a financial necessity—as is true for most mothers who work—she is not so likely to feel she is shortchanging her children. But if one consequence of economic hard times is that we feel less guilt as mothers, another result is that we worry about job security and feel guilty about neglecting our careers! Probably some residue of guilt clings to every working mother. As one woman quipped: "Guilt is my co-pilot."

Even the most confident mother suffers self-doubt when her child develops a reading problem or has a small accident. Then she may share the anguish of Connie, a successful academic who's refused chances for career advancement, yet still feels guilty about not being home with her nine-year-old: "I worry," she says, "because he seems to attach himself to people so desperately. I keep saying it's because he never got enough mothering and so he's emotionally needy and he will be at twenty-five, and forty, and even when he's seventy." Poor mother, who sees her failures making her child miserable sixty years hence! What a painful load of anxious self-blame to shoulder!

Mothers we talked with had been through any number of problems with their children: a son who stole small amounts of money at school; a three-year-old boy who suddenly stopped talking; an incommunicative teenage daughter. Not one of the problems, when resolved, appeared related to the mother's absence during part of the day.

This is not to say that side effects of a mother's working—her tension or her fatigue, for example—can't be part of a larger picture in which behavior problems develop. But the simpleminded equation of mother works = child's-in-trouble, is simply not true.

Handling Guilt

The best way to begin ridding yourself of guilt is to ask yourself: *"How reasonable is my guilt?"* Looking at research findings is likely to be reassuring. (See also pages 93–95, on how children of working mothers turn out.)

SOME OF THE THINGS YOU MAY FEEL GUILTY ABOUT

- missing your child in the middle of a business meeting
- not missing your child at all
- forgetting to bring a birthday present for your daughter to take to a party
- watching TV when you feel you should be making a big hearty stew
- falling asleep at a PTA meeting
- your child's toes turning in because you haven't had time to shop for new shoes
- being too tired for sex with your husband
- not having a clean tablecloth when your mother comes to dinner
- not having the beds made for two weeks
- going to your office when your child lies in bed with a 102° fever

How Does the Parenting of Working Mothers Stack Up? Pediatrician Mary Howell notes that homemaker-mothers report they spend six-plus hours a day in childcare, compared to employed mothers, who spend four-plus hours. While two hours a day may seem like a lot, Howell estimates that the difference in "attentive care" is probably not significant.

By the time children reach adolescence, even time differences disappear. Working mothers spend the same amount of time with their teenage children as do at-home mothers. And significantly, adolescent daughters of employed mothers are more likely to name their mothers as "the person I most admire."

Researchers Lois Hoffman and Ivan Nye, authors of the definitive *Working Mothers*, point out that "if a mother's work is gratifying, if she does not feel unduly hassled, or if she deliberately sets about to do so, she may even spend more time in positive interaction with the child than does a nonworking mother."

Probably the one finding that most mothers will back up from their own experience is the overriding effect of a mother's own attitude and satisfaction in her work. Hoffman and Nye concur with the women we talked to in concluding that when a mother enjoys her work, "she does a better job" as a mother. They cite studies that indicate that the satisfied working mother is often a better parent than the dissatisfied nonworking mother. Indeed, in one study, the full-time mother who avoids employment because of her "duty" to her child obtained the lowest scores on "adequacy of mothering." In another study comparing professional women with college graduates who had chosen to be full-time homemakers, the stay-at-home women viewed themselves as less competent in most areas, *including that of childcare.*

"The data, on the whole, suggest that the working mother who obtains personal satisfactions from employment, does not have excessive guilt, and has adequate household arrangements is likely to perform as well as the nonworking mother or better; and the mother's emotional state is an important mediating variable." Hoffman and Nye warn: "Mothers of young children . . . may mar employment satisfaction by too much guilt."

And so we come full circle. How we feel about what we do—and thus about ourselves—has a profound effect on our children. If we are anxious or unhappy about working, we communicate this dissatisfaction to our children, just as the dissatisfied housewife sends out danger signals about her boredom and depression. Excessive guilt can wreck the very benefits that a working mother hopes to bring to her family.

Handling guilt, then, is a matter of more urgency than your mental comfort. This nagging anxiety calls for two strategies so universal they can be set down flatly as rules.

> *Rule 1.* If you really are guilty of something, stop doing it. If your child truly is suffering under your present childcare arrangement, perhaps you should consider lowering your lifestyle and paying for better care. If your child is undergoing hardship that you can clearly trace to your absence, maybe you should consider working part-time.
>
> *Rule 2.* Don't instantly jump to the conclusion that your working is the cause of every problem that occurs. Guilt has a way of blinkering us, bottling in our normal sensitivity, so that difficulties seem insoluble.

Who Makes You Feel Guilty?

Of all the garden varieties of guilt the most poisonous is guilt fed by someone else. Sometimes the older generation is the culprit.

Mothers and mothers-in-law often become protectors of their grandchildren. They see themselves as combining the infallible wisdom of experience with the seasoned judgment of distance. ("After all, my daughter's never had a child before, she can't see what she's doing, leaving that child.") If the disapproving mother baby-sits for you, she has a double-whammy hold. First, there's the martyrdom of doing your job: "My daughter works, so I keep her children," these willing do-gooders sigh to friends. And second, she becomes the expert on your child, and you can be sure she'll report all the bad news. Kathryn, returning to graduate school at twenty-nine, asked her mother to take over at home. To her distress, "When I'd get home, my mother would say, 'Jonathan has been sitting at the door waiting for you for the past hour.' Maybe he was, but *she* should have been doing something to amuse him. Of course, I didn't see it that way for a long time. She made me feel guilty as hell."

Learning to trust your own instincts with your kids is an essential step in your growth as a mother. One woman expressed what we think is the healthiest attitude about grandmother guilt. She said: "My mother doesn't approve of me, but that's her problem."

Letting Grandma see how well her grandchild is developing and how happy he is may brighten the picture. At the Park Center for Pre-Schoolers in New York City, director Susan Weissman regularly schedules a Grandparents' Day for just this purpose. "They think we're an orphanage," she commented, laughing. "Or a zoo. I think they expect to see bars. But when they visit they see how cheerful it is and how the children are thriving, and all I can say is they're relieved." Knowing little Johnnie doesn't spend his day confined to a cage may not get your mother off your back, but at least it will give her less ammunition with which to bombard you.

Doctors. These are just a notch below grandparents in their power to induce guilt in us. Switch pediatricians if yours doles out guilt along with his medical advice; his job is to help you raise your child in the best possible way within the life-style you've chosen, not to make you feel guilty about your choices. This doesn't mean he shouldn't caution you about times that a baby might be especially vulnerable to your absence or that he can't suggest that you cut down on your social life if he thinks your child seems sad or lonely. But if all you hear is disapproval, your doctor's negative attitude may be standing in the way of his helpfulness. Seek out a physician who is more sympathetic to your views. You can find this out by asking direct questions when you interview a doctor.

The same holds true if you consult a psychiatrist or other mental health professional. Guilt is the last thing you need when you have a problem serious enough to warrant professional help. Marilyn and John discovered this when they went to see a psychiatrist about their six-year-old son Michael's fear of going to school. The doctor, a child psychoanalyst with a distinguished reputation, immediately labeled the boy's problem "school phobia," a serious disorder, and then proceeded to address a barrage of questions only to Marilyn. When she mentioned that she had returned to work a few months before, the doctor leaned back in his chair with the air of a detective who had cornered his prey. "Wait a minute," said Marilyn, starting to feel uncomfortably guilty, "Michael's father shares equally in his care . . . we're both very involved with him. Why are you talking only to me?"

"With school phobia," the doctor explained patiently, "we look to the mother. With arson," he added, turning to John for the first time, "we look to the father." "I see," said John. "And who do you look to if the child wants to burn down the school?"

Understandably disenchanted, Marilyn and John decided to take matters into their own hands. It turned out that Michael was terribly frightened of his teacher, whose bantering, aggressive style just didn't suit his shy nature. A meeting with the principal, a change in teachers, a few days of daddy lingering in the new classroom, and the dreaded "school phobia" was cured. Once again, parents turn out to be the real experts.

Nonworking Mothers (and their husbands) can also shake your confidence, although nowadays it may be the stay-at-home mothers who feel guilty for not being out in the work place. If they realize your income is crucial to your family's welfare, they probably won't criticize you directly. But if you encounter hostility, remind yourself that you do as much with your children as they do, and that yours are turning out as bright and well behaved as theirs are.

Kids. One source of guilt may be right under your nose. Children are uncanny at finding our weak spots. Your ten-year-old son, his voice dripping with sarcasm, says: "That's okay, Mom, I don't mind that you spent the whole night trying on clothes and you never spoke to me once." Wallowing in your guilt will punish you, but it won't do your son any good. Instead, remind yourself of Rule Number One: "If you really are guilty about something, stop doing it." In spite of the sarcastic front, this boy is really saying that he feels neglected. Consider yourself lucky he's as direct as this, and trust his motives. Kids only resort to outright manipulation when they fail to get what they want from being direct.

If you think your son or daughter is using guilt to get something you aren't inclined to give, try not to be taken in. When your daughter complains that "Jenny's mother lets her have two ice creams in the afternoon, and she's home when Jenny gets there," you can say, "I guess you wish I were home, too . . . but I still don't like you eating two ice creams." Next time, she'll find a less underhanded means of persuasion.

Trust yourself to know your child. Listen carefully to what he says and watch what he does, and you'll have no trouble telling the difference between "extortion" guilt and honest "I-need-you" guilt. If you're not sure, err on the side of honesty. No child's character was ever ruined by a few extra treats.

Setting up. In the final reckoning, the antidote to guilt that mothers find most reliable is their belief that working helps them be better mothers than they would be if they stayed at home full-time. The great majority of mothers we interviewed believed this to be true:

A head nurse: "Staying home all the time would not be good for my relationship with my children. I would get frustrated and not really be loving and caring with them."

A computer programmer for a banking system: "I come to my children mentally refreshed and dying to see them. When we spend time together, it's quality time."

A majority of mothers come to feel that less intensive mothering is a benefit to both them and their children. Certainly the identification of a woman's success with her children's success that occurs in exclusive motherhood is calculated to produce an overinvestment of mother in child (much as a man's overinvestment in success at work is bound to produce a narrowed life experience). But perfect mothers do not necessarily produce perfect children, as many a mother discovers.

Says Sandra, a thirty-four-year-old Kansas lawyer: "I think my children were relieved when I went to law school and wasn't hovering around them every day, organizing their playtimes and naps. Whatever kind of craziness I pass on to my children, at least it won't be like my mother's. She was the classic smothering mother, who made me feel I had to excel at things for her sake and if I didn't, she wouldn't love me. I'm proud of my kids, but they don't feel they have to do things for me."

Chapter Fourteen

Keeping Your Marriage Strong

> When you're pressed for time, you take it from the
> two people you know can take it—you and your
> husband.
>
> —AN EXPERIENCED WORKING MOTHER

You had a thousand hassles at your office and worked late. Your daughter greeted you with a skinned knee and in tears because her brother wouldn't let her use his computer all afternoon. You got supper on the table and supervised your son's loading the dishwasher and your daughter's bath. You sink on the couch after they go off to bed, and your husband looks up from the TV, hurt, "You're always tired. When are you going to have time for me?"

Until recently, social researchers found a higher degree of conflict in marriages where the wife worked, and, in the fifties and sixties, "working wives" were popularly blamed for the rising divorce rate. Newer studies reflect a new reality: Middle-class families where both husband and wife work do not seem to experience more marital conflict than those where the wife does not work. Indeed, some evidence suggests that women who enjoy their jobs appear more satisfied with their marriages than wives who stay at home.

Women we talked with were frank to credit working with positive benefits for themselves in their marriages. "Working," mused Abby, a secretary for a small TV station, "makes me a more interesting person, more attractive to my husband, and gives me more power in the marriage."

None of the women thought having a job would directly cause divorce. Carmen, a Chicana government worker, reflected on the dissatisfactions she was experiencing with her husband: "Working hasn't broken up my marriage. It's given me the option not to have to *stay* in the marriage. And that's encouraged me to look hard at him and try to make us find a way to get along better."

Here are two more findings to console yourself with when your mother-in-law sighs over seeing her son load the washing machine or your husband fails to be thrilled over a sale you've just achieved.

- Faye Crosby, Yale professor of psychology, found in a recent study that working women who are married and have children seem to enjoy their work more than women who are not wives and mothers.
- A broad-based 1972 study concluded that while working wives experience more conflict with their husbands, they also express more satisfaction with their marriages. Conflict and tension are not necessarily incompatible with marital happiness.

In fact, talking with women who had been nonworking wives and then gone to work, we got the strong impression that the very areas where the women said their marriages eventually improved—shared decision-making, more trust and respect, a healthier emotional balance for the wife—*at first proved the worst areas of fighting and conflict with their husbands.*

It's hard for a couple today to know exactly what to expect of each other, as traditional roles become less viable. But don't be afraid of change or even conflict. Neither change nor arguments with your husband means that your relationship is falling apart. On the contrary, couples who live happily together for many years achieve their happiness only by being tough enough to confront and work through differences, even trivial ones. Who loads the laundry after you've both worked a forty-hour week may not seem like an issue that should determine marital happiness. But a wife who feels that her husband is responding to her needs and is showing his commitment to their family by pitching in is likely to respond by greater commitment to him.

Sharing Financial Decision-making

Ask many women why they work and you'll get a fast "for the money." Ask what their greatest moment of satisfaction is and they'll answer "when I get my paycheck."

A paycheck confers more than the money. It bestows power on you—tangible proof that society declares you a useful person. It engenders feelings like these:

"My paycheck is proof that I'm a productive person, that I can earn my way in the world."

"It shows I'm pulling my weight in the family. We have four kids, and before we were terribly strapped and my husband was always nagging 'I have to carry all the responsibility, you don't help at all.' Now my paycheck is my contribution to our family and I feel respected."

"It gives me a right to a say in the decisions. Now I feel I can make decisions with my husband—and even disagree with him— about what to buy and how to live."

Shared financial decision-making is one of the most common results of a wife's working. Research studies of working wives in almost every Western country show that a woman who earns increases her power in decision-making in the family's economic choices—everything from what color to paint the house to whether the husband should replace his car, where to go on vacation, and what clothes to buy.

But working through to shared management of your family's money can be full of argument. It's never easy for two people, even with the same aims, to agree on their spending styles. Money is not only a critical practical matter of living but a highly emotional component of how you like to cope with life. Whether you're a spender or a saver, your personal style of handling money represents emotional security for you.

Maybe you like to carefully budget every penny, so you'll have the cash to splurge occasionally when you really want something . . . while he hates daily budgeting and condemns you as "small-minded." Or maybe you're the free spender, and he's more controlled.

Here are a few simple ways to give each of you breathing space and autonomy.

Agree on different areas of responsibility. If you are like most couples, the areas may split along traditional sex lines. For example, Anne and Larry, whose combined earnings of $32,000 are almost equally split between them: Anne, a teacher, pays for the groceries, the household expenses—from light bulbs to new slipcovers—and the childcare for their two sons. Larry, a salesman, pays all the major shelter expenses: the house payments, car, medical bills, life insurance. They both contribute to vacations.

Formalizing your separate areas of responsibilities by setting up separate checking accounts. Sometimes this simple step can produce peace overnight. Lucy's husband earned $40,000, and his salary alone should have spelled financial comfort for their family, but instead he complained constantly about her alleged extravagances: "He's always under a lot of pressure on his job. And just after the baby was born, we had a whole new scale of expenses: a sitter for the three days a week I work; a new house; and all the baby expenses. He kept nagging at me: 'Why do you have to pay the sitter so much? Can't you get someone cheaper? Why did you buy steak last week?' He was driving me crazy, until I put my foot down and opened my own checking account where I deposited my salary and paid for our groceries and the sitter out of it. Almost overnight when he stopped writing the checks and counting the money as it went out, we stopped quarreling."

THREE WAYS TO DEFUSE MONEY QUARRELS

1. *Suggest trial periods.* Most spouses' sense of fair play will make it hard not to agree to at least a short period of trying another way to handle the money. Six weeks is usually the minimum period necessary to find out if a new way works.
2. *Avoid making sweeping character judgments based on money behavior.* Try to avoid such angry statements as "That's just like you, you're a cheap person" or "My mother was right when she said you'd never be a responsible person." When you're angry, it's natural to leap from the particular situation to a wounding generalization that condemns the whole person. And then you're no longer arguing about money but about larger issues.

3. *Take small steps if you can't take big ones.* Sometimes small changes are the best, surest way to move ahead when a big change in money management is too threatening to your husband or to you.

Sometimes the only way to get your mate to compromise on his style of handling finances is *to neutralize the process* for a while with separate accounts or areas of responsibility and let him grow to respect your money-managing facility. Linda, a twenty-six-year-old computer console operator, describes how she worked through her husband's refusal to share decision-making. "He would never listen to me when I told him we should wait to buy something. So finally, I put part of my salary in a separate savings account and refused to show him my passbook. When he'd ask how much I had, I lied and said it was less than it was for fear he'd go on a spending spree. But lately, maybe because my account is the only savings we have, I seem to have become more important in his thinking. He's listening to what I say—like our TV is wearing out and he wants to buy a fancy new one and I keep saying no, no, we need other things more. And he surprised me—he hasn't bought it. I think the way I've budgeted and saved part of my salary impressed him. Now I've decided I don't want to ever have to lie about my savings book. It's a whole new step in our marriage."

Take the next step to full sharing. Oddly enough, it's often women with limited income who participate fully with their husbands in planning what their housing will be, how the daily budget will be spent, and how they'll work toward more financial security. "When you don't have much," says a nursing aide, "you sure as hell better have your say about how it's going to be paid out."

Women with sizable salaries of their own often fail to take the next step and share major financial planning with their husbands. One reason lies in the fact that, traditionally, the notion of finances and investment are shrouded in the myth of masculine expertise. Charlotte, a gifted teacher who feels that as a forty-five-year-old woman she missed the benefit of the independence of the woman's movement, confesses she plays no part in her family's financial management. "I sign my check and turn it over to him, and he gives me a certain amount back. I pay for my own expenses, the baby-sitter, the children's clothes, and food out of that. I would never dream of asking him for more."

Charlotte is equally reluctant to press her husband, who earns half his income from fast-moving real-estate transactions, to tell her their total financial worth, exactly what investments he has, or whether their assets are going up or down. "Sometimes he's very irritable, and when I ask what's wrong, he just snaps, 'The property; don't ask.'"

If you're ignorant about your family's financial resources, you're sure to feel incompetent and unqualified to speak when it comes to jointly making plans like where you should live, whether you can risk a job change, how to plan your children's schooling. A husband who refuses to explain why "we can't afford it" or insists "let me worry about that" is pushing his wife to become either frivolous with money or needlessly anxious (*not* knowing your financial situation can be worse than knowing, no matter how shaky it is).

Couples can also fall into a his/hers separatism in various arrangements that seem to be fair to both but, in fact, limit the woman's say in financial decisions that affect her and her children. Audrey, a dynamic midwestern woman lawyer who had just masterminded a million-dollar settlement for women workers in a discrimination suit, is typical. She told us that her husband had a large amount of savings and investments when they were married ten years ago, but to this day, she still doesn't know how much or where the money is. And while she's politely asked her husband, she's never insisted he tell her. "I accept that what he earned before he had a family is all his. I think of his earnings as his, too, and I'm careful to live on my income for my personal expenses, the sitter, and the children's needs. I would never dream of asking him to pay for a dress for me."

Both Charlotte and Audrey—highly aware and successful—were astonished as they heard what they were saying. If you realize you've been backing off from making decisions about your family's finances, are you using these excuses?

1. *You really don't know anything about money.* That's easily remedied by taking one of the many free courses in money management being offered to women at your local Y, church,

or brokerage house. One woman started her education by investing $1000 with a broker. She soon became familiar enough with Dow-Jones averages and other market terms to talk knowledgeably with her husband.

2. *You really hate talk of money and hate pushing your husband about it.* There are no excuses for being incompetent or ignorant when you must make decisions together affecting yourselves and your children.

3. *You really think money is one last preserve of identity and you're reluctant or afraid to take it away from your husband.* Maybe so. But unless you test the waters, you'll never find out.

Staying Emotionally Close

My base, my center in life, is my marriage. My core is to be happy with my husband. When that feeling isn't there, I'm desolate.

—MARY, YOUNG CREDIT OFFICER

Mothers who share wage earning and parenting often report a greater closeness and companionship with their husbands. This closeness develops naturally when you come to understand each other's concerns. Let a father stay two hours with a baby on a regular basis and he'll understand why you are exhausted. Let him be responsible for getting your twelve-year-old baseball-crazy son to do his homework and he'll grasp the psychic strains of being a parent. Let a wife put up with the givens of earning a living: coping with a boss, performing when you'd rather be home catching up on your sleep, competing with others in your office—and she can understand his strain when problems arise at work.

Sociologists offer a sound explanation of why wives and husbands who share in each other's worlds can be closer emotionally. Distinguished sociologist Lee Rainwater and others have long hypothesized that role sharing between spouses is related to close, warm, rewarding relationships. Role segregation—where the two sexes seldom share work or pleasures—is associated with social distance and a lack of positive emotions.

Many husbands oppose their wives' taking a job, assuming that she'll be too "independent," or not pay enough attention to him. Yet the fact is that many wives who stay home report they put too much emotional dependence on their husbands. And too much emotional dependence can be as damaging to a marriage as too much independence.

Carrie, a twenty-eight-year-old secretary who took her job two years ago, remembers that when she was housebound with her two young children, she put heavy demands on her husband for emotional excitement. "My whole world centered on him. Every night at six when his key turned in the door, it was the start of my day. I depended on him for everything—my information about the world, for opinion of myself, my support. It was just too much. He turned away from me, and looking back, I can see why. Anybody is afraid of someone clinging like that. Now that I have my job, my own sphere, I'm much more balanced. And we're closer."

In a strange turnabout, many women who have babies in mid-career express fears of what would happen to their marriages if they *stopped* working. "I'd feel very funny taking money from him," said a bank manager, a thought echoed by many other career women. "Everything's been worked out equally—I think maybe he'd take charge too much if I wasn't out in the world, too."

It may be useful to remember when you've been too tired to talk to your husband for four nights running that full-time intimacy is not necessarily a better alternative.

Can't You See I'm Talking to Your Mother?

A working wife describes her homecoming, that dangerous falling-apart of the household that occurs when mother's foot hits the doorstep: "The kids are all over me. My husband is already there and he's dying to tell me about his day. And the kids are dying to have me all to themselves. And it always ends up with me dancing around like a Marx Brother trying to talk to everybody and then my husband shouts at us all, 'Will you be *quiet,* can't you see I'm talking to your mother?'

"And then I feel so guilty. Because he is an adult and he can hold it in and wait until later. But my kids are little and they don't know about 'later'; it's just 'now' and they want to be all over me.

But he gets furious and it's a terrible problem. Who do I pay attention to?"

Working adds more tension to the pull between being both wife and mother. But don't forget that *all* mothers, working or not, must juggle a basic conflict in their double roles. Just as having a child forever alters your life, having a baby forever changes your marriage.

Having children is both the most uniting and the most divisive experience you and your husband can undergo. Alongside all the joy that children bring, many couples will also date their children's arrival as the beginning of the greatest strains in their marriage.

The conflict starts with pregnancy, when your body balloons from the young bride's he's loved to a new instrument housing another being. No matter how interested he is, no one can deny that child-bearing is definitely your act, and normally you will be self-absorbed as you confront the physical and emotional changes of pregnancy.

After birth, the sensual joy you and your baby share in nursing or through simply touching each other shuts your attention off from your husband again. And your baby, equipped with keen survival instincts of his own, is sure to find other ways to thwart your turning your attention elsewhere. Couples are amazed at how uncannily the baby wakes up to howl in the middle of the night just at the moment when his parents begin to make love. Some authorities even believe that sexual arousal stimulates an odor from the mother's breasts that rouses the baby to this threat. Danger! Mother is loving someone else!

Whatever the actual mechanism, husbands usually complain that a new sexual adjustment must be made with their wives.

And a different overall relationship emerges between you. Your husband must accept that from now on phrases like "the baby needs me" or "I want the children to have . . ." will forever be on your lips, reminding him that he's no longer first in your life. If he's skittish about responsibility, he may feel you're forcing him into a corner, tying him down and calculatingly looking on him as a breadwinner for your child.

Your job will be one more competitor for your time and attention. If your husband's been used to having his favorite dishes served on request, being greeted at the door by his loving wife with a drink in hand to wash away his day's labors, and commanding your full, wide-eyed attention whether he's pontificating on ballgame scores or the new tax laws, you can expect he won't adjust easily to having less of your time. This is true even of husbands who have been known to rustle up a plate of eggs for themselves, cheerfully take over the kids on the night you chair the PTA meeting, and loudly profess that they believe in women's rights.

Having time with you is *still* a problem. Mark, a twenty-eight-year-old civil-liberties lawyer married to a social worker, explains: "I couldn't be married to a woman without a mind of her own. I'm very proud of Jennifer. She's very good at her work, and I understand why it's important to her. But I feel left out a lot of the time. She comes home tired and upset. She's always busy with the children. We don't share enough together. I appreciate that she had to do what she's doing, but that doesn't make me feel any happier about it. I've begun to fantasize about a wife who'll just be interested in me."

The pressure of this-is-our-time-together can poison the time you do share. One man, married to a highly efficient woman who manages a pressured job and mothering three children, confesses: "I feel I'm just part of her program, even though she always finds time for me. We always have coffee after dinner on the patio, while the kids take their baths and get ready for bed. But I hear this clock ticking off in her mind while we talk. . . . 'In ten minutes, I'll go up and get the children to bed.' "

Women are used to juggling different sets of needs in their minds, but men can be upset by this wifely capacity. Making things even more difficult is the separate view of parental duties that most mothers and fathers possess. A husband has trouble understanding why his working wife can't just leave the children with a sitter and instantly turn back into the carefree creature he used to know and run off for a weekend of fun and sex together.

Finding Time Together. Most working mothers do feel that their free time belongs first to the children, even though they admit that sometimes such an attitude is either selfish or foolhardy. The first step is to realize that intimacy requires an ongoing exchange of feelings, of being aware of the other person's thoughts and emotions, of being concerned about each other's moods, no matter how passing they may be.

Wives who have hectic schedules can sensitize themselves to a husband's "neglect signs." One woman knows her husband is feeling neglected when he accuses: "You're not spending enough time with the children."

Another wife of fifteen years knows her husband is angry when he starts planning outings they'd both enjoy *without* her. And, of course, many husbands stay in touch with their feelings well enough to simply let you know in no uncertain terms: "I never see you anymore"; "You're too wrapped up in that job"; or "I don't want to hear another word about what's going on in your office."

When that happens, says a woman realty agent, she forces herself to turn off work temporarily. "Once I even refused to handle the biggest house I'd ever been offered, but it turned out to be a white elephant, so I didn't lose a thing." She concentrates on her husband until the relationship restabilizes.

Short trips together can be a marvelous tonic. A boutique owner takes her husband along on business trips. "It's terrific—tax deductible and, since it's absolutely necessary, I don't have to feel guilty about leaving the children. We never had time like this alone before."

A Connecticut couple has her mother come for the weekend and check into a motel only two miles down the highway, guaranteeing forty-eight hours free from domestic duty.

Make the effort to find some unpressured time together, however artificial it seems, however disastrous the first try. (Says one young wife who took a weekend off with her husband. "I ended up crying and worrying obsessively about the children; he had too much to drink and spent all the second day in bed nursing a hangover.")

And don't confine your time together to weekend trips. You may get the same resurgence of the wonderful, unmatchable "us-two" bond from a half hour shared over a cup of coffee after work, or an hour driving around together after dinner. Not only your husband but you, too, may feel the warmth of Tender Loving Care if you manage to fix a tray and both enjoy breakfast in bed—or lock yourself off in a room separate from the children for a drink together.

It's easy to grow apart when you're pressed for time, when the moment you want to tell your husband something important, he's not around or you're rushing off to work. It's easy to have separate angers, separate hurts that never get faced. Keeping in touch requires great effort—though you may not want to go as far as the couple who told us they were having trouble but were too exhausted to quarrel at night. Instead, the husband set the alarm for five A.M. "so we could have time to argue before the children woke up. We had some roundhouse fights before dawn, and it wasn't long before we worked things out!"

Making sufficient time to feel that connection and to enjoy each other—which, after all, is why you got married in the first place—is one of the great open secrets of couples with self-renewing marriages. Investing energy in finding space for that will pay you back many times over.

But Will He Love a Strong Woman?

Working couples today are leaving behind traditional notions of relationships based on the husband's unquestioned authority in the house. But the transition is littered by secret doubts and the absence of new models that carry the weight and reassurance of tradition.

In a more equal marriage, you may wonder how far equality can go before it becomes a dry, contractual exchange unleavened by love. He may worry that you won't respect him if you don't look up to his authority and think he knows more about the world than you do. No matter how much you appreciate his wanting you to grow and expand, you may sometimes wonder if he isn't so broadminded only because he doesn't really care about you.

Even the most self-confident woman can have these thoughts. For all of us have been shaped by the ideal of a love in which the male is magically superior in affairs of the world, leadership, and sexual knowledge.

Consider that timeless love story, *Gone With the Wind*. After single-handedly carrying her family from poverty to wealth, strong-willed Scarlett O'Hara eventually succumbs to the domineering but all-wise father figure Rhett Butler.

We might think we're living in more progressive times, but

today's best-selling paperbacks still present the same fantasy of lover as father. Typically, the woman plays a masochistic role, being raped in the early pages by none other than Mr. Right himself (who's so overcome by passion that he forgets himself). Immediately, he sails off over the seas, while the heroine suffers a Perils of Pauline series of rapes, beatings, tortures, and close brushes with death before being once more clasped in the strong arms of Mr. Right. Though the spunky girl has managed to survive on her own wits through all this, the last cloud of prose shows her being carried off by her powerful daddy figure, who will make everything all right in the future.

Behind much of this romantic tradition—even including such classics as *Jane Eyre*—lies the Victorian reality in which women were as economically dependent on men as were children. Lacking the right to own property, vote, or even control the dowries handed over to their husbands, a Victorian woman could do nothing better than attract the loyalty of a fatherlike husband, who would take care of her for life.

Even a contemporary study, *American Couples* by Pepper Schwartz and Philip Blumstein (Morrow, 1983), reinforces traditional stereotypes with the assertion that couples in which the woman is "feminine" have sex more often than couples in which she is more "masculine." And yet a closer look at how the authors rated people as "feminine" casts their finding in a different light. Persons who rated themselves or were rated by their spouses as "tender, compassionate, understanding" were labeled feminine. Surely women don't have a monopoly on tenderness or understanding! It could as easily be that a man who has an active sex life with his wife finds her "tender and compassionate" rather than simply "feminine," as the sociologists choose to call such loved people.

With all these messages from the past and present bombarding us, we'd scarcely be human if we didn't take some of them in. No matter how much a woman enjoys her increasing confidence, she may secretly fear that there's something unnatural about her, that maybe she's castrating, aggressive, or doesn't love her husband.

It helps to analyze what you *really* feel, not what you're supposed to feel. Do you feel closest to your husband when you're sharing a pleasure, when you're pursuing a goal together, when he listens to what you say? Or when he's coming on like the macho head of the family, you're saying yes-dear, or in more subtle form supporting the male ego?

Certainly there are times you appreciate being able to draw on his strength. But the exchange is evened when you can offer him strength, wisdom, and confidence at the times *he* needs them, as well.

If you feel conflicts about being strong in your relationship with your husband, consider the roots of this dilemma that psychologist Ellen Berman has traced. As counselor to troubled couples visiting the University of Pennsylvania Marriage Council, Berman discovered that many a high-achieving woman unconsciously demands that her husband be superior to her. This is because, although she is likely to see herself as intellectually competent, she still feels somehow unfeminine. Her need to feel desirable as a woman depends on her attracting the love of a man she regards as in some way superior —older, smarter, or more popular. As she starts to attain professional success and finds herself on a more equal footing with her husband, she begins to doubt her husband's superiority. And if he isn't superior, how can his love for her prove she's loveable?

Much as a man unsure of his masculinity feels the need to prove it with a string of conquests, she looks around for a superior man who can assuage her feelings of unworthiness as a woman by bestowing his love on her.

The irony, says Dr. Berman, is that the woman who goes looking for a strong man to "prove" her desirability is often in a marriage of real equality—surely a situation that proves her strength and worth far more than plunging into a new dependent relationship.

Sometimes the ways in which we persist in thinking our husbands are stronger and brighter conveniently deny reality. Joan, an accomplished pediatrician, demonstrates this point unfortunately well. She and her husband jointly head a large diagnostic clinic located in Pennsylvania. They have arranged that her husband works forty hours a week, while she works twenty-five, spending more time with their three children. Despite Joan's popularity with her patients and the respect she commands among nurses and other assistants, she insists her husband "is a better doctor than I am. In school, I was better at manual things—like drawing specimens," she concedes. "But now that we're in real practice, he's much better than I."

But doesn't she have a slight edge in talking to mothers? Well, she admits, she might be more patient, more intuitive in understanding their problems. Probably mothers ask her questions more easily, are less afraid of appearing stupid with her than with a male doctor. But, Joan declares firmly, her husband is better at diagnosis, brilliant at theory, and a far better doctor than she will ever be. Her colleagues disagree, but Joan sticks to her guns. Clearly she's more comfortable playing a secondary professional role.

Unlike Joan, many women *are* learning to get their own heads straight about being successful, decisive, and in charge. Do their mates then feel threatened by the new woman who's no longer the sweet little thing he married?

Increasingly, women are discovering that the qualities that make successful men attractive also seem to make women attractive, too. A woman who's alive, interested in the world and in her work, is likely to generate interest in both men and women. As a divorced Tennessee boutique owner says, "If you're attractive, you go through life having men say things like 'You're very pretty tonight' or 'You look very sexy.' That only goes so far with me since I've gotten absorbed in my business. Now, when a man is impressed with how well I do my job, it makes me feel terrific. That's the kind of admiration I need. The men who date me like me because of *all* of me, and that goes a whole lot deeper than just being the pretty-looking girl they want to show off."

Sex—Too Much or Too Little

Of all the doubts and anxieties expressed about working mothers, none is so paradoxical as the fear that a job will undermine her marital fidelity. Paradoxical, since not long ago, the secret feeling about the career woman was that what she really needed was a good dose of sex. *That* would put her back in her place, at home in the kitchen and nursery. Now the fear is that a mother going out to work is sure to be lured away from her marriage by having too great an opportunity for sex.

The common thread running through both fears is that *women can't handle sex*. Too little or too much—either way, anything above or below a standard controlled portion is likely to drive us bananas.

All these contradictory feelings reflect a double standard that is still widely accepted—the feeling that a woman's infidelity is far more dangerous and explosive in a marriage than a man's. This double standard lies behind many a husband's objection to his wife's working. Even while he protests that taking a job will mean that you won't have time for the children, that the house will be neglected, that his friends will think he's no provider, his real objection may be the prospect of sexual competition. And the question must be confronted: Is a working mother more likely to have an affair?

Realistically, working usually does place you in an environment that offers more chance for getting together with interesting men. The housewife has good reason to spend time with the pediatrician, the plumber, the washer-repair man—and that's about it.

But working, as a thirty-year-old woman college professor points out, "legitimizes your spending time with men. It's even expected that I will spend hours talking to men, attending meetings with them, working together on projects. And if something does spark, it's much easier to arrange the unaccounted-for time to do something about it. You can always say you were at a meeting."

A recent *Redbook* magazine study of 100,000 women produced this startling picture of greater infidelity among working wives. Here's how the percentage of women who confessed to having affairs broke down according to age:

WOMEN WHO HAVE HAD AFFAIRS

Age of woman	Employed	Not employed
Under 25 years old	21%	17%
25–34	40%	23%
35–39	53%	24%
40 and over	47%	33%

By the time employed wives reach their late thirties, they are more than *twice* as likely as housewives to have affairs!

These are startling figures, and some of the women we talked with told us how they became attracted to men and how the experience affected them. But their experiences were so different that they do not add up to any stereotyped pattern.

Watch Out for the First Year.   For some women, the first year back at work seemed to be a time for indiscretion partly because they lacked any anticipation of what the work world would be like.

Rosemary, thirty-two, returned to work two years ago as a magazine-space salesperson after having spent ten years at home raising children. She fell into two successive affairs as a result of what she now sees was naiveté about how to handle herself in business socializing.

"All I knew about being with men was what I knew from dating fifteen years before. I didn't understand the etiquette of business or how you maintain your distance while being friendly. All I knew was here I was all dressed up in the middle of the day, taking these successful, self-assured men out to lunch on my new expense account. I would have a drink and carry on this social conversation simply because I didn't know the language of business conversation. One of the men I had to see regularly was going through marital problems and I listened and was sympathetic. I didn't really mean to push it that far, but the talk and everything finally brought us together in a hotel room."

Rosemary's affair was not based on a deep attraction and didn't last long, but the next time she was deeply attracted to the man she had an affair with. Unfortunately, word got back to her boss, who called her in and told her this wasn't good business and to choose: the man or the job. "I chose the job and I realized that I had been dumb about myself and my own reactions and everything. I would advise any woman to make a little rule to herself—don't let yourself get involved in *anything* for the first year."

The first year back at work was also a dangerous period for Patsy. A twenty-eight-year-old mother married five years, she was smitten with hero worship for her architect boss when she resumed work as a draftsperson in his office.

"He is a very gentle, loving man and all his staff adores him. At first, I was overwhelmed just to be working there—he's already recognized, a name written up in the architectural magazines. I felt part of this fantastic work and that he was leading us all.

"When he started paying attention to me, I figured he was just being extra nice. And when he began to tell me little things about himself or squeeze my shoulder or brush my hands, it was like a dream. Here I was loving my job and having a wonderful man to boot. The whole physical affair was like a fantasy it was so wonderful."

The fairy tale didn't last. Patsy discovered that her dream lover runs through some kind of flirtation with every new person in his office. "He needs to know we all need him. And I finally opened my eyes and saw that our wonderful hero turns his charm on and off as it suits him. And how he woos clients. And that he's even taken credit for a talented junior's work on occasion. *And* that his work is the only thing that means anything to him. I crashed down to reality in about three months."

Interestingly, she adds this reflection: "I became much, much wiser about the world as a result. I don't regret that."

Monogamy Isn't Dead.   But stacked against the statistics is the conviction of many couples that the *quality* of a woman's marriage determines her fidelity far more than opportunity. Husbands repeatedly told us, "I figure if she wants to do it, she will whether she's home all day or in an office. Housewives run around, too." In many marriages, just being aware of the potential for attractions leads wives and their husbands to take extra care to maintain their closeness.

Sandra, a twice-married nurse who heads the intensive-care unit of an important Washington hospital, describes her decision to avoid sexual byplay on the job. A vibrant woman who loves her work and is strikingly attractive, she says candidly: "People assume that doctors and nurses are always jumping into bed. Well, it's true. When you work with people intensely in life-and-death situations, you develop strong emotions toward each other. Sometimes when you've lived through a tense night together, you can't just say good night and end it there. You have to share something physical. During my first marriage, which was unhappy, that happened easily and it happened frequently to me. In fact, I still stay in touch with one man and I'm sure we will always care for each other."

But Sandra has been happily remarried for four years. "This second marriage is a deep commitment for us both, because we survived terrible times in our first marriages."

She looks across the living room of her apartment to the terrace where her muscular husband lies stretched before the Sunday football game. "We still have a very physical thing between us after five years. I truly do not believe that Bill has anything going on the side. I certainly don't, though guys do cute things constantly and I have to discourage them. At times, it becomes a hassle. But Bill knows he can trust me and I plan to keep it that way."

Neither frequent advances from attractive men nor a history of affairs shakes Sandra's determination to remain faithful. That same deliberate decision was expressed to us by many women, both for business and personal reasons.

Linette, a hard-driving film producer, acknowledged the sexual temptations in her job. "My husband and I realize that mine is a very sexual business. You get intensely involved with your crew and you go off on location, where the spirit is anything goes. That's why marriages don't last long. If men want to stay married, they bring their wives along on location. But my real affair is with my work. If my husband's jealous of anything, it's certainly not other men, but the turn-on I get from work."

But surely attractions do bud with men even when she's obsessed with work? "Sure. About three years ago, my director and I were very sympatico. We worked together fantastically. It was a real high for us both."

After spending six weeks intensely working side by side, Linette did end up one night in bed with her director. "I felt so guilty about what I'd done that I flew home for the weekend across the country. I decided to end it right away. The man was bewildered and hurt. But I controlled it. I didn't just let things happen. I expect to do exactly the same if that situation comes up again."

Jeanette, marketing director for an Oregon firm, travels with her male salesmen, and last-minute show preparations often involve working late at night in hotel rooms. Jeanette is plainly irritated at being asked what happens.

"*Nothing* happens. I simply don't think about it and neither do they. I read somewhere that Margaret Mead suggested that we develop an incest taboo banning sex among women and men who work together. I endorse that. That's exactly what I've done. If you start with the attitude that your husband is important to you, you just use a little sense and don't let anything compromising or dangerous develop."

Sandra, Linette, and Jeanette have different occupations, but they all share the quality of being highly self-aware women. They are in control of their work and their emotional lives. They don't "just let things happen."

Other women may be less iron-willed than they. But one thing's for sure: Failing to think about what you want and value will lead to drifting. As we move from the ideal of monogamous marriages to a society that encourages sexual variety, as women break out to lives that allow them more experience and choices, each of us will have to develop the awareness of her own sexuality and values to steer a course that seems personally right.

And there are plenty of good reasons why a woman may well decide that a few moments of excitement hold little appeal in comparison to the unity of her family life. Nor is every attraction between you and a man necessarily momentous. Says a woman who owns her own crafts business: "Every woman knows that there's a certain kind of harmless attraction and flirting that just makes you feel good about yourself and men. It doesn't stop just because you're married. I call them my Subserious Attractions."

A woman may also decide that her family responsibilities have been too hard-won to endanger for an attraction. Says the same woman who enjoys flirting, "Marriage is a responsibility. It's not the most exciting life in the world but it works. Everybody is relatively happy—the kids, me, him. Marriage satisfies all our needs and it allows us to grow and change as well. Why destroy that?"

Others may find that the effort her husband and children make to adjust to her working create an obligation she won't break. Says one woman, "My family and I have worked so hard together to establish a work life for me. I could never betray that."

Hard business sense can also tell you that getting involved with the men you work with is not only dangerous to your marriage, but also can jeopardize the career you've fought so hard to have. Most businesswomen have seen the double standard at work when a man and woman in the same office have an affair. The man (who's usually superior in seniority or position) gets a wrist-slap or good-natured ribbing. The woman gets fired if the situation becomes awkward for management.

Finally, one of the biggest advantages of your working is that you just may discover it acts as a turn-on for you and your husband. All the stimulation and excitement that go with working can produce changes in you that improve the quality of your sex lives. "None of this happened overnight," says Penny, a twenty-nine-year-old mother and store buyer, "but our sex life has become much better."

She explains: "Before, I was a *mother* first and foremost. There's something very antisex about that. You're surrounded by diapers and burped orange juice and you have a saggy body and couldn't give a damn how you look. Even if you dress up, there's always something that makes you feel dowdy—your hair's not fixed or your panty hose runs. I was going through a lot of personal turmoil. I had wanted babies and had them and still I didn't feel grown-up. Under this pressure, I lost interest in sex."

Penny's experience reflects many women's experiences after returning to work: "My life took on structure. I had an excuse to get up and fix myself up. I began to realize I could do something, I wasn't just a little gray wren that was the helpmeet at home. And gradually that began to spill over into sexual interest. At first, I was just pleased with myself. I felt attractive, and so I wanted attention. But that kind of sex was replaced by something deeper. I feel free now to express myself if I want sex. And I feel confident enough of myself to experiment."

The relation between a woman's sexuality and her work fits no simple equation. Going to work can have no effect at all. Or it can lead you to important changes.

How Your Husband Feels

Make no mistake, a husband who's behind you in your work, who truly appreciates the efforts you're making to help out with family finances and make it all work, is worth his weight in gold.

Most women say it simply: "I couldn't do it all without him. If he weren't with me in this all the way, I couldn't handle it."

Husbands who give this kind of support earn a wife's gratitude and loyalty, and are well repaid. Those who lend a hand, understand why a woman wants to work, and don't assume she's slighting him or the children, have taken a big step toward creating a new kind of family unit in which no member's needs are served at the expense of another's. These husbands express their feelings like this:

"I saw how unhappy she was when she was at home all the time.

Things get pretty dusty around the house now, but we all seem to get along."

"She's very smart, and I'd be a fool to try to tie her down. So long as she's doing what she's good at, we'll get along."

"Sure I pay a price for her not being at home and doing all the things she could for my ease and convenience. And sometimes I get mad because she's tired or not with me when I want her to be. And I get jealous of how much she enjoys her office. But what I give up in return for having an active, involved wife is worth it."

Chapter Fifteen

Surviving As a Single Mother

One of the advantages of being a single mother is that your life, for all its strains, may be markedly better than what went before. Some women feel that it's easier to be a single working parent than half of a bad marriage.

Elka, thirty-eight and a receptionist since she divorced her husband one year ago, says, "When I rush home from work there's no longer that *lump of contention* sitting in front of the TV. Sure, I have three kids to raise and I'm the only human being in the world responsible for them, but at least it's not like when another adult was sitting around in the house not helping you one bit and you were mad all the time, resenting it because he was a dead weight."

Molly remembers she had much more to do when she was married: "I was taking care of two babies—my baby and my big-baby husband. When I came home, I had to feed three people and clean up for three and manage all these emotional needs. Things are 100 percent easier now."

Ginny reveals another source of strength for many single mothers: "I thought, I can't *possibly* raise the children alone. And then I suddenly realized—I've actually been making all the decisions about them for years. The only difference is now I make the decisions . . . and no one yells at me that I'm wrong."

The first message is clear: Doing it all by yourself is easier than doing it with a husband you're clashing with. But so is the second: Don't assume you *must* manage it all alone. The best strategy a single mother can adopt is to *establish a support system* to replace the traditional two-parent family. Over the years, most single mothers put together a support system of sorts. Save yourself a lot of wear

ADVICE FOR THE NEWLY DIVORCED

Carolyn, twenty-seven, has been separated for seven months and living with her five-year-old daughter, Erica, in a small apartment. In that time, a friend helped Carolyn get her first job in six years—as a public relations assistant. Carolyn's glamorous-sounding job actually consists mostly of typing and photocopying publicity releases and calling up bored newspaper editors. Despite this progress, Carolyn wonders if she will ever be up to running her own life.

For the first months of her separation, Carolyn was so wrapped in a blanket of fatigue that she barely got up. Some days she simply lay in bed, unable even to order in groceries by phone. When she first got her job, she'd fall back into bed as soon as she got home, worrying over the past until the next morning. But one morning, she got up and dressed, met an attractive man, and exploded with restlessness. Since then, she's been going out three or four nights a week, leaving Erica with a succession of baby-sitters. Five-year-old Erica had regressed to babyish behavior, crying whenever her mother leaves in the morning and even harder in the evenings. Carolyn's mother, who comes over every single day, is convinced that her daughter is on dope and goes around peeking into the pill bottles when Carolyn's not looking.

Carolyn doesn't really enjoy the men she's seeing—the novelty has worn off. And hiring the sitters takes up a lot of her time at the office —something her boss is complaining about. Carolyn still feels in a fog, and while she knows she should protect her job, she somehow can't deal with it. When she has those awful middle-of-the-night awakenings, Carolyn feels a rush of consuming love for Erica and worries about losing her. But when they are together, she can't seem to pay attention to her daughter or cope with her demands for reassurance and love. Their evenings together often end in tantrums and tears and a feeling of distance between them.

Is Carolyn crazy, weak, cracking up? No. She is going through stages of recovery that are universal enough to be predictable. If only she could find a wise friend, Carolyn might rouse herself from her circle of guilt, self-destructiveness, and self-pity to see ahead—and work toward the next stage. Try these simple but effective steps and you'll be on your way to recovery and establishing a new life.

1. *Expect to be a little crazy for a while.* Mary, an attractive thirty-nine-year-old auburn-haired woman who one year ago ended a twenty-one-year marriage to her high school sweetheart, says, "I

went out four or five nights a week with a different man. I couldn't stay home." Carolyn's reaction of total collapse for a month or so is more typical. Says Betty, a teacher and mother of three daughters, "I hired a live-in sitter and then I collapsed. For eight months, I couldn't do anything." Expect a full year before you are really in shape to plan a new life. Realize that this is *natural* and *temporary*.

2. *Get out in the world.* The oldest advice in the world and still sound. No matter how dejected and worthless you feel, get dressed up, go out, meet friends. *Don't* put too high expectations on yourself or them—you're not likely to meet Mr. Right at the next turn. But putting yourself in motion and seeing that the world, despite your personal tragedy, is turning right along will help.

3. *Don't just get a job—find out what kind of work you want to do.* Two out of three divorced mothers work, and financial necessity makes it likely that you will, too. Even if you have to take a make-do job for the present, take the time to discover the work that you *want* to be doing. From now on, working is going to be an important dimension of your life. If you take the time to experiment and find something that you really like, your job will be a big part of your recovery.

4. *Make friends with women who've been divorced longer than you have.* No one can understand what you're going through better than women who've been through it. And if they are further along in making a new life for themselves than you, they can advise and inspire you better than all the therapists in the world.

5. *Be good to yourself.* Indulging yourself is not indulgence. If you feel you'll benefit from professional therapy, get it. If you've never borrowed money in your life and hate the idea of owing anyone, recognize that this is a time when you need help—and don't hesitate to ask your parents, sister, brother, or maybe a friend for it. Indulge some of your lighter whims as well—whether that means staying in bed until noon on Sunday, buying a frivolous dress, or eating crackers in bed—and enjoy the benefits of being on your own.

and tear by *consciously* surveying your available resources and taking specific steps to integrate them into your life from the start.

No matter how indifferent your husband was, how inadequate as a parent, when you were married, you did have another adult in the house to test your opinions on. And you had another adult to back up your authority, even if he only shouted the kids down on occasion. ("Now there's never anyone," mourned one mother of three adolescent sons, "to just stand up and say, 'Damn it, shut up.' I can say it, but they don't pay attention to good-hearted old Mom.")

As a single parent, you'll discover that being one-on-one with your children twenty-four hours a day robs you of perspective. You can easily become overly protective or overly dependent on each other. As for your children, having no other stable adult in their lives except you can be frightening. Certainly it tends to put too much pressure on their relationship with you. They need other adults to trust in their world.

You won't find that other people fit naturally into your lives as though made to order. But with openness and determination, you'll establish a new "family" of friends or paid helpers who will enrich the lives of you and your children.

Find a Supportive Community. Somehow the urge to get away from the world strikes many a newly divorced mother. She sees herself and the kids starting life all over on a Vermont apple farm (where, significantly, there will be no *people* to disturb their tranquillity). Before you plunge all your divorce settlement into a charming rural retreat, remember that there will also be no ready transportation for your children and baby-sitters, no superintendent to call when the furnace breaks down in a blizzard, and no corner movie to send the kids to when they're driving you up the wall.

Better to look for a place to live that will put you smack in a web of support services. If you've lived in the suburbs, moving to the city may simplify life. Your children won't have to be ferried around by a licensed driver. And in case of sickness, an urban working mother can usually dash home on her lunch hour. "I have a good neighbor just across the hall, so my five-year-old son only has to step outside our door to get help," says Beverly, who left a big suburban split-level with two acres of yard for a one-bedroom apartment near the hospital where she works as a clinical psychologist. "At our old house, he would have had to walk half a mile and cross the street, and I'd have been worried sick whenever I was delayed a half hour by a meeting at work."

Look, too, for a home that offers a pool of baby-sitting services.

Locating near a college provides you with a wonderful, ready-made source of qualified young people eager for part-time work. Ask yourself, too, How far is the school? Or daycare center or family daycare? Will you be able to come home at lunch in an emergency? How much time will you have to commute each day (there'll no longer be someone to put dinner on when you're late)? Can your children enjoy a social life in the neighborhood, or will all their friends have to be imported?

Your Family Can Help. The first resource many single mothers turn to is their own families. As you and your children begin to function as a single-parent family, your own relatives may experience a deepened emotional commitment to you. A grandmother or aunt or uncle, instead of merely being an indulgent visitor, can become another central adult presence in your children's lives— someone who is an acceptable cover for you at school events or trusted enough to help your child weather an emotional crisis. A grandfather or brother can be a sustaining male figure in your female-headed family, one who can take your son and daughter on traditional outings to ball games, fishing, or on other activities you have no taste for.

Don't ever overlook support from *any* relative. Adopt early the rule of successful working mothers, single or married: *Get all the help you can.*

Alexandra, an artist who was left by the father of her baby one month before her son Jason was born, found an unexpected father substitute in her sister's husband, Tony, a self-made businessman whom she'd had little taste for. "I hardly ever saw my sister after college, except at family holidays, because she was such a typical suburban housewife, spending her days shopping and koffee-klatsching. But she and Tony have never been able to have children and they've become real second parents to Jason."

Through her son, Alexandra has also become close to her sister and Tony. "Tony is the stable male figure in my son's life, whereas he's seen his own father exactly twice, for an hour each time." Tony is old-fashioned and macho, and he and Alexandra disagree about politics, religion, and a host of other things, but they have never had a cross word over Jason. "Maybe because I can see how much Tony thinks of Jason, I can tolerate his views. If you told me four years ago that I'd let my son grow up influenced by Tony, I'd have said *never*. Now I wouldn't trade him for anything."

Emily, divorced from a gynecologist, sends her ten-year-old daughter for a month each summer to stay with her ex-husband's maiden aunt. "The two just happen to hit it off." Ann made friends with her mother-in-law *after* her divorce, and contentedly sends her two children off for a weekend with grandma once every month.

But before you rush back into the family bosom and arrange to live with or near them permanently, test out their reactions. Despite their love for you, parents can be angry at a daughter for "disappointing" them with a marital failure. They can be full of reproaches, of "I-told-you-never-to-marry-him." Or they may see your divorce as a *moral* failure and take your ex-husband's side. At a time in your life when your self-esteem is at its lowest ebb, the last thing you need is your mother delivering a running lecture on how you've let the whole family down.

Even if parents mask open anger, they can still deliver their resentments in subtle messages that just as efficiently drive you up the wall. They may overindulge your children, leaving all the nitty-gritty discipline to you, for example.

Bonnie returned with her children to her family home after leaving a stifling seven-year marriage—and immediately started fighting with her mother over everything from how she dressed for a job interview to what time the children should be fed. "I didn't figure it out for a long time, but we were fighting over my right to have a new life. My marriage was miserable for nearly the whole time. But my mother invested everything in an unsatisfying marriage and she thinks I'm rejecting her whole way of life. Since I chose differently, she, along with my ex-husband, is praying I'll fall flat on my face."

Moral disapproval is sure to spur wounding fights between parents and an adult daughter who's in the uneasy position of having returned to her parents' protection. Bonnie, like many newly divorced women, went through an initial phase of seeing a different man every night. Her mother was ignorant of how common—and passing—this phase is. Shocked at what she saw as an outrageous sexual spree and convinced that her daughter needed to be saved from herself, she angrily screwed up phone messages from men and created awkward scenes when they came to pick Bonnie up. But she righteously felt she was only doing her duty as a mother.

Families can be wonderful sources of emotional, logistical, and financial support for the single mother. But it's up to you to set the terms on which you accept their help. Blaming, reproaches over your failure, or excessive meddling in your sexual life can't be part of the terms.

Help at Home. The smartest thing a single mother can do is to: (a) beg; (b) barter; or (c) pay through the nose for live-in help. For the first few months, when you aren't up to your usual energy level, having someone around twenty-four hours a day can be simply lifesaving.

Carla, a social worker, feels her live-in sitter made an enormous difference in her recovery in her first year alone. "Even though I'd instigated the divorce, for twelve months I was really so messed up that Susan was better with the kids than I was. I was locked in my bedroom wondering how the hell I was going to ever bring them up. Susan was really their mother and she gave them love, she was there for them all the time. I'll always love her for it."

Once your own motors are running, a live-in helper can free you from the prison of being the only adult on duty. Ginny, who struggled three years working and caring for two young children with only baby-sitter help, discovered new freedom when she hired a nineteen-year-old woman part-time student (who jumped at the chance to live with Ginny in New York City for a salary of $40 a week, room and board, and two nights off to attend classes). "I really have a wife," Ginny giggles, "which is what we all need. She takes care of everything the way I used to for my husband—the cleaning, the laundry, the dental appointments, taking the shoes to the repair shop. I've gotten rid of a whole world of strains. When I'm late at work, I don't have to worry. When one of the kids is sick, someone they know and trust is right there in the house. And I don't have the expense of a baby-sitter, so I can afford to go out a lot more."

Sara, a merchandise buyer who must travel regularly, likes the stability of having a live-in housekeeper, which allows her daughter to accept her frequent absences with equanimity. "I couldn't leave her with a succession of sitters. Of course, she'd much rather Mommy was at home, but she accepts Anita and I feel perfectly confident when I have to go off."

Living with Another Mother.   If your budget won't stretch to pay for live-in help, trade a room plus kitchen privileges for part-time baby-sitting—maybe to cover from after school to ten P.M. on the evenings you'd like to be free to go out.

Or consider teaming up with another single mother to share an apartment for both families. Splitting the rent can help you afford a better apartment than either of you could manage alone. (But watch out for landlord prejudice. In a strange twist of logic, landlords are happy to lease a high-rent apartment to a flock of single stewardesses, but they may refuse to rent to two mothers unless one of them can afford the apartment on her own. They just assume the arrangement won't last long and that one or the other of the families will move out. Your best ammunition to fight this prejudice can be the local agency that handles housing discrimination.)

Having another grown-up there to share cooking and discipline and generally give weight to the adult side of the ongoing battle between Them and Us can be great. Annette, a teacher, who shares a sunny nine-room apartment in New Orleans with another divorced teacher, says, "It's wonderful to sit down at the dinner table and talk about something besides 'Starsky and Hutch.' And our kids like having each other to play with. I get much less of 'Mommy, I don't have anything to do; play with me.' "

If the idea of sharing your family life with another person doesn't seem your style, consider other combinations. Sue, a Houston cocktail hostess who's on duty from seven P.M. to three A.M., happily lives with her son in an apartment shared with a secretary who works in the daytime. "We can't get on each other's nerves," says Sue, "because we only see each other for a half hour a day, from six to six-thirty." But thanks to their opposite schedules, Sue has someone on the premises to get her son off to school and to sleep in while she's away at night. Her roommate can count on Sue to pick her twin sons up from nursery school in the afternoon and cover until she gets home.

You can arrange for more privacy but still get the support of sharing by renting two apartments in the same building or sharing a two-family house. Agree on alternating nights to cook dinner or be in charge of the children. Iris, a mother of four children who is divorced from a police officer, rents a two-family Queens home with another woman who has four children of *her* own. "With eight kids, there was *no way* we were going to share one house. But with upstairs and downstairs, and our own entrances and areas, we get along fine."

Women Friends. The most reliable source in your budding support system is likely to be women friends—particularly divorced women who are further along in making a new life. Invariably, women who've been there can be the most empathetic and selfless friends. But don't overdo this source of sympathy. Avoid using your friends as spectators at the ongoing soap opera of what-he-just-did and what-he-told-my-lawyer. Gain strength from their genuine concern—but don't cross that thin line where you turn sympathy into an exercise in self-pity. You can't afford it. Instead, use your friendship as an emotional support for moving on to new experiences.

When you take your kids on outings to the zoo, on a picnic, out to eat, you may be stuck by that blow-to-the-stomach feeling that you're kidding yourself, that the whole world is a Noah's ark, with man and woman paired, two by two, two parents to a family. Instead of feeling sorry for yourself or inadequate as a one-parent family, use your women friends to build up new rituals in your family life. Betsy, a Chicago personnel-agency worker, gets together with her friend Sheila for their family dinner at an inexpensive restaurant every Thursday night. "Our kids are different ages, but they knew each other back when we all lived in the suburbs. So eating out is both a nice familiar link with the past and our own new ritual. Our kids have a family feeling for each other that cuts across the usual friendships between kids the same age. Her Jacqueline, who's twelve, plays big sister to my two-year-old. Her six-year-old son looks up to my ten-year-old son as a big brother. The children get a real assurance from having this regularity in their lives."

Holidays can lose their we're-no-longer-a-real-family pall when you invite friends to share a pot-luck Thanksgiving feast. And you won't spend all your holiday trussing the turkey and making the mincemeat pies. These and other rituals can become enjoyable and valid on their own—not make-do substitutes for the old two-parent family Christmases and Sundays at the beach.

Married Friends. The usual script calls for a divorced woman's married friends to drop her as a Typhoid Mary, an agent of infection who'll spread the germ of marital infidelity among their content husbands. This is more often myth than fact. And there is a special value in cultivating and keeping up ties with married parents who can serve as models of stability to your children. "I moved into the city an hour and a half from the people I knew in the suburbs," says Greta, "but I've made a point of keeping up with them because I want my sons to know what life is like in a two-parent family. I make a huge effort to get my kids out to see them and to invite them to come with us to ball games at the city stadium. Some of the fathers continue to be very important and loving to my sons."

Support From Counseling. Your eleven-year-old daughter starts skipping school. Your son is driving you nuts with his negativism— he absolutely delights in dawdling while you shriek that it's his turn to do the dishes and your carefully worked out family-sharing chart might as well be a guide to the 1933 World Series.

Don't be hesitant to get professional counseling or family therapy when you and your children have emotional and disciplinary clashes. Lauren, a West Coast real estate salesperson, credits her good relationship with her ten-year-old son and twelve-year-old daughter to getting good professional help at crucial times. Lauren's family felt stress when her ex-husband remarried. "All of a sudden, things with my son got very rocky. Everything was my fault; if he lost something in his room, that was my fault, too." Just as troubling were the constant fights that marred Lauren's daily homecoming.

"Being a single parent makes it damn tough to deal with these things, because there's no feedback from another loving parent to say, 'Oh, take it easy, you're worrying too much,' or 'Okay, you people, you're getting hysterical, go to your corners.' There's no one to help break the intensity of what's going on."

Lauren was surprised at the simplicity of the techniques her family counselor suggested. "Some of the techniques were so simple that they ran against my grain at first, but they worked. First, we set up that if the kids went for just ten minutes without fighting, they'd get a check mark on a piece of paper and a reward of a nickel each. I didn't like buying good behavior, but it didn't take more than a few days and all of a sudden we would forget to record it when a half hour went by with nobody fighting. It was so amazing!"

Next, Lauren's counselor concentrated on improving understanding among the family members. "Another fantastic technique was one our therapist called 'Stop.' If an argument begins, or your kids escalate something and someone begins to take a potshot at someone else, you simply say to the other person, 'Stop.' That's the signal that the other person has to guess what you're feeling. They have to be precise—like you're feeling put down, or you're really angry, or really hurt. And keep coming up with adjectives that describe how they think you feel until you say, 'Yes, that's right.' Then the other person asks you to do it in reverse."

"When I'd get these teary calls at work, and Greg would be crying on the phone that Jennifer and her friends were doing such and such in the pool and wouldn't let him jump in, I would say, 'Greg, I think you ought to go play 'Stop.' '"

Along with other techniques to end fighting, "Stop" quickly brought peace to Lauren's household. "The interesting thing was that although we used 'Stop' a fair amount at first, we don't seem to need it anymore. It's a way of forcing you to see how you're affecting the other person, to empathize and understand that, though you may be speaking out of pain, you're also hurting somebody else. It takes away the argument and focuses on the emotional interaction, which is what's really going on when you're fighting."

Lauren urges other single mothers not to feel self-conscious about getting objective professional help. "Mothers need to feel comfortable about getting help, and to get it early. Don't wait until the situation is really rough."

Elka's son Chris became a disturbed twelve-year-old when his father moved out of their home. Although Chris studied conscientiously every night, his grades went down. He became withdrawn and refused to discuss his study problems with his mother. Elka asked Chris's school counselor to administer the usual tests, and the counselor promptly reassured her that, while Chris's mind remained bright as ever, she should seek a therapist with whom Chris could work out his feelings.

"When I told him he was going to go to someone to help him, he burst into tears—the first emotion he'd shown in months. As the months went by, I could see this terrible pressure lifting. I just wouldn't have been able to work it through by myself with him, because of his confused loyalty to my ex-husband and me. All the money I spent in those six months—I had to borrow every penny of it—was well worth it."

You don't have to spend a fortune to get good professional help. Lauren arranged for her family therapy at minimal cost through her religious group. Low-cost help is usually available from your local Family Service Association, church, clinics associated with a university, the outpatient clinic of teaching hospitals, and even your child's school. Ask for references from agencies like your local Family Service Association of America, Mental Health Association, or department of psychiatry at a teaching hospital.

Don't be afraid to shop around for a clinic or therapist that feels right for you. Counselors treat parents and kids separately and in groups. Or they may use the increasingly popular technique of family therapy, when all of you are treated together. (The idea is that a person doesn't develop his problems in isolation; they are reinforced by reactions of other family members.) Warning: Psychological counselors are not infallible, and some have even been known to harbor a grudge against working mothers. *Don't blindly follow orders from a counselor when they really go against your feelings.*

How Much Psychological Support From Ex-Husbands?

Can your ex-husband be part of your new support system? Or will he hang around like a blot from the past, impossible to ignore and always guaranteed to leave you in a state of fury when you talk? One thing's for sure, as Melody, thirty-one, divorced three years, says sadly: "You *never* get rid of your ex-husband. I thought when I walked out that I was starting a whole new slate—you know, big Joan Crawford scene, walking off into the night. Instead, I'm talking on the phone to him four nights a week! When is he going to pick up the kids, where should they go to camp in the summer, can he afford braces for our son? I never expected life after divorce to go on just like it was before."

Like it or not, you and your children's father will most likely be involved for the next ten to fifteen years. Putting that involvement on a sharing basis that will do the most for you and your children will require yeoman effort from you. The *amount* of involvement you encourage your ex-husband to have in your life is crucial. We identify three different levels of involvement: no involvement; limited involvement; and full involvement. Each has strengths and problems, but one of them is probably best for you and your need for support.

1. Daddy Loves You, But He's Far Away Right Now. If your divorce was particularly bitter, or your ex-husband is a predominantly destructive influence, you may opt for no involvement, even with a loss of child support. Josie, a vivacious thirty-four-year-old editor with a son, nine, and a daughter, eleven, left her husband eight years ago when he announced he was in love with a student from his college classes. "He was at the time an English instructor at a famous experimental girls' school in New England. The way he had his situation worked out so beautifully was that he didn't want me to work at all. He had his perfect family, ensconced in a beautiful old country house where I was baking bread and bringing up the kids. Only on too many of those long, snowed-in New England nights, he'd call to say he couldn't get home through the snow.

"I had no image of myself working, although I'd loved history in college and had planned to teach high school. But there were no openings up there in the country. I had nothing in the world to do, no one to talk to except nice country-neighbor ladies. He had a succession of affairs with students—all very pretty, very intelligent, very knocked out by him. When he finally decided he wanted to live with one, he gave me no choice. I had to get out.

"The only thing to do was put some space between him and me." Josie left her children with her mother in Iowa for three months and came to New York to search for a job and an apartment. She lived in an inexpensive hotel for women—a famous and famously depressing first stopover for New York newcomers—and one weekend, turned down for yet another job, she lost heart. She blew her savings on a plane ticket to Iowa and stayed a week, asking her mother, "Please mother *me* for a few days."

But since then, Josie's life has been all uphill. She landed a job as a secretary in a publishing house and moved up in double time. "I made a totally new career and life and I'm very proud of myself. Eric and Jennie are very together kids, and we get along better than most mothers and kids. I just moved into a new, better job where I'm making $19,000—more than my ex-husband *ever* brought in. We finally have a bigger apartment and some breathing space over money. But in all this time, he's had *nothing* to say about the way I bring them up, *nothing*. He sends very little money, so he has no claim.

"My marriage was obviously very bad psychologically for me, and I couldn't have recovered if I'd been forced to talk to him every week or so, or even once a year. And since he was never an interested father, I don't have to worry about the kids missing him."

With such a traumatic marriage, Josie chose well to support herself and cut off all contact with her ex-husband. Only by submerging herself in a totally new environment, job, and city was she able to carve out a new life.

The advantages of going it alone are highly appealing to some mothers. They have all the responsibility—but they also have the freedom to make all the decisions. Without harassment. Without argument. Without the emotional trauma that can ensue from that neutral-sounding standard divorce agreement, Parents shall consult on matters of importance.

2. Daddy Will See You Sunday. A more common arrangement, one that exists in the majority of divorce settlements, is the Sunday Daddy. Custody arrangements that grant Daddy Sunday visits don't necessarily lighten the mother's responsibility. Paula, an attractive forty-three-year-old woman who has been divorced for nine years (during which she founded and built an interior-design business) wearily reports: "I've had Sundays free from my two children—but *never* one whole weekend in nine years. I have a daughter who is a very demanding child, with many behavioral problems, and it was an unbelievable strain for me for a while, a terrific emotional drain. But my ex-husband said, 'I am not here to make *your* life easier.'

Once a week, and he never misses. And what I've wanted for years is just *one* weekend to myself."

Some divorced fathers put in their Sundays with punctual regularity, determined no one's going to say *they're* welching on the bargain. They're just as determined as Paula's husband that their *wives* aren't going to get a break, either. But negotiating a more flexible arrangement for your husband's taking the children *can* be done.

Paula got relief when their daughter's emotional problems threatened to become disabling. Paula, her ex-husband, and the children all went into family therapy. One outcome was the father's realization that he could easily arrange his schedule to trade two Sundays for one whole weekend—a block of time that, the counselor persuaded him, would give his daughter time to settle down and become accustomed to him, and for them to share better interaction. Paula finally got her weekends.

Another problem of Sunday-only arrangements is that the mother is often cast in the role of disciplinarian. "Daddy appears for the fun and games. I'm there for the real-life times to say no, you can't, wipe your mouth, say please. I get tired of being the bad guy."

Innovate to give your children and ex-husband a chance to know each other in a natural parent-child situation. If your child is under two, having Daddy take him out for the day involves complicated logistics with diapers and food. And few toddlers can retain good temper under the stress of change. Instead, you might try getting out of the house yourself for the day and letting your ex-husband visit the child on his home turf, where daily courtesy and discipline are in order. Older children can benefit from the same at-home visiting. Their father gets to see them in their native milieu, and the firsthand encounter may make him sympathetic and supportive of your efforts in dealing with them.

Hallowed by custom and legal tradition if nothing else, the Sunday-only visiting arrangement does have undeniable advantages for some mothers. They assume most of the control and spend most of the time with their children. But all of them are naggingly aware of the problems their children have in maintaining an emotional relationship with a father who appears once a week. Recently, two Brandeis University sociologists shed light on how the amount of time a father spends with his children affects his parenting. They compared parental competence and overall satisfaction expressed by four categories of fathers:

1. full-time or full-custody fathers
2. half-time or joint-custody fathers
3. quarter-time fathers (defined as those who spend between seven and thirteen days a month with their children)
4. fathers who visit one day a week at the most

The most satisfied fathers were the half-time group, as opposed to the weekend father and the full-time father. Weekend fathers tended to feel alienated from their children. Because they spend what time they have with their children on unnatural, aren't-we-having-a-good-time entertainment, they had little chance to take an active parenting role or build experience in handling the emotional problems of their children.

Full-time fathers, on the other hand, felt overwhelmed by their responsibilities. No surprise to any single mother!

Half-time fathers felt more secure in their roles as parents; they tended to speak more confidently of their parental "rights," not "privileges," as the weekend fathers regarded their visits with their children.

Half-time fathers also managed to stay on better terms with their ex-wives. Both weekend and full-time fathers spoke of very hostile or mixed relations with their ex-wives. Those who shared the parenting more often described themselves as being "friendly" with ex-spouses. Which brings us to emerging arrangements that recognize the need of both parents to be actively involved in bringing up their children—variously called *split custody, joint custody,* or *co-parenting.*

3. Daddy's Always Around. At its most formal, sharing of parenting is legally arranged as *joint custody* or *split custody.* More informally, a mother may maintain legal custody but agree for the children to spend a significant amount of time with their father. They can carve up the time in half-week periods, giving one parent charge from Thursday through Sunday, the other, Monday through Wednesday. If the father lives far away, the mother and father may agree to six months with her, six with him. Parents may alternate weeks. Or, as one New York couple arranged in a new twist, the children stay in one spot and the parents move in and out every other week! (Both parents are architects with offices that double as living quarters.)

The obvious benefit of co-parenting is that you share the arduous responsibility of parenthood. You get time to yourself to develop your own life with adults, your ex-husband feels less isolated from his children, and the children benefit from having two actively involved parents.

On the negative side, some professionals still feel that having two homes is simply too confusing to a child, especially to one already beset by his parents' divorce. About half the women we interviewed who were trying co-parenting found the arrangement was good on the whole. But they were frank about problems like jealousy.

Ruth, divorced from John, a high school teacher, reveals her efforts to deal with competition for her older daughter Patty's affections. "It used to tear me apart to see how eagerly Patty went with her dad every weekend. He really has the advantage because he has the girls on weekends when he's relaxed and there're no schedules to meet, no dressing for school on time. The days I spend with them are consumed with all these duties of homework and getting up in the morning and off to the baby-sitter and to bed—all these mother-do things.

"This bothered me for about a year. I'd be hurt if Patty didn't run in and eagerly hug me when she got back Sunday night. And I'd come down on her real hard about discipline. Sometimes, she'd be overly loving, trying to manipulate me. Then, other times, she'd be stubborn about not helping in the mornings, especially when she just came back from her dad's. She'd complain that she was overworked, getting up and getting herself dressed and helping with the lunches. She never had to help clean up over at her father's because he had a maid.

"I talked it over with John and asked him not to make all their weekends such fun and games. He agreed that they should have chores at his place, too—mostly fun things, like helping him trim the hedge. But that helped. Their experiences with him now are pretty real."

Ruth is firmly committed to the principle of open communication with her children, and she finally solved the tension by talking it out with Patty. "I sat her down and told her, 'It's okay if you love Dad more than me. That is really okay. I know you love me. You don't have to feel guilty about that.'" Ruth's openness cleared the air and relieved her daughter's guilt over her ambivalence.

Would Ruth rather keep her daughters all the time? "Oh, no, this is best for all of us. The jealousy is just something I had to become aware of and stop acting out. I need this time by myself. And they need their father. It's a price I'm willing to pay."

Suzanne, a government career officer, and her husband John worked out an enlightened joint custody as part of their amicable divorce. Their eight-year-old daughter and four-year-old son spent four days with Suzanne, then packed their toys and schoolbooks to spend the next three days at their father's two-bedroom apartment across town.

"It worked out great for their father, me, and our daughter, who's very attached to her father. But the shuttling back and forth was too much for my son. All of a sudden, he wasn't sleeping or eating well, and he was obviously in distress, telling me he didn't want to go. They were used to John's traveling, so Michael got the idea when he went to Daddy's that I was off traveling. One day he asked me where I was going this week while he was at Daddy's, and when I told him nowhere, he was furious: *'You stay in the house and I have to go!'* "

That realization triggered an acting out of Michael's distress. "One day at nursery school," says Suzanne, "he got sick with a stomach virus and I left work to pick him up and stayed with him the afternoon. It was the twenty-four-hour kind, but the next day I got another call—Michael's having stomach cramps. As soon as I got him home again, the cramps disappeared. Then, on Friday, when I reminded him his daddy would be picking him up from nursery school, he got stomach cramps again."

Suzanne was alarmed enough to force a change in custody. "I had to threaten John with legal action to void our joint custody, because it was obviously detrimental to Michael. He finally agreed, though with a lot of anger. But Michael's settled down. Right now he needs one home."

Jan, a Tennessee social worker, came to an unusual sharing arrangement for her thirteen- and eleven-year-old sons. "I knew I'd never be able to take care of the house on alimony and my salary, and that Jim would never pay for us to live there. So I left the kids with him and moved to a small apartment a mile away. I'm not asking for alimony. The kids stay with me Monday through Thursday."

Jan has some anger because her husband is doing all the things she'd never have been able to afford. "He hired a housekeeper to help him. But she does free me from chores like doing the kids' laundry. And I'm still a suburban mommy. I drive them three nights a week to dancing class and Little League and Sunday School. I'm very much in their lives."

How does the arrangement work out? "We have perfect reciprocity. I went to Europe recently on a work trip and that happened to coincide with Jim's break from teaching. But he stayed home and kept the children. Then, at Christmas, I had a chance to go skiing and he kept them. If he wants to go away on a Sunday with his girl friend, there's no problem. I take them, so long as I have advance notice. He's a very good father, and although it sounds complicated, I think this is the next best thing to our all living together."

For women who've struggled for years shouldering the lion's share of parenting, who've sacrificed their personal lives to devote themselves to bringing up their children with only Sunday relief, coparenting may sound like a dream—but, unfortunately, a trend that's come too late to help them. On the contrary. If you're to make your ex-husband part of your new support system, don't regard your present childcare arrangements as binding forever. As your children grow up, changes in your individual responsibilities may be in order, either because of their needs, your ex-husband's growing willingness to assume charge, or other pressing responsibilities in your life (like going to graduate school to get a better job).

Josie, for example, after managing solo for seven years, was amazed to get help from her ex-husband. "Now that the kids are older and more interesting as people he's gotten interested in them and wants to see them. We experimented last Thanksgiving, when they took the bus by themselves to spend three days with him. He has several motorcycles and cars that he's always working on, and my son thinks that's really neat. So they now visit regularly. I can even see, at some point, one of them announcing that they want to go and live with Daddy for a while. And I can see myself emancipated enough from the past to say okay, good-bye."

Formal co-parenting may not be wanted by many husbands. But without relinquishing your legal rights, you might agree to let a child spend an entire summer or other extended period with her father. And co-parents, as Suzanne and John discovered, also have to be flexible enough to change if children are confused or insecure in joint custody. Whatever the arrangement you started with, be open to experiment and change if you want to get maximum support from your children's father.

Chapter Sixteen

Establishing a New Life As a Single Mother

Part of establishing your new life is learning to handle yourself as a single parent. One of the happiest results of being single can be a deepened companionship with your children. Married mothers invariably feel the difference in their parental stance when their husbands are away for a while. Frances, married thirteen years, observes, "When my husband travels, I slip into a different relationship with the kids. We're less formal. They're less well behaved, but they help me more, too. Maybe I'm a little looser, too. When there's not two of us adults against them, I have to save my authority for when it really counts."

Single mothers often enjoy a greater comradeship with their children. Without another adult to share their problems, many single mothers discuss their thoughts more freely with their children. "My eight-year-old daughter loves to know just where I stand with my latest boyfriend," says Annie. "And you know, she has better instincts about them than my adult friends."

Children learn to share chores and responsibilities—after all, who else is there to go to the grocery store and help Mom lug home the heavy bag of groceries and that extra bag of kitty litter so they can all survive the weekend? Single mothers say the job of surviving together blurs the line between Responsible Adult and Carefree Child as well. "If we don't get it together, if they don't help me with the laundry in a responsible way, if I get sick, well, we're all in one big mess. Maybe I even count on them to be grown-up *too* much."

Here are common problems with children and solutions some single mothers have found.

Post-Divorce Anger. All children feel anger and guilt when their parents are divorced. This is hard to deal with because of the difficulty children may have expressing how they feel to you. How can they be loyal both to you and to their father? One way to help them work through their emotions is to put them into contact with other children of divorce. Elka, whose twelve-year-old son Chris was disturbed by his father's departure, discovered real healing came from Chris discussing his thoughts and feelings with other teenaged boys whose parents were divorced. "I would slip around and hear them talking about these things—does your mom do so-and-so, does your dad have girl friends, do you think they'll get back together? They can talk to each other better than to any grown-up about things they could never, never bring up with you. I would advise any mother to see that her child has friends of the same sex whose parents are divorced."

Angers will be worked through faster if your children don't cling to any illusions about you and your ex-husband getting back together. If, after a day with Daddy, your daughter asks, "Are you and Daddy ever going to live together?" reply with a firm, "No, we're not." Sometimes children dream of having their families reunited and never express the thought. Avoid any actions that might encourage the hope that everything can return to "normal."

And lest we worry unduly about the children's reactions, Dr. Lee Salk reminds us that divorce may even be emotionally liberating for some children. "Not *all* children love their parents," he writes. "Sometimes a divorce helps a child come to terms with his true feelings about a parent." If a man has in fact been a tyrant in his household, it's a good possibility that his child fears and resents him. If divorce rids him of the parent, "the child has a sense of relief and affirmation that he is not alone with these feelings." The notion of holding-the-marriage-together-for-the-children has long since disappeared from most people's thinking. But few of us take the next step to realize that divorce can be *good* for children in some cases.

Masculine Figures. "My son is five years old, and between his older sister and me, I'm afraid he's overwhelmed by women. I asked him what he wanted to be when he grew up and he said, 'a girl. So I can boss people.' How can I provide a male figure in his life to model himself after?" This mother's concern is not unusual.

Single mothers consistently worry about the absence of a steady male figure for their sons to pattern themselves after. Will he grow up homosexual if he only knows women? Will he have trouble getting along with other little boys? Who'll teach him to throw a baseball and those other American male things?

Scout around and enroll your son in those still scarce grammar and nursery schools that boast male teachers. "I've gone out of my way to find first a nursery school, then a kindergarten, and now a grade school with male teachers," reports a suburban California mother steeped in Freudian theory. "I didn't want my son to grow up in this hothouse of women only. He's adored all his male teachers and frankly they've responded by adoring him. I don't think he's suffering one bit. I think he's a healthy kid."

If male schoolteachers are missing in your community (though at least one mother we talked with got herself on the school board and changed that absence), try enrolling your sons in after-school recreational activities led by men. You'll find courses at the Y, your church group, or paid recreational groups that offer instruction in hockey, baseball, and many other sports.

Your own family may provide a strong male figure. Make the effort to stay in touch with married friends, too. Married fathers can show a special tenderness and interest in children who don't have a two-parent family. And they're likely to prove more permanent figures than men you are dating. In fact, unless you have a fairly stable, long-term relationship going, it's best not to count on men you're seeing as male role models for your son. That can lead to sticky situations where you're reluctant to stop seeing someone because he means so much to your children.

So long as your son is exposed to images of both women and men as authority figures, the chances for his healthy adjustment are fine. The pervading influence of movies, books, and the culture in general in driving home male behavior to your son ensure that your own role will be well balanced.

Overdependence. This is one of the knottiest problems that single mothers face. Here are some comments:

"When it comes down to the bottom line with my daughter, there's just me. We have a symbiotic relationship. It's very mutually dependent."

"Our relationship is very intense. He's an only child. I'm an only parent. We've been an island, the two of us."

"I was spending too much time with my kids—all the time, in fact. They were too dependent on me and the relationship between us was not good. I knew I had to do something to change it."

"After my divorce, I spent literally all my free time with my two sons," recalls Jane. "And we had and have a very close relationship. Most of the time, I think that's the way it should be, the best way I can make up for their father not being there. I want them to feel loved, that Mommy is always there for them. But at times, I worry. My younger little boy will never stay away from home as all the others in his class do. So I worry, am I making them cling to me?"

Emma, a thirty-year-old M.B.A., explained the symbiotic relationship between her and her daughter. "Mine was never a happy marriage, but when Jill came along, I hadn't yet really realized that. So I lavished all my emotions on her, and that intensity has never left our relationship. All her life, I've literally been up every night with her, even when I was in graduate school. My husband slept through everything. He has never been there for her in any way. Even now, my parents live very close, so you would think we have an extended family. But emotionally, it doesn't work that way. I never can leave her with them for very long. I know she counts just on me."

Emma is aware of the bad side effects that can result from this kind of symbiotic relationship and thinks she's making progress. "Jill is nine and she's only this year beginning to sleep through the night. It's no question that she's had a sleeping problem and other problems because I lavished all my time on her. But somehow I can't believe it's really destructive. I think we've helped each other survive."

Emma is wisely loosening the emotional bonds of what has been an unusually intense mother-daughter relationship. "I know I have to find a way for her to grow away from me. It's beautiful and satisfying now, but it won't be for her forever. I wanted her to go to camp this year and I talked it up big. But at the last minute, she decided she didn't want to, and I couldn't see forcing her. Better for her to stay at home than to think I don't want her with me."

After the shock of divorce, it's natural that you and your children draw together in your own tight emotional world to regroup yourselves. They will demand more of your time, love, and patience than ever before. And it's likely you'll feel pained and/or guilty for them having lost their father, whether that's reasonable or not. Still, there's a thin line between giving each other all the love and reassurance you feel welling up in you as you fashion a new life together, and becoming so tightly bound that you crowd out other relationships now and in the future.

There are three constructive things you can do to fight unhealthy clinging between you and your children. First, encourage your kids to develop a social life of their own. When they can draw love, continuity, and emotional response from their own friends, they will be less jealous of your adult social life—and create fewer of the screaming-at-the-door scenes and cries of "Mommy, don't leave" when you go out. Second, build up your support system so that other adults are part of their lives. And third, develop work and other interests that you enjoy and through which you can express yourself.

Being a single parent carries stresses and strains that are unique. Learning to trust yourself as sole disciplinarian and chief source of love takes time. But there's a good chance you were the primary parent when you were married; you may have had more practice than you realize.

Relationships With Men—Are You Ready for Involvement?

> *I have a friend who said after my separation, "Joyce, you're one of the few people I know who was really sensible when she separated. You didn't go off on some wild, totally inappropriate kind of relationship. Everybody I know has gone off with a hippie or an artist who was totally irresponsible. I really admire the way you maintained your sense of perspective." And I looked at her and said, "Well, the truth is, nobody asked me."*

—A DIVORCED MOTHER

Married mothers complain that they have to give up their social lives for their families, but single mothers lack time not only for friends but for social life with men. "If you're home every night after your children finally fall asleep, collapsed in front of the TV screen, you're not likely to meet any eligible men. Where are they? Maybe home collapsed before *their* TV sets," says one mother.

Not the least reason for lack of involvement for some women is that they put up their own blocks against too much intimacy—natural for a time, but a stage that can last for years in some women.

Jane, a forty-four-year-old Manhattan lawyer who's been divorced for sixteen years, brought up her son and daughter on her own. A few years after ending "a very destructive marriage," Jane pulled herself together and enrolled in law school. Only a few weeks later, her ex-husband suddenly died. Now Jane and her children were truly alone.

But her control of her life slowly increased. She progressed in her law-school work and began to date. One of the men, Robert, a divorced businessman, became important. Their relationship deepened into an arrangement as stable as marriage: he took her out on Wednesday and Saturday nights. She stayed at his place on Wednesday nights, when she had a sitter. Each summer, when the children went to camp, he moved in for two months. When the children returned on Labor Day, he moved out.

"After the wreckage of my marriage, which left me so broken, I can't tell you how much Robert has meant to me. But he always understood that I wouldn't marry him when the children were young.

"I wouldn't because I knew they were happier when they were the center of the house. If someone else comes in, they have to move over. My marriage was very disruptive and my ex-husband was a bad influence on the children, so I thought I owed it to them to have a place where it's peaceful and where they are central.

"Now my son is thirteen and my daughter is sixteen, and Robert is talking again about marriage. But I don't think I want to do it. Because I'm used to being independent now. God knows, I've worked hard to get to that state, professionally and personally. And while there's never any suggestion when we're together that I'm expected to do wife things, I know he's the kind of man that would expect to come in at six-thirty and have a beautiful meal on the table, and there's no way with my practice that I can do that."

Jane's determination not to let anything stand in the way of doing her best by her children is shared by many women. Her hesitation to marry, now that they're adolescent, is more unusual. Is she masking some other reason?

Jane says: "Am I just using that as an excuse to avoid the commitment—and possible pain—of marriage? I know I couldn't live through another divorce. And after all the energy I've put into developing myself, I couldn't see my career go down the drain. For a long time, I feared if I married Robert, I would give it up. But now I'm earning enough that no man can say your job is just secondary, we can get along without your salary. So I think essentially my decision is not made out of fear of that. I think it's an honest decision that I'm reasonably self-sufficient and I want to keep what I've worked for so hard."

By the time Jane felt free to marry, her pleasure in her own career and in her independence made marriage less appealing. Others are fully convinced that the prospective intimacy of a second marriage is too much for them to handle.

Lee, a forty-year-old divorcee, says, "I didn't unconsciously put marriage off; I was *consciously* scared of getting married. A lot of women really don't want to get married again. They seriously wonder whether they would have anything really to offer in the second marriage. You wonder if I'd done this or that would it have lasted. You feel guilty."

Other women stave off commitment by dating only unsuitable men. Annie, a vibrant twenty-eight-year-old photographer with a crown of curly brown hair, has been separated since her daughter was six months old. She admits frankly that she used her daughter to postpone intimacy with men. "I had this baby at home and it was a very good excuse for not doing anything that scared me, whether that meant going out with someone new, or taking a job. My husband was only the second man I'd ever slept with, and I knew I had a whole sexual life to discover, so what I did was go out with younger guys. We had really nice sexual relationships, but basically I couldn't get involved. They were like second children in the house. We would take my daughter on picnics and it was like three kids out together. I didn't feel guilty toward my daughter this way. It was just easier."

Choosing partners with whom you won't be deeply involved can be a stepping-stone to trusting yourself once more to survive emotional contact. And, as a way of avoiding feeling bereft and out of contact with all men, it can serve you well. Annie, for example, now feels ready to take her dating more seriously.

But no partners at all is a more familiar story. You're busy with your kids, you have limited social time, and many men shy away from women with responsibilities.

Joyce is a brilliant woman who, in her mid-thirties, has achieved an outstanding position in the academic world. She was married to a childhood sweetheart who fell short of her remarkable intellectual capacity. When her husband, a Vietnam veteran, went to college, Joyce took a battery of vocational tests as a lark, and was surprised that the vocational counselor was excited. "These are the best test scores I've ever seen. You have too much to give," he told her, "to stay home and be nothing but a housewife." When her two children were old enough to go to nursery school, Joyce enrolled in college, and within five years, graduated with honors and won a coveted fellowship. Her marriage, however, was finished.

Since then, Joyce has established herself professionally and set up her single-mother family in a Western university town. She's weathered behavior problems with her children, and while devoting much time to them has launched a glittering career. She has not run off with a hippie. She has barely had any dates. She has some ideas why:

"Statistics for women with children who remarry are incredibly lower than for men. I had my children early, and the fellows who are about my age—mid-thirties—see this woman with a grown family, and it makes them feel as if you're older. And you *do* feel older; you've been through a lot. You're not the dewy-eyed happy-go-lucky young person that you would be if you hadn't had to cope with so much responsibility. I think when you've got kids, you really no longer feel comfortable in the social swim with a lot of men your age.

"And, of course, if you're working and raising a family, too, you've become tremendously independent, you are used to making your own decisions. One fellow who called me for a date was sort of concerned that I was going to wear a pants suit rather than a skirt. You think, where does this guy get off? You're not used to having to accommodate so much to someone else, you're used to making the decisions yourself, and maybe it makes you a little less pliable. . . .

"It's so lonely, the lack of companionship really breaks you up, but I think, realistically, you are much less eligible as a date because you're not seen as free—either emotionally or sexually. I mean, you're not just going to be able to take off for a weekend, as a childless woman could. And even if you could, there's so much logistics involved, it loses spontaneity."

Hurt . . . responsibility to your children . . . your own independence . . . the physically heavy load of working and parenting jointly—all these realities may make relationships with men so difficult that you're willing to declare a vow of chastity. It's a role that has some comforts. And with financial and emotional debts to work off every day, you may think it's all you can manage. Finding the emotional calm to start feeling for others is hard. As Annie described her five years of friendships with younger men: "Part of it was that I really didn't want my daughter to have a man who would take her away from me. Her father had abandoned us both, and I've made our lives go on. With all the pain it cost me, I didn't want some man waltzing in to take her affections back."

Getting Back into Relationships: Friends and More

Once you do start seeing men and feeling ready for emotional involvement, you will, of course, have a tricky new equation to manage in your household: (1) how he feels about the children; and (2) how they feel about him.

Josie, like many women, simplified her romantic life after dating a string of men who disliked or were indifferent to her children: "I'm not interested in a man who can't accept dealing with my children as part of being with me. For the next ten or twelve years, that's the way it's going to be. After that, maybe there'll be somebody who won't care that I have children nineteen or twenty years old. But for now, that's the way it has to be." She has her priorities firmly in place and feels better for it.

On the other hand, avoid pursuing perfect understanding between men and your children. Ginny warns: "One thing I've had to learn is to stop dreaming of the Perfect Family. I used to dream of Mr. Rich Texan, this handsome, understanding widower who would fall in love with my children, marry me, and take care of us. Stop thinking you're going to find this wonderful man who will love you and be a father to your poor little kids. *It is not going to happen.* No matter how great a guy he is, he is *not* going to be just like a father is. No stepfather is. So you try to date guys who like your children, but don't insist he *love* them."

The man in your life may turn out to be warm and loving toward your children; they may develop a terrific relationship. But *don't expect to produce a wonderful new father to heal your children's wounds and your guilt.* That's a fantasy, and not a very useful one. If you date with that ideal in the back of your head, it's going to distort from the start relationships with men you can like and enjoy being with. As stepparenting becomes more prevalent in our society, some of the illusions are being stripped away. Even the most loving stepparent rarely becomes as close as Mom or Dad. "There is always a difference," says a successful stepfather whose family consists of his own children from a previous marriage, his wife's two children, and their own baby. "You are always making tiny mental adjustments about 'her' kids and 'mine.' "

Any woman who's planning to marry to give her children a new father should carefully reexamine just what she thinks "father" will entail. If she expects the same degree of responsibility toward the child that she feels, she's expecting too much. And if the children already have a father who's even moderately involved in their lives, her expectations become all the more inappropriate.

Here are some of the conflicts between your men and children you'll have to iron out.

Jealousy. Soon after divorce, children have especially strong fears of abandonment and they react intensely to men as potential rivals.

Sandy, thirty and divorced for six months, did free-lance typing to supplement her salary and when she took along her son to deliver a job to the apartment of a client, Arthur, she was mortified that her son suddenly turned into a demon. He darted into the bedroom, dragged out a toy Arthur was saving for his own son, and promptly tore it to pieces. He calmed down only when Arthur picked him up and plopped him firmly on the sofa with an angry *"Sit* there." Sandy says, "I didn't understand why he was so bad until we were driving home and he asked, 'Is Arthur going to be my daddy?' " In the beginning, children will fear that every man who crosses your path is going to marry you and displace them. Handle their fears by saying firmly: "No, he's not your daddy. Your daddy will always be your daddy. He's Mommy's friend."

Some women keep children's resentments at bay by setting rules about how often they go out. They almost sound like high-schoolers on probation: "I can never go out two nights in a row." "I limit myself strictly to dates on weekends." These rules can be reassuring both for you and your children.

Another way to enjoy men's company without pushing your children to the background is to discover the joys of men as *friends.* Your whole family has fun if you're able to integrate men friends into your life. Elka spent the first few months after her divorce going out with a different man every night. "Then when I decided this *isn't* what I want to be doing, I discovered how nice it is to have men friends drop by." She thinks it's important for her children to see men not only as people who come and take her away. "One man friend of mine takes my son swimming. Another one comes by occasionally to take us all to the beach or a movie, and we have a great time. My kids used to be jealous because I kept all the men separate in our lives. Now I'm bringing them more into the family and it's working better."

Making time for your children to chat or visit with your date before you go out helps them feel more a part of your dating life. Leaping further along in a relationship, remarrying couples nowadays are asking their children to take part in the marriage ceremony. When children become an active part of the marriage, they are better able from the first to put aside jealousy and become part of a new living unit.

Sex Roles. "I almost die of embarrassment when Jim comes over," says Elaine. "My daughter is in his lap, all over him, Little Miss Coy dying for a daddy. She's only six, but she woos him, and he can't kiss her enough. While my son, who's eight, sits in the corner glaring at this man in the house."

If a child reacts negatively or with excessive affection, the motives may lie in his normal sexual development. Don't be too miffed or worried when your four-year-old daughter leaps into your boy-friend's lap—after all, she's trying to emulate *you*, in however crude a fashion. Youngsters in their teens, struggling to come to terms with their own sexual identities, can be particularly trying, running through the gamut of negative emotions from open disgust to insulting indifference. Before you and your man take offense, consider that their reactions are part and parcel of their own effort to come to terms with their own sexual lives.

Discipline. Few areas draw battle lines between mother and boyfriend more quickly than the discipline of her children. It may be fine for you to deal out smacks to misbehavers, but let your man do the same and you are likely to rush to protect them.

Keep the peace and a reasonable amount of order by setting firm guidelines for other adults. If a man is living with you, most of us agree that he has to have *some* disciplinary powers. "You can't have a man around the house and not have him interact," says one mother. "He has to exercise discipline and he has to be able to tell them when they're bothering him and to be quiet, turn down the TV, stop running around, and wipe their mouths and wash their hands. On their side, the kids have to feel free to tell him when they're tired of his teasing or whatever."

You may want to definitely draw the line at the physical discipline your friend exercises. Polly, who has a nine-year-old daughter and has lived for five years with Jim, complains that discipline is their biggest battleground. "My theory is that if a child requires disciplining, you handle it in a manner that is not repulsive to the child or yourself. Unless it's a life-or-death matter, handle it quietly, calmly. If it's something that requires definite action, I isolate her for a period of time or temporarily restrict her privileges. That's all that's needed, because if you make a child believe she's a good child, she *will* be good."

Jim is of the old spare-the-rod-spoil-the-child school. "He assumes children are bad, that they do bad things for their own sake or specifically to irritate him—like when my daughter chews with her mouth open, which he hates. The biggest hassle in our life is physical discipline, which I refuse to let him use. My father physically disciplined me and I hate him to this day. I don't believe spanking works. Sure, it may relieve your frustration for a moment. It does *nothing* for the child. Discipline is a real problem in our household, but I think we are painfully working it out because I insist on my way."

Insist on *your* way with your children. You are the person primarily committed to them, and your values—even if misguided—should be applied unquestioningly.

Your Own Sexual Life. Sooner or later, you'll resume your own sexual life and face one of the more painful dilemmas that confront single mothers: How do you explain the strange man at the breakfast table? How open mothers are on this delicate subject is split right along a generation gap as clear as the San Andreas Fault.

Women over forty consistently told us they put a seal of secrecy over all their sexual lives. Samantha, forty-one, divorced ten years and mother of sixteen- and eleven-year-old boys, is typical. "I know these are the seventies and everything's much looser, but I would never, never have a man live with me. I know there are no more birds and bees anymore, the kids know more than we do. The other night my eleven-year-old was arguing that I should let him go see *Saturday Night Fever*, and he blurted out, 'Mom, I know all about screwing and sex.' And I gulped. But I think seeing their mother with a man in their own house would be destructive to my sons and I've never done it. I *have* arranged to go away on a weekend and I haven't hidden that I was going with a man."

At the other extreme, Francine, a twenty-four-year-old pediatric nurse well versed in child psychology, lives in a one-bedroom apartment and has frequently had a man stay over. "My four-year-old daughter has waked up to see me in bed with a man, and I think it's perfectly okay. She understands that when people like each other, you sleep together. But she doesn't understand just what that involves."

You should handle those aspects of your sexual life that affect your children in the way that feels most comfortable to you. Younger women, committed to great openness with their children, have fewer fears about letting their children know that they have sexual needs even though Daddy is no longer around. To a certain extent, their openness is merely realistic. As one young mother says, "Don't think they'll buy that old story about how he slept in the extra bedroom." True, children's sophistication nowadays guarantees that they will see through elaborate stories. As one forty-four-year-old divorced mother discovered to her chagrin, after years of fabricated excuses about why she had to be away at night, "My teenaged son blurted out one night when it turned icy outside, 'Joe, when are you going to stop this playacting with Mom? Why don't you just spend the night?' "

Most women distinguish between caring relationships and an indiscriminate parade of men. "I would only let a man stay over if I had a real feeling for him. I think it would frighten and confuse my children to see a number of men spending the night. And those are not the values I want to pass on to them, that you sleep with everyone."

We feel some precautions are not only prudent but essential. Be discreet. There's nothing wrong with a closed door to Mom's bedroom; letting your child in for a snuggle with you and a man in your bed may seem like innocent good fun on a Sunday morning, but even this could prove disturbing to young children.

Adolescents call for extra wariness and restraint in the physical affection you show with a man. A teenage son, working through normal Oedipal attractions to his mother or acutely aware of his own trigger-quick sexual responses, should not be exposed to the sight of his mother fondling another man. A teenage girl who sees her mother in physical intimacy with a man can easily misconstrue what is a normal, natural show of affection as an act of female rivalry. These are tinderbox times, and a little restraint need not cramp your own life.

Success and You: I Can Do It!

If you're a single mother, chances are your paycheck is essential to your family's welfare. Only about 20 percent of all divorced, separated, or single women receive any regular financial assistance from the fathers of their children. Despite the fact that women are handicapped as earners in the job market, most single mothers must shoulder the support of their children.

For all the grim financial problems faced by mother-headed families, there *can* be a positive spin-off from the money squeeze. Necessity galvanizes many a single mother into a career she would have put off until the kids were grown or maybe never have had at all.

And many women make the decision early on that being financially responsible for herself and her children is going to mean more security and peace of mind than waiting for a check or haggling over it every month. Emma's husband decided he wanted to drop out of corporate life, and his checks dried up overnight. Her decision: "I sat down and considered my options. I could go to the courts, scream, cry, or get aggravated. No, I thought, it's easier to do without."

With family courts set up as they are—"a shrine to bureaucracy and injustice," said one woman bitterly after seeing her husband, a $50,000-a-year man, walk out from the fifth court appearance without coughing up a penny of the two years of child support he owed—your decision to become financially independent just may be the one that sets you on your way to success. And you will be in good company: Many single mothers decide to seize financial fate in their own hands.

Says Annie, the photographer: "My husband announced he was reducing my child support from $100 a week to $25. I decided not to fight him because I'd be better off spending my energies getting another client and finding another job. And it was only then, that moment, that I truly accepted that *I* was going to be financially responsible for me and my child. . . . And I can tell you, it was the greatest motive to succeed a woman ever felt."

Your work will probably have even more urgent meaning for you than for a woman who can count on her husband's paycheck. And even if you're currently provided for by your ex-husband, don't forget that circumstances change—if he loses his job for whatever reason or if he remarries and has other children, your children are likely to be squeezed out. Here are some special tips for the single mother whose job will be vital to her family's security and to her identity in her new life.

Take Yourself Seriously. You're going to be working for a long time. Take this investment of your time and life seriously. Many women say that being a breadwinner forced them for the first time to think realistically about their career options and to set goals and ways to work toward them. Use the upheaval in your life to reexamine what you *want* to be doing.

Don't expect to find the answer to your vocational problems overnight. Lynn remembers: "I spent two years after the divorce in the playground with my daughter trying to figure out what I wanted to do. My ex-husband was starring in a Broadway show and I'd pass his picture on a poster every time I wheeled our daughter along and think there he is fulfilling his dreams, what do I want to do with *my* life? Finally I decided I'd been having such a hard time deciding because I was fighting the fact that I wanted to be a writer. That was the one thing I liked to do in life and was good at. I had worked at a publishing house as an editorial assistant when I was married but it was like I was just playing—I didn't take it seriously. Now I got down to work and persuaded a new paperback house to let me read books for them free-lance. I got my toe in the door and said let me write your advertising, I can do it!"

Lynn's first step led three years later to a copywriting job in an advertising agency where she's making $30,000 a year and loves her work.

If the career you want requires that you go back to school, *do it!* Don't be afraid of the commitment, if you can possibly swing the finances. Divorced women who have clearly focused goals are surprised when their concentration puts them ahead of younger students. As Aline, a single mother who began law school in her late twenties, recalls: "You go back to school with a whole different attitude. I had been out of college five years, three of which I spent at home taking care of an infant. So naturally I had a different attitude from someone who goes directly from college. I had a goal and I wanted to succeed at it desperately. I was surprised when I discovered I could do it."

Says Louise, who earned her master's in computer science at thirty-six, "I went back to school at thirty-two, when everyone else was twenty-two. I was very much aware of the generation gap and very nervous about it. But I found I was a much better student, more able to concentrate than the younger students. I had life experiences to draw on that the kids didn't. The whole experience of studying and thinking was richer for me than for them."

Believe in Yourself.   This simple bromide is the key to success for many a single mother. And the first step to achieving this is simply to *act* as if you do. Present yourself confidently to employers. Keep in mind that your experience, maturity, and ability to handle responsibility make you an attractive candidate for many sought-after jobs. Summon the will power to start seeking jobs that will offer you the personal and financial rewards you deserve.

Learn to value yourself and how to convey that feeling to the world. You don't have to come across as an aggressive go-getter; simple enthusiasm and quiet confidence can do the trick. Molly, soft-spoken and gentle, had put in three years of nursing night shifts, and her young son was tired of kissing his mother good-bye every night at six-thirty P.M. as she left for work. When she learned of a daytime opening in the research department of her hospital, she nervously scouted it out. Qualifications were fuzzy—the job seemed to call for an intern or nurse practitioner, but that requirement wasn't stated. She recalls, "I had been carrying out duties similar to those of a nurse practitioner on the skeleton night staff, though I didn't have that actual title. But I steamed myself up and went in to the director and was very enthusiastic about his project. I asked a lot of questions and I said, 'I can do this job.' And they hired me!"

Molly underscores a good strategy for any woman looking to move ahead fast: Pick a new occupation where qualifications aren't rigidly established and say, "I can do it."

For Ginny, a legal secretary, positive thinking helped her put together a totally new job image. "I'd always felt inadequate because I never got a college degree, and, of course, my resumé revealed that. It didn't even seem worthwhile putting down that I was enrolled in a night course at Columbia. I'll never forget one personnel director for a big company who yawned over my resumé and told me they had no openings." One year later, feeling stronger about herself in the work world, Ginny redid her resumé, "omitting all mention of marital status and children. And I listed at the very top: Enrolled in Columbia University. Then I put down all the five colleges I'd attended all through my checkered educational career, without once mentioning dates. And this very same personnel director—he didn't remember me at all—looked at it and said, 'I can see you're a very educated person!' And he wanted to hire me."

No matter what your job level, going armed with a well-written resumé will put you a step ahead in conveying the image you want. Often, with a resumé, you won't have to fill out an application form at all, and that's in your favor. Remember that old lawyers' rule: Avoid answering other people's questions. It's better to make up your own questions to put yourself in a favorable light.

Set Financial Goals. Now that you're the chief breadwinner, don't drift. Take control of your financial future. You will want to take out adequate life and medical insurance—without going to the other extreme of being insurance poor. (See insurance information on pages 174–175.) You may want to invest in a home—if so, bone up on credit antidiscrimination laws before you go to the bank. Some lenders regard single mothers as poor risks. Increasing your understanding of money can help you find unsuspected fat in your earnings or help you invest or work toward a financial goal. And while you're learning, don't hesitate to seek professional advice—good old brother Bill may have your best interests at heart, but that doesn't make him an expert on financial juggling. Try a reputable accounting firm or the trust department of a bank if you have a sizable settlement (over $10,000). If you have a smaller nest egg, the bank officer where you have a checking account can help you set financial priorities, arrange for a loan, or otherwise help you untangle your budget. Or you can get reasonably good counsel from some free agencies run by Parents Without Partners, church or government groups. Cover yourself by getting advice from several sources.

One typical money hang-up: Many women feel uneasy about borrowing and owing money. If you insist on paying every bill on the first of the month, you may not be getting the most leverage from your money. A professional adviser or a good book on money management can help you figure out how much credit you can handle.

There's no mystery about money. And no reason you can't take charge of your financial future along with the rest of your own life.

Living Alone and Liking It

"I get mad at myself for wanting a man sometimes. Why can't I just accept that this is my family, my kids and I, and that we love each other, and that's enough?"

Every single mother knows moments like these—moments when she feels lonely, unable to cope, longs for Mr. Rich Texan to come bail her out . . . and at the same moment, hates herself for feeling that way.

For some of us, it's hard because it's our first chance to experience that scary yet quintessentially human condition of being alone. Bonnie realized how little preparation she'd ever had to be alone a moment in her life. At first, she hated being by herself, especially sleeping in her big king-size bed after she and her husband split. "There was a point when I felt I couldn't deal with being alone. I would have moved in with a man if there'd been anybody around. I really thought: I'll never do well alone."

Bonnie realized she'd never been on her own in her entire life. After growing up in a close two-parent family, she moved directly into a college dormitory with two close friends. She married on the day of graduation, and since then "never slept more than two nights alone. But now I no longer wake up in the middle of every night in a panic; I'm determined to hang on and find out what it's like. There are things I want to do that I don't want anyone to tell me I can't, like dancing all night or buying a pair of $65 jeans. Utterly impractical. But I'm finding out about myself."

Given time and space, most women discover that the pleasures of being alone are real—and they're not eager to give them up. A single mother can pick her own friends—no more seeing people because of "couple ties." Your children, too, can sometimes pick friends that Dad didn't approve of. And without another adult questioning your values, your child-rearing methods, or your wants, you can come to treasure the sense of being in control that you've worked so hard to achieve.

Being single calls forth a daily churn of emotions: loneliness, fright, joy at succeeding on your own, relief that you're still able to keep going. But as you establish a new life, you'll enjoy more and more moments of feeling high, charged with the confidence you've earned from being on the line—and coming through. Being alone, you're forced to become your own judge of your worth. And when a woman reaches that happy state of independence when she can decide herself how she's doing in the world and what she wants, she's reached a heady new freedom.

These are the good moments, and they're worth fighting for.

Chapter Seventeen

Taking Care of Yourself—
Coping with Stress and Burnout

For each of us trying to combine achieving and loving, there are no givens, no guarantees. We have to trust our own instincts in order to nurture our families as well as ourselves. "You're always trying to strike a balance," said a woman lawyer as we talked over coffee. "And you're never quite sure it's struck." Tears welled up in the eyes of this controlled woman, who habitually freezes opposing lawyers with her calm self-assurance.

You may not think of yourself as trying to play supermom, but you may be on a treadmill nonetheless. The compulsion may come from some lingering uneasiness about playing a "male" role—holding a job. To minimize conflict between parenting and working, many of us try to be as good in both our jobs as possible—so good that *no one* can criticize us. The result is we wind up tired and tense, worried that we are not doing either of our jobs as well as we'd like to.

You can take your first step off the treadmill by asking yourself two questions: (1) Do I always expect a perfect performance?; (2) Can I accept less of myself some of the time? Mothers who cope well learn to reduce the demands they make on themselves.

Next, recognize that working parents' lives are intrinsically stressful. Psychologist David Elkind leaves no doubt of this when he says, *"Parents who go to work—which is to say, almost all fathers and many mothers—are under more stress than at any time since the Great Depression."*

The pressure of economic hard times—the very pressure that has sent so many women into the work force—accounts for much of the stress that parents suffer from today, as jobs become harder to get and harder to hold onto. Stress comes, too, from rapid social change, from roles that shift and relationships that develop problems as we try to balance job commitments and personal satisfactions.

What Is Stress?

Stress in itself is neither good nor bad. It is merely a bodily sign that our systems are being taxed by an unusual or strong demand. Any intense experience, positive or negative, produces stress; surprisingly, your body adapts in much the same way to good news like a job promotion as it does to a disaster like a death in the family.

Generally, when we speak of stress and the working mother, we mean the reactions we have to our overpressured lives. Excessive demands and conflicts strain our ability to cope. Of course, "excessive" means different things to different people. Some women thrive on dawn-to-dusk productivity and get tense if every minute isn't filled. Others become anxious or sick when they have to make many choices or take on a lot of responsibilities. Being aware of your own tolerance for stress in a variety of situations will help to keep it from becoming a problem for you.

You know the symptoms of excess stress: exhaustion; irritability; a pain in your head; a knot in your stomach; and, in its extreme form, the panicky feeling that you can't hold on anymore. Stress has been linked to heart disease, high blood pressure, and serious mental disorders. It's important to remember, though, that we need some stress to motivate and challenge us.

Stress in small doses is energizing. While you keep on the go eighteen hours a day, while you use weekends to catch up on your family, when you haul yourself out of bed on Sunday morning to take the kids on an outing when you'd love to just lie there, remind yourself that working mothers, statistically, enjoy better health than nonworking mothers (better than men, too!), and that you are less likely to have severe emotional problems than housewives.

Don't take these advantages for granted. Build on the strengths of your busy days, not on the weaknesses. The stimulation of a career . . . the deep satisfaction of raising your children . . . the pride you feel knowing you're doing two jobs as well as you can—these are the rewards of a full and exciting life.

Begin coping with the pressures that every working mother—

indeed, every working person—falls prey to by examining what makes you feel stressed.

What Causes Stress?

Are you starting a new job? Getting a divorce? Have you just had a baby? Many people believe that life events like these are the main causes of stress. Not so, say the experts. While it's certainly true that the circumstances surrounding major changes do cause stress, it turns out that what people suffer from most is a *build up of hassles*.

You cope with a new baby because your mind and your body prepare you for the difficulties. But a morning that starts with a five-year-old's fever and ends with your boss giving you a black look as you creep into the nine-thirty meeting at eleven-fifteen can cause a migraine by midday. And it doesn't have to go that far. Strong women have been known to weep over misplaced keys; losing a child's shoe has given more than one mother hives or a headache.

Laying out clothes, keys, and lunch boxes the night before, allowing extra time for calamities, lightening your load of responsibilities—all these measures will help prevent undue stress. But no amount of planning can make your life totally hassle-free. In fact, overorganization itself can cause stress, because if you believe that staying in control will give you the power to manage your life perfectly, you will be in for a rough jolt when the inevitable problems crop up. Not even the successor to "superwoman"—what some people are calling the New Improved Woman—can ever be so fit in mind and body that she always copes flawlessly. No matter what you do, you can't keep kids from getting sick, sitters from quitting, jobs from turning sour, and busses from running late. Instead, direct your energy toward areas of your life you *can* control, and try to ride with the hassles. Be on the alert, too, for the following special stresses of a working mother's life.

Basic Conflict Between Mothering and Working.   Shifting back and forth between the demands of two worlds can cause tension. One woman commented: "Every time the phone rings my priorities change." Psychologist Marilyn Machlowitz suggests that you handle this kind of role conflict by resolving not to make these decisions on a daily basis. You will do better to acknowledge that you have two roles and then get on with each. She says: "You can't get up in the morning and ask, 'Am I a mother and a manager? Or a manager and a mother?' You should just get up and go to work."

Vacillating between priorities is bound to make you anxious. If, for example, you make up your mind not to go to meetings after five P.M., and then you allow yourself to be swayed from this decision, you keep imposing difficult choices on yourself, instead of making a hard decision once.

Too Many Jobs at Once.   Interestingly, people who take on many responsibilities have been shown to function at a higher level and more happily than those who have only a few. Nonetheless, there is such a thing as spreading yourself too thin. Working mothers—bedeviled by self-imposed perfectionism—are especially vulnerable to this stress-producer. A systems analyst recalls a holiday season when her sons were seven and nine:

"Every Christmas we'd go to a party that close friends give; we would bring the children and I always made a few dishes. I love to cook, and I like it when people praise what I make. Last year, my younger boy had a three-week bout with pneumonia, and then I had crisis after crisis at the office. When it came time to do the cooking—I was planning to make my specialty, green-apple cake—I simply couldn't mobilize myself. The thought of buying the apples, much less peeling them, the mess in the kitchen—everything was suddenly horrible. I couldn't even drag myself to the market. But I felt terrible, like I let my friend down. My husband suggested I buy a cake. I worried I wouldn't get the pats on the back for being a good cook. Finally, I gave in. He was right, of course, and I felt relieved. But why couldn't I have let myself off the hook myself?"

Letting yourself off the hook when mental or physical fatigue overwhelm you is your responsibility: Only you can know when your energies are flagging. If you find yourself catering the office Christmas party, baking the class cookies, and chairing the school-board meeting—besides your regular duties as wife, mother, and worker—you may be heading for *role overload*. Rethink your priorities, and learn to say "no" to peripheral responsibilities.

Many women find it hard to say no. They worry that people won't like them if they are not accommodating all the time. Yet endless self-sacrifice can make us dislike ourselves, and in turn can harm our relationships with others. If you think of saying no as a coping skill instead of a cop-out, you will find it easier to order priorities and set goals.

First, figure out what you *must* do. If you're going to have to work overtime to finish that memo by tomorrow, say no to the overnight baking job. If you've got two weeks in which to prepare the sales report, you can still squeeze in the school-board meeting, but a shopping trip with your daughter may be just too tiring. Say no to her, but give her a raincheck, and stick to your commitment.

Practice saying no before you reach a state of emergency. If we were to be absolutely honest, few of us would describe our life goal as "cramming as many activities as possible into every single day." Yet this is how many working mothers live. Ask yourself each time: "Does this new responsibility add anything to my life?"

Say no to extra responsibilities, unless you can see a long-range gain. Many employers will pile on tasks with little regard for who's doing them. If you're already carrying a full load, turning down some assignments won't hurt your career. If your mother-in-law insists on coming for dinner to see the new baby, ask her to bring the dinner. Limiting your entertaining is appropriate when you have a job and a baby. (If you must feed a visiting relative, see the box on quickie dinners, page 112.) You don't have to have a fever to refuse your child's request for a bedtime story once in a while. Even mommies are allowed to falter before they're at death's door.

Needing to Feel Dependent. As women, we learn from childhood that our job is to care for other people; in our service-minded economy women even find themselves tending to the needs of others on the job. Rarely are we encouraged to seek nurturing for ourselves. But letting someone else care for us is more than a luxury; sometimes it's a necessity. As one woman put it, "I'm out there working like a trooper. It's lonely. Sometimes I want to crawl into a warm lap. I want someone else to take care of me."

It's not hard to find a warm lap, once you admit that you need one. Ask yourself who are the most caring people in your life. Your husband? Your mother? A good friend? Perhaps even your children. Ask for their help. Chances are your best friend will be delighted to take you to lunch when you're at the end of your rope. Your husband's caring can be especially meaningful, but don't expect him to know intuitively when you're most needy. Tell him directly. Be frank with your children when you're tired or overwrought. Give them the chance to care for you occasionally, whether it's serving you breakfast in bed, or just giving you a warm hug. Be careful, though, not to burden them with your problems. You can say, "I've had a hard day. How about heating up some of that nice soup for me?" without going into detail about your troubles in the office or the strains in your marriage.

Take Care of Yourself—Your Way

There is no one source of stress, and there's no best way to cope. During the heyday of the "feminine mystique," bored housewives were told to "take a day off . . . go to a museum." Poor Rembrandt —forced to be the guardian of our mental health! Today's working mothers are also handed panaceas. But no all-purpose remedy can relieve the pressure of your life. Instead, find out how other working mothers handle stress. Then choose solutions that suit your temperament and style.

Barbara, a research chemist, recalls her graduate school days: "I wanted desperately to be with my kids, but I needed every single minute to study, so I took the books to the ball game and sat in the stands studying. Yes, it made me a little crazy, but I'd have been crazier if I'd stayed home and cut myself off." An afternoon in a museum would probably have given Barbara the jitters instead of the peace of mind she needed.

Surprisingly, a lot of working mothers find housework relaxing. Women have the advantage of two ego-supporting roles, our work selves and our domestic selves, and when things go badly in one place we can turn to the other for solace. One woman remarked: "At work, I'm an administrative assistant, but at home I'm an administrator." And a newspaper editor told us: "There are days when I want to scream or cry at work. My boss is unsympathetic . . . I get frustrated. Nothing seems to go right. At home, I feel competent again. Believe it or not I iron my husband's shirts; it's a peaceful, nice thing to do. Cooking makes me feel creative, like I'm in control. The kids ignore me sometimes, but they still love me."

Other women find cooking and cleaning anything but a comfort.

"I need mindless time," says an advertising copywriter, "time to read, or to listen to music, not to accomplish anything at all." Hobbies are therapeutic for some working mothers. One calls her weekly pottery class "psychoceramics." Another says, "This is my Valium," as she holds up the sweater she is knitting for her son. A woman who gardens for relaxation says jokingly, "The worms in the garden don't talk back; the ones in the office do."

Whether you soothe yourself with a soufflé or simply take to your bed to stare at the ceiling, be sure to reserve some time just for you.

Selftime

"Sometimes I feel I have no personal life. There are points where I feel I don't exist anymore . . . I feel as if everybody is asking everything out of me. There's nothing left."

"I realized I'd gone four weeks without shaving my legs . . . a simple thing . . . I just never found the time."

"There's so much to get done . . . the first thing to go is you."

Selftime—emotional and physical privacy to play or think or retreat—is a basic human need.* Men, it has been said, take time for themselves; women must make time.

Set aside time away from both work and relationships. And don't let yourself get sabotaged like Marcia, who described the following scene:

"One night I announced to my family that I was completely exhausted and was going in to bed at eight o'clock. About ten minutes later, one of my daughters came in and said, 'Do you mind if I just quietly lay here with you on the bed and watch the TV?' I said, 'Okay, but quietly.' But then the dog came in. And then my other daughter came in saying, 'I'm going to just quietly call my

---

* Our thanks to Judith Langer, president of Judith Langer Associates, for sharing this concept with us and for allowing us to quote here from interviews she conducted.

friend on the phone.' Then my husband walked in and saw the dog lying across my chest, one kid across my feet, another kid on the telephone, and said, 'I'm so glad you're relaxing.' "

Marcia's family could have felt a threat in her bid for solitude. Or she herself may have communicated some ambivalence about her right to privacy. (Saying no to companionship is hard for women to do; it goes against the feminine ideal of warmth and friendliness.) Had Marcia said simply, "I am going to bed early tonight; please do not disturb me," she might have gotten the rest she deserved.

Selftime is different from pleasant moments with family and friends. As one woman explained, "Time by myself puts things in perspective. It reaffirms the fact that this is my life and I control it, not someone else."

Coping With Stress

Successful working mothers cope by managing stress, not masking it. Instead of popping tranquilizers to calm themselves down or working double-time to upgrade their accomplishments, they recognize the symptoms of pressure as a sign to reorder priorities and take stock.

Women are especially susceptible to thinking that everyone is coping more effectively than they are. Reminding yourself that most people—men and women—are not doing any better than you are will help you feel better. And if something is bothering you, action is usually the best course. As Marilyn Machlowitz points out, "Worrying is more stressful than working."

In interview after interview, working mothers used the same words to describe their lives: "It's very, very hard," they said. Accepting this is your first line of defense against stress. Here are some other, more specific preventatives and remedies:

Bodily Comforts. Ten minutes with your feet up in a dark room . . . yoga breathing . . . a warm bubble bath with the door locked against all comers—these proven relaxers can be adopted by every working mother. Train yourself to recognize your personal signs of stress and overwork. Whether it's a neck pain or a cold that puts you in bed for three days, learn to pick up your signs early, then slow down for a day or two and avert the big sickness. Sleeplessness, an extra measure of fatigue, listlessness—all are common body warnings.

Many women start the day tension-free with an early-morning swim or exercise class. Others wouldn't think of going to work without first running a mile or two, rain or shine. For the less ambitious, walking to or from the office is the perfect way to loosen up mental and physical kinks. If that's not possible, try getting off the bus a stop or two early; brisk walks will energize you in the morning, help you unwind in the evening.

Don't overlook office tension-relievers. If you spend eight hours at a desk, the physical tension can lead to emotional fatigue. Force yourself to move around: don't use interoffice phones; go to the storeroom for supplies instead of keeping them in your desk. Try deep breathing at your desk every few hours, and especially at the end of the day before you plunge into home routines. For a handy guide to in-office exercise, see *Do It at Your Desk* (order from Tilden Press, 1737 DeSales Street N.W., Washington, D.C. 20036).

For some of us, nothing less than hands-on nurturing will provide relief. One suggestion: Have your hair and nails done at a beauty school (prices are so low you can do this every week and even throw in a facial or a massage) join a health club with a friend and indulge in after-work "steam and sympathy."

Friendships.   Friends are good for you. Being a working mother can be isolating, and a few carefully chosen kindred souls—what market researcher Judith Langer calls "highly cherished friends"—will help you validate your feelings, solve problems, and cope with the self-doubts that plague so many of us. One woman jogs on Sunday mornings with the mother of a boy her son's age: "We get our exercise, we get away from the house, and we talk and talk and talk mostly about our kids. I couldn't have gotten through last year's marijuana crisis without her." Another has a "regular telephone friendship" with a trusted colleague. She says, "We're both worried about our jobs, and we need each other to test realities and sometimes to test the waters of change."

If you think you don't have time to keep up with friendships, consider this: Studies have shown that good personal relationships actually contribute to better physical and mental health. The benefits come from sharing your feelings with someone who won't judge you or become enmeshed in your personal life, as family members or job acquaintances might. Supportive friendships should not be an "extra" in your life; seek them out and use them as valuable assets.

Support Groups. Parent groups (see pages 11–13) are especially valuable for new parents, but even more experienced mothers can gain confidence and insight from a sympathetic, nonjudgmental group of people in the same boat.

If stress stems more from your job, a networking group of people in the same industry may help. Here again, sharing concerns and connections, knowing you are not alone with your problems, will help you cope more effectively. One caution: be careful seeking support on the job for personal problems. When you talk to your superiors or your colleagues you may expose vulnerabilities that are better worked out elsewhere. Although some people are quick to praise the value of office friendships in a crisis—we all know women who cried through a divorce on the shoulders of co-workers or even bosses—in general it is safer to look outside the office for family-type support.

Reorganizing Your Time. Analyze your day. When is the most stressful time? Is it the morning when you're trying to get your army fed, uniformed, and out to meet the school bus? The split-second timing of most mothers' mornings can leave even the most super-organized woman frazzled. Recounts a high-school teacher, the mother of a three-year-old daughter: "Mornings are the bottom line of everything. No matter how hard I plan, something happens—her shoelace breaks—where can I find a shoelace at seven in the morning? By the time I get to school, I feel as if I've worked a full day." Another mother described a morning so hectic that she arrived at work with only a half-slip and a sweater under her coat—in the rush she'd forgotten to put on her skirt!

You might try getting up an hour earlier; the relief of stress will more than compensate for the loss of sleep. If this is too horrible a thought, consider using checklists to jog fuzzy early-morning memory. Be philosophical—and realistic; you can't control everything. Share morning chores with your husband, or take turns so that one of you can sleep through.

If evenings are your worst time, try hiring a teenager to help with night-time chores and children. Or put your husband completely in charge of bedtimes a few nights—and put yourself to bed.

Separating your workday and your home day can be a key to relieving the stress of role conflicts. You have real worries at work and real concerns at home, and carrying them back and forth only doubles their intensity. A mother who commutes told us: "On the train in the morning I worry about David's sore throat and whether the center will send him home. At night on the train I worry about whether I'm going to get laid off if business gets any worse. But I've learned to keep these worries on the train. I don't think it's fair to be with David and be thinking about work or be at work and thinking about David. I force myself to cut off."

Be Good to Yourself. Give yourself a present—a package of little soaps, a bottle of bubbling bath oil, a bouquet of flowers—that says you care about you. "It's sort of like a parent giving you a reward," comments a woman who's addicted to this practice, "except that you're the parent and you know what reward you want." You can reward yourself for the report you finally finished or console yourself for the job interview that didn't go quite right. One woman comforts herself with a cup of hot milk and honey, just as her mother did for her when she was small.

A particular peril of the working mother is "having it all—and no time to enjoy it." Try to set aside time just for play, whether alone or with family or friends. A well-planned vacation is a terrific stress-reliever, of course, but don't overlook the value of the impulse getaway, the long weekend without the kids, the afternoon at the seashore.

SIX SIMPLE STRESS-RELIEVERS

1. *Keep a diary.* Stress can come from not knowing what you want. A diary is a wonderful tool for self-discovery, because when you record your emotions and experiences—the good as well as the bad—you start to see important patterns emerge. One woman said

that finding the word *tired* on every page finally made her realize why she had been so cranky. Another was able to improve her relationship with her employer by keeping a running description of their meetings. You needn't write in your diary every day, but be sure to reread your entries regularly.

2. *Learn to meditate.* You'll cope more easily with stress and conflict if you practice a simple form of deep relaxation for fifteen minutes twice a day. The easiest method—the Relaxation Response—goes like this: (1) sit in a quiet place; (2) assume a passive attitude (do not use this time to compose a letter or plan a dinner party—the idea is to clear your mind); (3) close your eyes but don't sleep; (4) repeat a "mantra"—any word or syllable—over and over at a regular rate (try the Sanskrit mantra "Om"). For a more in-depth view of meditation read *The Relaxation Response,* by Herbert Benson, M.D., and Miriam Z. Klipper (Avon, 1976).

3. *Play hooky.* A "nonsick" day off will pay you—and your employer—back in revitalized physical and mental energy. Use it to catch up on chores, visit an out-of-town friend, or just to rest. Give your child a special treat—play hooky on a school holiday.

4. *Go home for lunch.* If you live close by, this is the perfect stress-reliever. You can share a sandwich with your child, wash your hair, take a nap. Other lunchtime possibilities: visit a museum; read magazines in the library; take a dance class. The break in the day will leave you refreshed for the afternoon and evening ahead.

5. *Spend a weekend in bed.* There's a well-kept secret in the world of working mothers: Many top executive women retreat to their bedrooms for two days of rest and renewal. You can do this, too; all it takes is a little planning and the conviction that you're entitled to this luxury. Prop yourself up on pillows, catch up on your correspondence, read a mystery. It's okay for your kids to visit, but keep your passive pose; don't take charge or make big decisions. You'll emerge a new woman on Monday morning.

6. *Get a checkup.* Don't wait for Big Problems. Let an understanding doctor help you pay attention to your mind and body, whether it's the nagging headaches you've been ignoring or the lack of sleep that leaves your nerves jangling. Two cautions: (1) choose a physician who will take the time to talk with you. Careful probing can uncover causes of stress; (2) don't use your gynecologist as a general practitioner unless he or she is willing to perform a thorough checkup.

What Is Burnout?

The tension of stress reaches its acme with burnout, which signals total physical and psychological collapse. But whereas stress can propel us toward positive change, burnout, like depression, flattens out our emotions. When you are burned out you feel listless, hopeless, and unmotivated.

If "supermom" was yesterday's slogan, "burnout" is today's trendiest buzzword. In New York City, one YWCA even combines the two, offering a course in "Coping with Superwoman Burnout."

A BURNOUT CHECKLIST

Look over your life at home and at work over the last six months. Have you noticed any changes? When you answer the following questions, rate yourself on a scale of 0 (for little or no change) to 5 (for a lot of change). Then check your score on the scale shown below.

___ 1. Do you tire more easily? Feel fatigued rather than energetic?

___ 2. Are people annoying you by telling you, "You don't look so good lately?"

___ 3. Are you working harder and harder and accomplishing less and less?

___ 4. Are you increasingly cynical and disenchanted?

___ 5. Are you often invaded by a sadness you can't explain?

___ 6. Are you forgetting? (appointments, deadlines, personal possessions)

___ 7. Are you increasingly irritable? More short-tempered? More disappointed in the people around you?

___ 8. Are you seeing close friends and family members less frequently?

___ 9. Are you too busy to do even routine things like make phone calls or read reports or send out your Christmas cards?

___ 10. Are you suffering from physical complaints? (aches, pains, headaches, a lingering cold)

___ 11. Do you feel disoriented when the activity of the day comes to a halt?

___ 12. Is joy elusive?

___ 13. Are you unable to laugh at a joke about yourself?

___ 14. Does sex seem like more trouble than it's worth?
___ 15. Do you have very little to say to people?

THE BURNOUT SCALE

  0–25   You're doing fine.
26–35   There are things you should be watching.
36–50   You're a candidate.
51–65   You are burning out.
over 65 You're in a dangerous place, threatening to your physical
            and mental well-being.

Burnout has been called the "superachiever's sickness," but working mothers don't have to be high-powered executives to experience it. Just juggling a full load of work and family responsibilities is achievement enough to make you vulnerable. Burnout is also traditionally associated with people who work in the "helping professions," whose ability to care for others gets strained by the constant pressure to give to their clients. Working mothers experience many of the same demands and report a similar sense of depletion. Margaret, a West Coast marketing manager, who returned to work three months after her second daughter was born, comments: "After the baby, I began to question the meaning of my job; no matter how hard I worked, I never felt I was doing anything right; I always felt overwhelmed. Nothing made any sense."

Margaret felt exhausted, used up—burned out—because she expected too much of herself. *Perfectionism* is a key ingredient in burnout. If the goals you set for yourself are so high that you can't realistically achieve them, you will feel driven and disappointed—"nothing will make any sense." The antidote, notes burnout authority Dr. Herbert Freudenberger, lies in self-awareness and self-acceptance. Had Margaret reminded herself that the strains of a new baby were bound to affect her job performance, she might not have been in such despair. Had she been willing to take credit for her accomplishments while temporarily putting her job on hold, life might have made more sense. Instead, she kept pushing herself harder and harder. The result was a classic case of burnout.

Avoid burnout by making a conscious effort to appreciate yourself—both your achievements and your limitations. One woman, a highly competitive copywriter and the mother of nine-year-old twin boys, hangs a sign over her desk that says in bold letters GOOD ENOUGH. When she's tempted to drive herself over the edge, a glance at her wall helps put her back on course.

Lack of feedback is another cause of burnout to which working mothers are especially susceptible. Motherhood, after all, is a long-range enterprise; no matter how much energy you devote to your children, it is a fact of life that no one ever says, "You did good mothering today." And there are, as well, many jobs in which daily accomplishments go unnoticed by everyone but you. The danger, of course, is that without feedback, even you will stop noticing. Fight the isolation that can lead to burnout by keeping track of your achievements, even writing them down if necessary. Talk yourself up at home; let your family offer praise and encouragement if none is forthcoming from your employer.

Fatigue is also a major cause of burnout. Mothers of babies whose sleep is constantly interrupted, and even parents of older children, underestimate how much their emotional and physical well-being is taxed when they miss out on sleep. Every decision, every task, becomes harder when you're overtired. And if your nutrition is under par, if you're grabbing sweet buns and sodas on the run, this only compounds the problem.

It's not hard to upgrade your eating habits. Try to eat regular balanced meals, take a multivitamin every day, avoid overstimulating soft drinks and too much coffee (try soothing herbal tea instead). For sensible advice on nutrition consult *Jane Brody's Nutrition Book* (Norton, 1981). Fatigue is a trickier problem. You can try brief catnaps during the day (frequent breaks actually improve performance), forego evening chores to get to bed early, cut down on your social life. But there will always be times in your busy life that you cannot be well rested. Again, self-acceptance is the antidote. Don't look for a star performance at the office the morning after your child's all-night earache. If you can be kind to yourself, others around you will take their cue from you.

Lack of enthusiasm on the job when you used to feel a high sense of drive is a signal to assess the situation. Don't rush to blame your dual roles: not only working mothers feel burned out; just plain working people suffer from this, too. Decide to structure your work more effectively—delegating more, taking frequent breaks, looking closely at your goals. If these strategies don't succeed in breathing life into your work situation, you may have to consider changing jobs or shifting your attention elsewhere for a while. One secretary who started to find her job tedious tried creating new ways of managing her employer's reporting systems. When this didn't make her feel any better, she decided to concentrate more on a nonwork part of her life, distance running. A side benefit of training for a ten-mile run was that she was soon able to approach her job with renewed vigor.

Burned-out feelings spill over into your home life. The routines of childcare and housekeeping can sometimes be boring and burdensome. And when the strain becomes too great, women find themselves asking, "Why am I doing all this?" A change in routine can help: This is the time for the trip to Bermuda you and your husband have been discussing. Whatever you do, don't ignore these feelings and don't try to whitewash them away. Paying attention to your own state of mind—without imposing "shoulds" or "musts" on yourself—will help you move out of the burned-out state.

Profound feelings of despair, especially if you can't mobilize yourself in any direction, may call for professional help. Don't make the problem worse by telling yourself, "I ought to be coping better." If you could, you would. A good psychotherapist can help you identify the roots of your depression and to make changes in your life that will restore your equilibrium.

To Each Season . . .

As time goes by, we come to realize that we have to live with stress, not hide from it. We learn to monitor our reactions, to tell the difference between the natural pressures of job and family and the squeeze play we perform by asking too much of ourselves. The balancing act becomes less shaky as we draw support from friends and family and share our experience and our problems. And, as we put aside outworn prejudices against self-indulgence, we find that nurturing ourselves renews us to care for the people we love.

No matter how well you manage, you're bound to end up busy and harassed some of the time. Most of us accept this pressure as simply a part of the motherhood season of our lives. And we are aware that a modern woman's life will span many seasons. Says a marketing executive who works long hours yet still manages to spend lots of time with her fourteen- and thirteen-year-old daughters, whose values she has worked hard to help shape, "I'm so busy now, I wonder myself how I keep such a pressured schedule without collapsing. But my own inner psychology is that there's plenty of time ahead just for me. I am thirty-nine, and in four years, both girls will be out of the house. There will be a whole other life then, when the kids are gone, and plenty of time for reading poetry and making strawberry preserves, long before there'll be any grandchildren."

She enthusiastically adds: "Forty-three is young these days, and my husband will be forty-six and into the new career he's preparing for. I don't know exactly what it will be like when our child-rearing ends. But I know it will be better and more exciting because of this season being full and rich."

I'm a Success!

Not so long ago, Margaret Mead could speak of an ambitious woman being faced with the grim choice between becoming either "a loved object" or "an achieving individual." Some choice.

And in *Passages* (Dutton, 1976) Gail Sheehy direly concluded that women simply can't integrate marriage and career before the age of thirty at best, and probably not until thirty-five.

We found that women—single and married, committed to feminism or indifferent to it, from seventeen to sixty—are changing these realities. We don't want to skate over the difficulties. Even though more than half of the mothers with young children are now in the work force, we still have no public commitment to childcare. Many parents feel they are scaling a glass mountain, climbing one step up, sliding two steps back down.

For most of us, though, the deep satisfactions convince us we're on the right track. "I am a wife and mother," says one woman.

"That's about 82 percent of who I am. But there's this other 18 percent that's just me alone, and if I didn't do something with that, I'd feel I was failing myself. To me, working means the difference between being a success and not being a success."

Take time to look over what you *are* accomplishing. Chances are, when you add up the pluses and minuses, the things you do and the things you wish you could get done, you'll come to the conclusion that makes it worthwhile: I'm a success!

Index